MW00610620

TUCSON
Memories

Happy Memories!
Bonnie Henry
2 08

by Bonnie Henry

foreword by Bruce J. Dinges

Published by the Arizona Daily Star, a Lee Enterprises Newspaper,
Tucson, Arizona, 2006

ISBN 13: 978-1-59152-034-4
ISBN 10: 1-59152-034-7

Tucson Memories is published by the Arizona Daily Star 2006

Book design: Farcountry Press

Cover Illustration by Dave Castelan: Arizona Inn, early 1930s.

Library of Congress information:

Henry, Bonnie. 1945-
Tucson Memories / by Bonnie Henry : foreword Bruce J. Dinges
p. Cm.
Includes index.
ISBN 13: 978-1-59152-034-4
ISBN 10: 1-59152-034-7

1. Tucson (Ariz.)-History. I. Title.

Acknowledgments

As Tucson hurtles toward 1 million souls, it behooves us to slow down from time to time and reflect on how we were not so very long ago.

Thanks to all of you who helped me in this pursuit — telling your tales of car races and marathon dances, amusement parks and plane crashes, boxing matches and dude ranches.

Decades later, the stories still resonate — in our memories and in our hearts.

To all who shared your stories with us over the years — those still with us and those who've passed on — a heartfelt thanks. This goes out tenfold to Roy P. Drachman, who died in 2002.

Thanks also to all those who worked so hard to bring this book to light, including Star Publisher & Editor John M. Humenik, who barely six months in Tucson had the confidence in this project to make it a reality; Star reader advocate Debbie Kornmiller, who edited the stories and whipped the book into shape; Star visual team leader for photography Rick Wiley and his crew; Star librarian Elaine Raines; Star research assistant/photo Ermelinda Gutierrez; copy editor Mark Stewart; and the San Miguel High School interns, who typed about half of the stories in this book — stories created before the Star went to electronic archiving.

Thanks, as well, to those who staff the reference desks of the Arizona Historical Society and the University of Arizona Special Collections. Whether it was printed material or photographs, you were always ready to help.

As with my first book, "Another Tucson," a special thank you to Bobbie Jo Buel, the Star's executive editor. Without her support, neither book would have happened.

And finally, thanks to you, the readers, who love Tucson — past and present — as much as I do.

Foreword

I vividly recall my first view of Tucson. It was late June and at the end of a two-day drive from Houston. I was rolling into town to take a job at the University of Arizona. The air conditioning had conked out just this side of Fort Stockton. From I-10, the town was barely distinguishable from the dry landscape. I thought to myself, "OK, I'll give this five years." That was almost 30 years ago, and I am still here. In fact, I can't imagine being anywhere else.

The point is, we are almost all from somewhere else. When I arrived in 1978, Tucson was a modest city of not quite 300,000. Today, we are tickling the 1-million milestone. And we all crave, or should crave, a sense of belonging. We want what Bonnie Henry has.

The Old Pueblo is Bonnie's hometown — its history, and, especially its people, are her passions. For 20 years she has been leading a guided tour in the pages of the Arizona Daily Star, introducing us to our neighbors, bringing back memories of bygone days and commenting on the day-to-day foibles of life in our desert community. And she does it all with grace, charm and self-deprecating wit that makes firm friends and intimate confidants, even of people who have never met her. From Bonnie, we learn what it feels like to be a Tucsonan.

In 1991, the late Jim Officer and I met with Bonnie Henry and the Star editors to talk about gathering together some of Bonnie's columns in a book. That collection, titled "Another Tucson" and with a foreword by Jim Officer, appeared the following year and sold out almost immediately. Even then, we knew that someday we would need another collection of Bonnie's columns. Fifteen years of good reading later, that day has finally arrived.

"Tucson Memories" is vintage Bonnie Henry. Through Bonnie's sparkling eyes, we take in dances at the Del Rio Ballroom and enjoy ballgames at Hi Corbett Field, sample Dave Bloom and Son's menswear and Porter's western garb, relax at the Arizona Inn and celebrate UA victories at the Varsity Inn, meet legendary barber Johnny Gibson and remarkable teacher Maria Urquides, and rock to the music of Elvis Presley and Buddy Holly. Articles on Depression-era life in the Tucson Mountains and the day Kennedy died remind us of the impact of the outside world, while stories of the VA hospital, Fourth of July celebrations, the Desert Museum, Sabino Canyon and the Gem and Mineral Show explain the things that make us unique.

History is, after all, about stories; and stories are the threads of community. They bind us to one another and connect the present with the past. No one tells Tucson's stories better than Bonnie Henry. So, sink back into your easy chair, relax and enjoy.

Bruce J. Dinges
Arizona Historical Society

For my children,
Laura and Robert

TUCSON
Memories

Table of Contents

Let the Good Times Roll

Yvonne Pain-Jakimowich, 3, Shirley Pain-Webb, 2, Bryan Lance, 5, and his father Frank Lance, thrill at Kiddyland.

Who says there's nothing to do in Tucson? Not the folks who danced away the night at the Silver Slipper, took in a baseball game at Hi Corbett Field, or rode the roller coaster in a magical place called — what else? — Kiddyland.

LET THE GOOD TIMES ROLL
1

Gay Alley

Sabino Street was the official name of Tucson's red-light district.

Mae Palmer lay low that night.

Dubbed by the Arizona Daily Star as "The Queen of the Tucson Underworld," she kept her house of ill repute, otherwise known as No. 12, "as silent as the grave and as dark as the tomb."

John Law will sometimes do that to a person.

Dec. 13, 1907. Tucson's City Council and mayor order the town's chief of police to resuscitate a 4-year-old ordinance outlawing "any bawdy house or place of ill-fame or room for prostitution."

That evening, several enterprising Star reporters stroll through the entire Tenderloin district, dutifully checking the level of activity.

They are not disappointed.

"Still The Red Lights Gleam," proclaimed the next morning's paper, which went on to recount how "night cabs were doing a quiet but steady business. All through the night women were abroad in Gay Alley and McCormick Streets and visitors were admitted to the rooms on the row."

Noticeably absent from the scene, noted the Star, were any policemen.

Sabino Street was the official name for Tucson's red-light district, a two-block lane that ran between Ochoa and McCormick streets, Convent Street to the east, Meyer Street to the west.

But most called it Gay Alley — named not for its ambience, but for Tucson pioneer Mervin G. Gay.

As red-light districts went, it was relatively new. Up until the 1890s, Tucson's prostitutes conducted business on Maiden Lane, a three-block road that ran between Stone Avenue and Meyer Street, just north of Congress.

By the turn of the century, however, the "sporting district" — saloons, gambling halls and ladies of easy virtue — had moved south of Congress, slopping over into the streets surrounding Gay Alley.

Here, according to historian Dick Hall, as many as 250 women conducted business from "cribs," or rooms barely large enough to hold a double bed, table and chair.

This was their "office." During the day, the girls slept at the old Belmont, Red Front or Cosmopolitan hotels.

"Every race, including Orientals, was represented on the line," wrote Hall, who interviewed several old-time Tucsonans for his article, which appeared in the winter 1979 Journal of Arizona History:

"The girls, their faces heavily painted, sat or stood near the doors. Some wore bright kimonos or short dresses. They sat in chairs with their feet propped up on tables so that a passing customer could see their pink lingerie."

The going rate for a "good time": Anywhere from $1 to $3. Being a whore, however, "was not a romantic way to make a living," wrote Hall.

Every Friday, the women were checked for disease by the county doctor. Certificates signed by the doctor were posted by the door of each crib. Girls whose tests proved positive had to leave the alley.

More bureaucracy lay in wait at the south end of the alley, which joined McCormick Street. Here is where the Madam of Madams lived. To her fell the task of collecting the monthly $5 city license fee from each girl.

On the southeast corner of Ochoa and Gay Alley was No. 12 House, also known in Mae Palmer's time as the Palmer House. The large building housed a saloon and several bedrooms.

This was a high-class whorehouse, featuring not only a 10-cents-a-tune piano player, but also a stable of girls who fetched the top $3 price, plus tip.

Into this sporting district around 1910 strode Jesus Camacho, who for the next 33 years would serve with the Tucson police force.

"The Mayor of Meyer Street" they called this Tucson native, who patrolled by horseback the very streets where he had played as a boy: the area south of Congress Street between Church and Meyer.

Initially greeted with jeers, Camacho — who had kicked up his heels in the same saloons where he was now required to keep order — soon earned the respect of every pimp, gambler and trollop in his district, as well as the decent folk who also made their homes in the area.

"The criminal element had great respect for him," said Roy Drachman, who was born in 1906 in a home less than two blocks away from Gay Alley.

Drachman's route to school took him down McCormick Street, right past Gay Alley. "It was all row houses," said Drachman, who had to pass directly under the Madam of Madams house. "It was two-story. The madams would look down on the street."

When Drachman was 10, the family left the neighborhood. "Mother said we had to get out. The drunks were literally lying in the gutter."

Not long after, a campaign to rid the town of bootleggers and prostitutes was launched. Churches and women's clubs petitioned Tucson Mayor O.C. Parker to close the strip. To which Parker replied:

"There are more single men in Tucson than married men. Under the Police Department's supervision the alley is tightly controlled. As long as I am mayor, it will stay open."

However, when rampant prostitution cost Tucson consideration as a site for a military aviation camp, the mayor and council passed a 1918 ordinance that required all Tucson women to have a visible means of support.

Policemen fanned out through Gay Alley, telling the girls they had to clear out. Most did. Some set up shop in other parts of town, including at least one well-known madam who happily settled into Snob Hollow.

But within months, many were drifting back into their old familiar haunts along Gay Alley.

For the next 10 years or so, Gay Alley and the rest of the town existed side by side. An occasional raid would be launched. Fines would be paid. And business would continue as usual.

"The police recognized that this kind of thing was going to go on one way or the other," said Drachman.

In the 1920s, a blue ribbon committee headed up by a prominent University of Arizona faculty member came to the conclusion that no matter what action the City Council took, the world's oldest profession would, alas, continue to prosper right here in the Old Pueblo.

As a bow to respectability, however, a tall fence was erected at the entrance to Gay Alley during its final years. "You could walk around the fence; you just couldn't see through it," said Drachman.

By the '30s, several of the madams, grown prosperous through hard work and savvy investments, were contributing generously to Tucson's worthy causes.

But during the World War II years, town officials — with an eye to the huge influx of military personnel stationed in and around Tucson — began a crackdown on houses of prostitution, by then scattered all around town.

After the war, an organized prostitution ring tried to muscle its way into town. Bowing to the Red Scare then sweeping the country, the Tucson Police Department and the FBI responded by investigating possible links between organized prostitution and the Communist Party.

All through the '50s, raids were dutifully launched from time to time. Several occurred not far from the old red-light district where Mae Palmer and others of her ilk once plied their trade.

Today, the row of adobe cribs where women in pink lingerie once lounged by their windows is no more. Gone too is Gay Alley — obliterated, all of it, by urban renewal.

Ironically, much of it lies directly underneath yet another edifice dedicated to entertainment — the Tucson Convention Center.

LET THE
GOOD TIMES ROLL
2

Silver Slipper and Plantation

The Plantation was one of the first joints to take advantage of legalized liquor in the 1930s.

Hard times and temperance be damned. When it came to kicking up our heels in this town back in the '20s and '30s, Tucsonans had many a place in which to make merry. Until the inevitable fire or wrecking ball had its way, that is.

In the meantime, let the good times roll.

And roll they did for a time at the old Silver Slipper and Plantation nightclubs.

Located, according to old city directories, on "East Broadway two miles east of the city," the Silver Slipper came into existence with a bang. Literally.

Front page headline, the Arizona Daily Star, Oct. 14, 1928: "Shots Halt Merry Dance in New Hall."

The story goes on to detail how just after midnight, one George B. Echols "fired two shots into the body of J.L. Mills, killing him almost instantly."

Bad blood did it.

It seems Echols and Mrs. Mills were good friends, so much so that two months earlier each had testified in the other's divorce trial.

A smaller headline over the story tidily wrapped it all up: "Tragedy Follows on Heels of Triangle."

Luckily, Pima County Sheriff Jim McDonald was among the hundreds there on opening night at the Silver Slipper. He quickly took Echols — "smoking revolver" still in hand — into custody.

The shooting did little, if anything, to dim the allure of this nightspot. Neither did Prohibition.

"It was not legal to serve liquor, so people brought their own," said former patron Roy P. Drachman. The club, said Drachman, supplied the "setups," such as club soda, etc.

There was no secret knock at the door, no "Joe-sent-me" routine, said Drachman. "Anybody could go. It was a nice place. They could seat maybe 150 for dinner. There was a dance floor and a small combo. This was no dance hall."

Macel Brothers, who remembered going to the Silver Slipper as a young bride back in '31, agreed. "Believe it or not, I had four long evening gowns back then. And yes, I wore one of those gowns when I went to the Silver Slipper."

Swell though it may have been, the nightclub could have passed for a dance hall at least once. That was the night a fire broke out at the old westside dance hall next to the Clearwater Pool.

Inside, a massive marathon dance had been going on for about a week. When the fire broke out, about 15 or 20 couples were still on the dance floor.

No problem. The couples, still dancing, were transported by truck to the Silver Slipper.

Though he wasn't sure of the exact date, Drachman remembered the night the Silver Slipper burned down, sometime during the '30s. Just hours earlier, the University of Arizona boosters club known as the Towncats had partied at the place.

The last group of Towncats left the Silver Slipper about 3 a.m., said Drachman. Ninety minutes later, the place was in flames.

Reduced to ashes more than a half-century ago, the nightclub lives on today only in the guise of silver-hued metal slippers. Passed out to the ladies as souvenirs, the slippers may still rest in a few trunks and dresser drawers.

On April 7, 1933 — eight months before Prohibition's repeal in December of that year — beer and wine again became legal in 19 states of the Union, including Arizona.

It took a day to get here, but by 8 a.m. April 8, legal beer was again flowing into the parched throats of customers lined up at Steinfeld's lunch counter.

Days earlier, an anticipatory Star had already begun running beer ads, along with merchants' urgings to: "Order your case today."

Not long after, ads for "Tucson's most exclusive night club" began appearing in print as well. Known as the Plantation, the nightspot, read the ads, was "four miles out on Oracle Road — look for neon sign."

Featuring "singing, dancing, drinking" and a private dining room, the Plantation was run by a former convicted bootlegger, name of Bob Nardelli.

The place was one of a dozen nightspots recently opened up in large old homes on the outskirts of town, wrote Drachman in his book, "Memories," which recounted his personal recollections of Tucson.

As a "first generation of joints to take advantage of the recently legalized liquor," wrote Drachman, the Plantation "was probably the pick of a poor bunch."

The main house on this 10-acre northside parcel had been converted to a saloon and restaurant. There was also a beer garden, Drachman wrote, "where customers could sit outdoors until either the bugs or the heat drove them indoors."

Though the Plantation offered "buffet service at all hours," the food, said Drachman, "was purely coincidental."

After years of swilling home-brew or doing without, it was the beer, said Drachman, that drew 'em to the Plantation.

"People loved beer, but you couldn't get it during Prohibition. They'd make home-brew. If you held it up to the light, you could almost see through it. It was very foggy, lots of stuff in it. To get legal beer was quite a thing."

In time, said Drachman, the Plantation became more of a nightclub. Even the food improved.

Still, just when you thought a veneer of respectability had settled down over the place, along would come some little news item, such as this disavowal from Nardelli in the Aug. 3, 1937, Star:

"There is no gambling at the Plantation now, unless you count a couple of slot machines in which slugs are played."

Former patron Opha Probasco remembered it otherwise. "There were rumors gambling was going on in the back room, and there were slot machines out in front. No slugs. They used real coins."

Call it the wages of sin, call it World War II. For whatever reason, by the early '40s, the Plantation had ceased to exist — at least as a nightclub.

The former home-turned-saloon became home once more, this time to apartment dwellers. In the years to come it would bear a collection of names alluding to its past, ranging from "The Old Plantation" to "Plantation Motor Court."

One of its later owners during the '60s was former Tucson Mayor Lew Davis, who in turn sold the property to a development company.

In July of '71, it all came tumbling down to make way for a new shopping center on the northeast corner of Oracle and Roger roads.

Next time you're driving by the spot, now anchored by Target, give a little nod to what was once "Tucson's most exclusive nightclub" — and beer garden. Cheers.

LET THE
GOOD TIMES ROLL
3

The World Series before radio

As you pop a cool one, settle back into that easy chair and get ready to watch this year's World Series, give thanks that it's not 1924.

Oh sure, the Giants' Frankie Frisch and the old Washington Senators' Walter Johnson were in there battling. Trouble was, there was no way fans here in Tucson could hear, let alone see, the crack of a bat.

Television, after all, was decades away. As for radio, that was something listeners had to stay up way past midnight to hear.

"You couldn't get transmission over the hot desert floor," said Randall Legler, a Tucsonan since 1914. "So the hams would stay up late, to listen to Phoenix or Los Angeles."

That's right, sports fans. Commercial radio didn't set up shop here until 1926, when KGAR (later KTUC) began transmitting from its studio at 30 S. Stone Ave.

Though the station, which was affiliated with the Tucson Citizen, did broadcast a play-by-play account of the 1926 World Series, it would take some time before a majority of Tucson households were listening to the games on their very own radios.

In the meantime, there was always the megaphone — and the news wires — clacking away down at the local newspaper office.

"The machine would relay the play-by-play, and some guy would sit in the window with a megaphone and yell to the crowd down below what was happening," remembered longtime Tucsonan Roy P. Drachman.

"Every play will be megaphoned to you in the Citizen bleachers by a leather-lunged human radio broadcaster," trumpeted the Citizen in its Oct. 2, 1922, issue.

The Arizona Daily Star was more circumspect. From a small notice in its Oct. 4, 1924, issue: "The Associated Press wire opens at 11:30. The game starts at noon, Mountain Time. So pick a soft place in the pavement and make ready."

"Soft place" in the vacant lot was the way Legler remembered it. For by 1924, the Citizen had considerably upgraded its World Series presentation.

Then in high school and working as a carrier for the Citizen, Legler would join the crowds at World Series time milling about in back of the old Citizen building at Stone Avenue and Jackson Street.

The object of the crowd's attention: a large wooden billboard propped up against a Citizen second-story newsroom window. On the side of the billboard facing the crowd was the outline of a baseball diamond, lit up electrically.

"All nine positions had a light; home plate had two lights — one for the batter, one for the catcher," said Legler. As the play-by-play came in on the wire, says Legler, someone would hand the plays out the window "to the fellows working the lights behind the panel."

Batter up. "The pitcher's light would come on. Then the batter's light. If the batter missed, then the catcher's light would come on," said Legler. A box score took care of showing runs, strikes, balls and errors.

"If the batter got a hit, say, to shortstop, the shortstop's light would go on," said Legler. After that, it was up to the crowd to follow the blinking — or unblinking — lights. For only the bases where runners were declared out lit up on the board, said Legler.

There was no sound — save for ol' "leather lungs" and his megaphone — and only one special effect. "There was a home-run light," said Legler. "When it went on, everybody would holler and cheer."

The crowd, which he estimated at around 300, was a rather fluid one. "Some die-hards would stay for the whole thing, but most of the crowd came and went," said Legler. "Maybe somebody would spend a lunch hour there."

Bring your own brown bag. "No, nobody sold hot dogs or soda pop," said Legler, though he did remember vendors hawking snow cones.

Meanwhile, the Star was struggling to offer its own version of up-to-the-minute coverage. In 1922, it hosted a "Star Baseball Party" at the old Opera House movie theater, then owned by Drachman's father, Emmanuel.

"Every fan in Tucson who wants lightning wire returns on the game is going to be at the Opera House this morning, where they can have comfortable seats while the returns are coming in," trumpeted a Star ad.

By 1925, the Star was no longer offering this service. But this time it had found something guaranteed to keep sports fans glued to the sidewalk in front of its offices.

"Never before seen in Tucson," the Playograph, as it was called, also offered up a baseball diamond on a large wooden sign. Unlike its electrical cousin, however, this apparatus was "entirely mechanical in construction."

As described in a 1925 Star article, the Playograph featured a regulation league-size ball "invisibly suspended in front of the playing field and as the ball is pitched, batted or fielded in the actual game, the ball on the Playograph travels to all parts of the playing field."

As for the runners, their progress was shown around the diamond via a ribbon of white metal, which ran underneath footprint cutouts.

And all of it operated by — what else — someone standing at the rear of the machine. "The Associated Press has installed special wires direct from the ballparks to the operator back of the Playograph, ensuring speed and accuracy," the Star assured its readers.

These mechanical marvels, by the way, were the rage everywhere for a time, including at New York City's Times Square.

Tucson's Playograph stood for only one World Series in front of the old Star building on West Congress Street. The following year it moved down the street to the Opera House, where it would make eight annual appearances.

"Every fan in the city is welcome to bring his wife, his cigar and the kids and watch every game," touted the Star. Admission was free. And no, the Opera House didn't make it up in refreshments, for none was served.

"My dad was a baseball nut," said Drachman. Football too, it would appear. "We used to do the same thing for the Wildcat football games. We had a big board painted green that looked like a football field."

1933 was the last year the Playograph appeared at the Opera House. The following year it moved across the street to another Drachman-owned movie house, the old Rialto Theatre.

There, Tucson baseball fans "saw" Dizzy Dean pitch the St. Louis Cardinals to a world championship over the Detroit Tigers.

By then, fans could also "hear" the game via an announcer, who described each play as it appeared on the Playograph.

Or fans could listen in to KVOA, the town's second radio station, broadcasting the play-by-play results as they came in on the Star's news wire.

The Playograph's appearance at the Rialto only lasted one year. When the Detroit Tigers and Chicago Cubs squared off for the 1935 World Series, no mention was made of the apparatus — at least in the Star.

There was, however, a small notice advising readers that a "play-by-play report of the World Series" would be broadcast by KVOA, both over the air and through amplifiers set up on Congress Street.

The die, it would appear, had been cast, as more and more Tucsonans relied on radio coverage of the games.

Randall Legler remembered his family's first radio — an Atwater Kent — bought back in the late 1920s. He also harbored fond memories of listening to baseball games on the radio, particularly after Dizzy Dean took to the airwaves.

In the days of televised sports saturation, however, Legler switched allegiances. "I watch more basketball and football," he said. "I don't watch that much baseball anymore."

LET THE
GOOD TIMES ROLL
4

Del Rio Ballroom

Celebration of Patricia Gutierrez's Jan. 10, 1976, baptism held at Del Rio Ballroom.

Speedway was two-lane and the freeway non-existent the year Mike Hernandez built his ballroom.

"Where the freeway is now was all greasewood," said Hernandez, who close to 60 years ago put up a rambling block building where two generations would romp and stomp the night away.

Known first as El Victoria and later as Del Rio, the blue ballroom at the corner where Speedway meets Interstate 10 shuddered its last cumbia in the mid-1990s.

"The state wants the building for right of way for freeway construction," said Hernandez at the time. His last booking — a quinceañera — was set for Saturday night, July 30, 1994.

After that, it was close the place down, strip it of all its fixtures and wait for the wrecking ball.

Asked how he felt about that, Hernandez said with a shrug: "I don't feel good or bad. I'm old now. I'm glad to get rid of it."

Ah, but he was singing another tune back in 1948. That was the year this truck driver by trade made an abrupt career change.

"I wanted to have a ballroom," he said without elaboration.

After plunking down $4,000 on four adjoining vacant lots, he found a general contractor who would give him what he wanted:

A large box of a building capable of holding 400 folks. Entrance and bar to the south, bandstand to the north, wooden dance floor in the middle, tables and chairs all around.

"I bought the tables and chairs from Reuben Gold's," said Hernandez, who soon ensconced either himself or his brother, Jesus, behind the bar.

Opening night came in the waning days of '48. Admission was negligible.

"It was 10 cents a dance, or they could buy a full ticket for $2," said Victoria Hernandez, Mike's wife, and early namesake of the ballroom.

As for why the place wasn't correctly named La Victoria, Mike explained: "Well, it was a bar. It had to be male."

Beer on opening night was 70 cents a pitcher, the band was Greg Estrada's six-piece combo and the dancers were decidedly formal.

"In the early days, they dressed up," said Victoria. "Not just for special occasions, but for any dance."

Still, it was a struggle at first getting 'em in the door. Enter the gimmick.

"One time we announced on the radio that a baby was going to be born, its mother didn't want it, and so we were going to raffle it off," said Victoria.

"We advertised this for a month. On the day of the raffle, I went to the store, bought booties and a blanket. When they were calling off the raffle numbers, I came onto the floor with the blanket and here came this bunch of cops."

The "baby" turned out to be a piglet. "It got loose and was running all over the floor and people were trying to catch it," said Mike.

Friday and Saturday nights the joint was jumping to live music. "Nobody wants to pay money to dance to a jukebox," said Mike.

Other days it was the working crowd that showed up. "People would come in after work, buy a bottle of beer or two."

For a brief time in the late '50s, Mike leased the place out to others. That's when the name change occurred — which was just fine with Victoria. "Gosh, I didn't want my name to go up there in the first place," she said.

Not that she wasn't down there in the flesh. "I worked like a maniac," she said. "Selling tickets on Saturday nights, then on Sunday mornings making snacks for the tardeadas" — afternoon tea dances.

So did they ever have to contend with those who preferred fancy fisticuffs to footwork? "Did we ever!" Victoria answered.

As a result, said Mike, "I kept six cops there — three inside, three outside."

More often than not, however, it was romance that kept this ballroom filled, weekend after weekend.

"I'm getting the children of the people who first had their wedding receptions here. Now their kids are getting married and having their parties here, too," said Mike at the time, pointing to a makeshift arch at one corner of the dance floor. "The people decorate it, and that's where the bride and groom always stand."

When Interstate 10 went in, said Mike, "I had 40 customers who wanted to buy the place. But I didn't want to sell. I was doing all right."

Sometime in the '60s, however, he did quit holding dances for the general public, preferring instead to rent the place out for everything from reunions to quinceañeras, benefits to anniversaries.

"They pay for the hall, arrange for the band and supply their own food," said Mike. He, however, continued to set 'em up from behind the bar.

It was also sometime in the '60s, he says, when an electrical short started a pre-dawn fire near the front of the building. "By the time we got down there, the firemen had it out," said Mike. Still, a new ceiling was in order.

Other changes were also reshaping the place. When Speedway was widened, it bit off a few feet from the front of the ballroom. "That's when we moved the bar to the west of the building," said Mike.

Ceaseless shuffling left the hardwood floor worn and creaky. As for the somewhat mysterious color of the bandstand carpeting where countless combos blared and strummed: "It used to be red," Mike said with a laugh.

Still, he took quiet pride in the paintings that lined all four walls of the rooms — all landscapes, all done in fluorescent colors, all his.

Most were painted right on the block, which means they would come tumbling down along with the walls.

The fixtures, however, were another matter. "I've sold it all to one woman, everything from the toilets to the ballroom light," said Mike.

"Yes, I've bought it all," said Theresa Tellez, owner of a southside party supply store. She, along with a silent partner, hoped to open another ballroom on the city's southside before the year was done.

Like many in town, Tellez was feeling a sense of personal loss over the impending demise of Del Rio.

"I had my wedding reception there," she said.

LET THE
GOOD TIMES ROLL
5

New Year's Eve with Wayne Webb

Wayne Webb leads his orchestra during a holiday dance in the early '50s.

He was never home on New Year's Eve. He was with you.

If you are of a certain age, you remember swaying to the rhythms of the Wayne Webb Orchestra.

For years, the trombonist and his orchestra — including four younger brothers — played everywhere from Wetmore's to the Blue Moon to a gaggle of society balls.

Earlier, he toured with such big band leaders as Guy Lombardo and Horace Heidt.

When he died in October 2000 at 92, his death hardly caused a ripple here.

Then again, he'd put down his trombone almost two decades earlier.

Still, his silky notes live on in the tapes his family plays — and in the memories of countless students he taught over the years.

Francis Wayne Webb was born on Christmas Eve 1907 in the state of Chihuahua, Mexico.

His parents were part of a Mormon settlement. "They were all friendly with Pancho Villa," said Monty Webb, Wayne's youngest brother.

Yet when Wayne was 2 years old, the family came to Tucson just ahead of la revolución.

They settled into the Mormon settlement of Binghampton, near Dodge Boulevard and the Rillito River.

Young Wayne, second-oldest of 11 children, taught himself how to play the horn, much as his own father had done.

Teachers at Davidson Elementary pitched in. But his real education came under Tucson High School music teacher W.A. Sewell.

After high school, he attended Brigham Young University for a year, as well as doing a summer stint at a music conservatory in Chicago.

In 1928, he married Josephine McGee in Salt Lake City.

The newlyweds started out married life in a cabin near the mountains.

"There was a nightclub nearby, and Dad became part of the band," said daughter Deanna Sims.

Soon, Wayne Webb was traveling with various bands.

"As he got farther and farther east, he played with bigger and bigger bands," said son Lanny Webb.

Wayne's first big band was Guy Lombardo's. "They played the Waldorf-Astoria," said Monty.

"I remember staying at hotels and apartments. My mother drove us across the country," said Sims.

While with Horace Heidt, Wayne made the 1941 flick "Pot O' Gold," starring Jimmy Stewart — a film Stewart later dismissed as his worst ever.

Never mind. The family proudly showed off an old studio shot of Wayne and Stewart — and the ever-present trombone.

Drafted, then classified 4-F, Wayne spent part of World War II in Hollywood, playing with the house band for Radio KHJ.

After the war, he and Josephine, who died in 1999, returned to Tucson for good.

One of his first gigs: the old Wetmore ballroom.

"We had a 15- or 16-piece band," said Monty. "But after everyone was paid, there was not money to pay ourselves."

So all five brothers — Wayne, Merle, Lloyd, Carlyle and Monty — enrolled at the University of Arizona.

All graduated and became educators, most in music.

"My father had a job laying tile, he played in bands at night, raised a family and graduated in three years with distinction," said Sims.

For the next 21 years, Wayne taught music in Tombstone, Tucson and Sahuarita schools before retiring in 1973.

In the early 1980s he suffered a succession of little strokes, said Sims — enough to put the trombone down for good.

Nonetheless, other Webbs would continue to toot their horns around town.

LET THE
GOOD TIMES ROLL
6

Tucson Rink

More than a half-century since anyone skated here, the maple floors were still visible — the ones Sue Suedkamp's family put in back in the '30s.

"The building was already there; we remodeled it," said Suedkamp, whose family once owned the old Tucson Rink at 1128 E. Sixth St.

Gladys Edwards, Ann Fee, Helen Nelson and Barbara McGee in '41 at the rink.

Its run was short — late '30s to mid-'40s — but it certainly made a memory mark on those who wheeled through here.

"They had four pillars there in the middle of the rink, with a shiny ball hanging from the ceiling," said Ann Fee. "If you wanted to do something special, you'd go and spin under the ball."

The rink began as an alternative to unemployment.

"Nobody had any work here," said Suedkamp, whose family settled in Tucson in about 1938. But her brother Jack "Pete" Berning had a dad willing to help start the rink.

"Dad said to my brother, 'How about trying this?' I was one happy teen-ager."

Open every day but Monday, the rink ran from 2 to 5 p.m. and again from 7:30 to 10:30. "My mother had supper promptly," said Suedkamp.

The cost to skate was 35 cents, with a free skate after 10 punches on your card.

In the beginning, most folks rented skates that were clamped to the soles of their shoes.

"I tightened up the clamps and fixed the ankle straps," said Travis White, who served both as skate boy and later floor manager at the rink.

Floor manager was better. "You wore a whistle and a cap," said White. His duties included slowing down the fast skaters and picking up the beginners.

He, like all the good skaters, could skate backward.

Wardrobe was also important. "You measured your confidence by what you were wearing," said Suedkamp, who favored short, flouncy skirts.

Music — organ, naturally — came from old 78 records.

"The automatic changer was always acting up," said Suedkamp, who did everything from cashiering to checking in coats and purses.

Her parents were also at the rink on a regular basis, serving as chaperons.

"It was an entirely safe world," said Fee, who used to work as an usherette at the old Rialto. "I rode my bike home at midnight and never felt unsafe."

Fellows from Davis-Monthan showed up at the rink on a regular basis. So did the kids from nearby Mansfeld Junior High.

That's where Fee was when she first started hitting the rink after school was done.

When she was 15, she hooked up with skating partner Gordon Nelson, 19 at the time.

Together, the two won the trophy for Most Graceful Dancers. "I'd go skating two or three nights a week after work," said Nelson.

He, too, served as floor manager from time to time. "We also had hockey games there after they closed the rink at 10:30."

No helmets, no face protection. "We put sponges on our knees and elbows."

After Fee graduated from Tucson High in 1943, she went on to college out of town.

Meanwhile, Nelson and White went off to war. So did Pete Berning.

Nelson and White came home from the war. Berning didn't. He was declared missing in action in 1945.

For a time, the rink limped along. "My dad helped; I helped," said Suedkamp. But in 1946, the family lost the lease.

For years, Eagle Baking Co. occupied the spot. Later on, Sunrise Silkscreen would hold the honor.

Fond memories aside, Suedkamp could point to at least one other long-lasting benefit from working at a roller rink:

"The only time in my life I ever impressed my teen-agers was when I showed I could still skate backwards."

LET THE
GOOD TIMES ROLL
7

Kiddyland

Mickey Mouse was only a cartoon and Anaheim was still an orange grove the night all our dreams came true.

The night Kiddyland opened.

A Ferris wheel, roller coaster, choo-choo train, merry-go-round, boats, airplanes, cars, ponies, and the tallest ice cream in town — slab after slab of it piled into a cone.

What more could a kid want in a town without TV?

Even Hizzoner got into the act. Oct. 7, 1949: Mayor E.T. "Happy" Houston officially opens Kiddyland by taking controls of the five-car train, chugging around the park. Hundreds stand in lines 20 deep for a chance at the rides, according to the next day's press accounts.

Kiddyland was a Tucson child's dream come true in the '50s.

"The weather was good, there was a hell of a crowd and everyone was happy. That's what I remember," said Jerrold Cohen, who was all of 5 years old at the time.

It was Cohen's parents, Sam and Ruth Cohen, who brought forth Kiddyland on a plot of bare land "way out" on Speedway — where the pavement gave way just east of Alvernon.

Those of us who spent many a happy moment with our behinds planted in one of Sam Cohen's rides owe it all to the fact that Howdy Doody had yet to come to the Old Pueblo.

"There was no television in Tucson, so he decided to open a kiddyland," said Jerrold, whose father had sold television sets back in the family's hometown of Chicago.

Illness brought the family to Tucson.

"My father had cancer, but he didn't know it. It looked like arthritis," said Jerrold. "Someone suggested Tucson."

Construction began in early '49 on 2½ acres, leased. "My father could have bought the land for $37,000," said Jerrold.

Neighbors included Soporito's market across the street, a lumberyard and a gas station. Jerrold also remembered Maple Leaf Furniture Co. "Their advertisements used to say, 'Right across the street from Kiddyland.' "

A landmark it was. "I used to dread the first day of school," said Jerrold. "We all had to get up and tell about ourselves. When I would say that my parents owned Kiddyland, the kids would get so excited. Sometimes the teachers would, too."

Built for $100,000, Kiddyland was open every afternoon but Mondays during school, longer hours during summer. "We'd stay open until the last customer left," remembered Stephen Cohen, Jerrold's older brother.

Rides were 9 cents apiece, 12 for a dollar. What were your favorites? Remember the planes on chains? Remember the boat rides — and fighting with your brother over who got to clang the bell?

How about the Ferris wheel? Remember how scary it was to stop at the top? You'd sit very still, while the machinery quivered and creaked and all of Kiddyland — kids, parents, rides — roiled beneath your feet.

Want a swell birthday? Only Kiddyland would do. "We had a special place for them to have cake and favors," said Jerrold. Twice a year the whole park had other parties: an October anniversary celebration, and a free party in December for underprivileged children.

Three years after he came to Tucson seeking a cure, Sam Cohen was dead of cancer. Kiddyland continued. Young Jerrold joined his older brother at the park, taking tickets, selling refreshments, and, when he got older, operating the rides.

A man who lived a block away took care of maintenance. So, on occasion, did whoever else was handy. "The train engine did two loops around the park," said Jerrold. "The cars were always jumping the track. Once in a while the engine did, too. We'd just get a bunch of people and put them back on the track."

In 1958, Ruth Cohen sold the business. "She just got tired," said Jerrold. "It got to be a headache." The long reach of the television antenna had also begun to cast a shadow over the little amusement park. "The kids — and their parents — were all staying at home to watch TV."

Kiddyland continued to operate for a few more years, then closed for good, its rides dismantled and hauled away. For years, the land stood vacant. Now commerce stands on the site. You want thrills these days, try the traffic on Speedway.

"A lot of people lost money under the merry-go-round," remembered Jerrold. "I used to say that when they closed the place down, I wanted to go back there with a metal detector. But I never did."

Never mind. For some of us, the coin of memory still burns bright. Of dancing pink ponies and train trips down a clackety track — to that place of childish dreams.

LET THE
GOOD TIMES ROLL
8

Beau Brummell Club

Duke Shaw, one of the founders of the Beau Brummell Club, stands in the back row, third from right.

Thousands rumble by it every day, a nondescript building near the northeast corner of Main Avenue and Speedway.

Few know its history, or the fact that it was once owned by the man who started up the Beau Brummell Club, an exclusive men's club for Tucson's prominent blacks.

The man was Duke Shaw and the building was Duke's Drive-Inn, later a gathering place for the club he and others started back in 1936.

"He was the type of person who wanted something better for the black man," said Shaw's daughter, Gail Shaw.

So exclusive was the membership, then held to 15, that potential members' wives were also scrutinized.

"Because I was a bachelor, they kept me out for a while," said attorney Rubin Salter, a member since the mid-'60s.

Besides professionals, the club also had a few members in service — as in butlers.

"Having been around rich and educated people, they were also leaders in the social life," said Salter.

For a time, he added, dinner parties were held in each other's homes on Wednesday nights. "That was the maids' and butlers' nights off," said Salter.

The club also held an annual formal dance at the old Blue Moon ballroom.

"I'm told it was the best between St. Louis and San Francisco," said Salter. "It was something to get an invitation to that ball."

Then there were the family picnics, also held once a year, said Gail Shaw. "We'd go to Mount Lemmon or Sabino Canyon, have midnight cookouts."

Duke Shaw, besides being a Beau Brummell, was also something of an entrepreneur, owning a dry-cleaning plant as well as the drive-in.

"We would eat there all the time. You could sit in your car and also at the counter. It also had a number of booths," said patron Cress Lander.

The drive-in was built around 1941. A few years later, Shaw built a 10-unit motel just to the south, named for his wife, Anne.

"The main reason my father chose to do that was entertainers would come here. They couldn't stay where they were entertaining," said Gail Shaw.

With the vestiges of Jim Crow still hanging on, Beau Brummell members also hosted other blacks, including members of the Cleveland Indians, in town for spring training, in their homes, said Salter.

In a little booth between the drive-in and the motel, a black disc jockey would spin records broadcast on radio, said Salter.

In 1954, the drive-in was expanded and the Beau

Brummell Club moved into a portion of the building.

Beau Brummell member Al Fowler leased the drive-in after Duke Shaw suffered a stroke in the early '60s, said Gail Shaw.

Meanwhile, the motel limped along until 1970, a victim of the interstate.

"Main Avenue used to be like the freeway. When I-10 went in, we went broke," said Gail Shaw.

Al Fowler also shut down the drive-in in the 1970s, with the Beau Brummell Club taking over the entire facility.

The club, which at press time had 18 members, still holds a dance every year, said Salter. It also sponsors an annual charity golf tournament known as the Ghetto Open. Some 160 turned out in 2005, he noted.

In early 2006, the motel was leveled, with plans to develop the entire block, said Salter, adding that someday the club will have to move.

In the meantime, members continued to meet at the old Duke's Drive-Inn — to reminisce and perhaps lift a glass to what once was.

"This is a history we want people to know about," said Salter.

LET THE
GOOD TIMES ROLL
9

Hi Corbett Field

Crowds have been filling the bleachers at Hi Corbett Field for three-quarters of a century.

Steinfeld's was selling a couch and two chairs for $145, and a new home in the Sam Hughes neighborhood would set you back $4,800 on April 1, 1928.

Meanwhile, those who cared less for real estate speculation and more for the crack of the bat could be found in the bleachers of Tucson Municipal Park.

There, opening day would find Johnny Kellner "hurling airtight baseball" for the Five Points nine, pitching a perfect game to shut out the Sunshiners 4-0.

What a swell time must have been had by all — well, except perhaps by the Sunshiners.

Two weeks later, same field, the Tucson Cowboys would trounce the House of David ballclub, beating the bearded "Davidites" 6-1.

It all began in May of 1927, when voters approved a bond election that allocated $35,000 for a municipal baseball park and athletic field in a place we now call Hi Corbett Field.

Ted Williams played spring ball here. So did Bob Feller, Satchel Paige and Willie Mays, here in the old ball field in the heart of Reid Park.

More recently, the Rockies moved their spring training to Hi Corbett in 1993, a year after the Cleveland Indians left for Florida following 46 springs in Tucson.

Baseball in this burg, however, goes way past the Tribe.

Old newspaper accounts dredge up games played as early as 1885, when the Tucson Nine took on the soldiers from Fort Lowell on a "rock-strewn vacant lot" downtown.

Equipment: one ball, one bat. Catcher's masks came later. Kind of. The first were fencer's masks, mistakenly ordered. They used 'em anyway.

By the early 1900s, baseball teams were swatting the ball over at Elysian Grove, about where Carrillo Intermediate Magnet School now stands.

The owner of the Grove and manager of the team was Manny Drachman, whose son, the late Roy Drachman, would get the name of Randolph Municipal Ball Field, as it was by then called, changed to Hi Corbett Field in 1951.

A ninth-generation Tucsonan, Corbett brought major-league spring training to town.

Ruth Corbett Cross, daughter of Hi Corbett, remembered going to the games with her dad when raw desert still surrounded the field.

"There wasn't even a wall," said Cross. "A home run was when you couldn't see the ball outside the lights."

She was also there when the Cleveland Indians came to town in 1947. "It was very exciting," she said. "The Cleveland newspaper reporters were in the press box, which was a long table with four or five chairs."

When the park was renamed for her father in 1951, Cross said, "He was so proud. He had tears in his eyes."

Plenty of minor-league teams also grunted and scratched and spit — and, oh, yeah — played ball here. Among them, the aforementioned Cowboys.

But in 1958, the Cowboys folded, and baseball was no more until 1969, when the Tucson Toros came to town.

In 1998, the Toros, renamed the Tucson Sidewinders, moved to Tucson Electric Park as the Triple-A affiliate of the Arizona Diamondbacks.

So ended minor-league play at Hi Corbett Field, although other endeavors, such as the Arizona Heat women's pro softball team, would continue to crack the bat here during the summer.

LET THE
GOOD TIMES ROLL
10

Louis Leon

Mambo, samba, cha-cha-cha.

If you know the difference, odds are your hips and toes once swiveled and swept to the rhythms of Louis Leon and His Orchestra.

"I played every society dance in town except the Angel Ball," said Leon, who in later years would make only rare appearances as a bandleader.

But for close to 40 years, he and his big-band orchestra were a fixture at just about every ball in town — ranging from the debs to the firefighters.

Jewish receptions, Mexican weddings, symphony cotillions, NAACP gatherings, the Highway Patrolmen's Ball — no matter the crowd, Leon got them up on their feet.

Louis Leon, front, right, and his orchestra kept 'em dancing for more than 40 years.

We're talking such swell places as the Pioneer and El Conquistador (both the old and the new).

We're also talking Twistathons at the old Congress Street Sports Center, as well as all-night gigs at mining towns sprinkled from Ajo to Morenci.

"We'd play the mining towns on Sundays and get home just long enough to change clothes before going to work," said, Leon, who retired as head of Pima County's revenue collections department.

A fourth-generation Tucsonan, Leon was born at his grandfather's ranch, where El Rio Golf Course now rambles along West Speedway.

Home, however, was his parents' ranch farther north, where the Breakers Family Water Park would eventually surface.

"It was all ranches and cotton farms out there," said Leon, who grew up one of seven children born to Antonia and Luis Leon.

"Everybody played music in the family," said Leon. "Mother and Dad played the guitar, and we'd have gatherings and big all-day celebrations."

But it was violin that young Louis would learn, at his father's insistence. "That's a mistake parents make — having their kids play their favorite instrument. My dad's was the violin."

So every Saturday, he and his parents would dutifully motor to town — they to shop, he to drag bow across strings. "I took lessons for three years," said Leon. "Then the teacher died."

Not long after his 1941 graduation from high school, Leon wound up in an Army uniform.

After the war, he worked in Mexico as a United States agricultural inspector for a few years. In 1953, he hired on at the county.

Meanwhile, this still-aspiring musician had taken up tickling the ivories — and playing with a few bands around town.

They in turn inadvertently inspired him to start his own group. "Some of them were awful, and so sloppy," said Leon. "They'd show up wearing T-shirts."

Not Leon, whose first shirt as leader of his own band was a ruffled affair made by Gloria, his wife of less than a year.

Conjunto Bahia was the name of that first band, a six-piece combo that could swell to 13, depending on the gig.

Before long, the group had caught the eye of Jim Sfarnas, owner of a popular Miracle Mile supper club, the Saddle & Sirloin.

"He saw us playing somewhere and said, 'Louis, I want to hire your band for every night.' I said, 'Jimmy, I can't. I work every day, plus we have other engagements.' "

Sfarnas did snare them for a month, however, playing everything from fox trots to bunny hops, tangos to polkas.

Little by little, this band was expanding numbers as well as repertoire. "The biggest band under my name had 20 members," said Leon, who clearly relished the big-band sounds.

By the mid-'60s, Conjunto Bahia had evolved into Louis Leon and His Orchestra.

Some were regulars in the band; others only worked from time to time, depending on the gig.

Albuquerque to Phoenix to Nogales — both sides of the border — this band would play. Then there was that memorable night in Casa Grande.

"We were going to play at the gym in Casa Grande," said Leon. "I had a car pulling a trailer, with a tarp to cover the instruments. I was going kinda fast. When we got there and got ready to set up, we discovered that everything had blown out except for one trumpet.

"We went down to the sheriff's office and told him what had happened. He opened up the music department of the school and got us some instruments. Then we went down to a music store and got some more instruments.

"Talk about weird sounds. I kept making announcements during the dance, apologizing."

The next day, the band organized a search party. "We were going up and down, picking up instruments from the side of the road."

Then the local media picked up on the story. Little by little, people started returning still more instruments, lost along the side of the road.

"One day I was at my job at the county and this guy called asking for 'Lee-on.' He said, 'My wife and I were driving down the road and I said, "Honey, I could swear that was a bull fiddle at the side of the road." She didn't believe me. So we turned around and sure as heck, there was this bull fiddle.' "

Leon got his bull fiddle back, along with every other instrument lost during that ill-fated ride. "The last instrument was a trumpet some kid at Marana found. And do you know, not one person would take any money from us as a reward."

On Dec. 19, 1970, Leon and his band were playing at the Pioneer Hotel to a packed ballroom filled with Hughes Aircraft employees. Around midnight, Leon smelled smoke.

"We had wires all over the stage. I told the guys to check their wires." Not long after, the Pioneer's catering manager came up to Leon at the piano. "He said: 'Louis, get 'em the hell out of here. The place is on fire.' "

Leon stopped the band, then made his announcement to the curious crowd on the floor. "I asked them to please evacuate the building as soon as possible." Never was the word "fire" mentioned.

Within three minutes, the ballroom was cleared. "By the time we got to my station wagon, the fire engines were coming."

From Glenn Miller to Elvis to the Beatles, this band played 'em all. "Winchester Cathedral," said Leon with a sigh. "They used to ask for that all the time." The most-requested song of all time? "In the Mood."

"That will never die," said Leon.

LET THE
GOOD TIMES ROLL
11

Tucson Boys Chorus

Eduardo Caso, right, directed the Tucson Boys Chorus from 1939 until he died in 1965.

Thank heavens boys minded their mothers back in 1939. Otherwise, Tucson — and the rest of the world — might never have heard what would later come out of that collective mouth we all know as the Tucson Boys Chorus.

It began with one man — and one boy. The man was Eduardo Caso, English-born tenor and music teacher who moved to Tucson in 1937 to recuperate from tuberculosis.

The boy was Jim Pfersdorf, who sang in the Mansfeld Junior High School Chorus.

Oh yes. There's a woman in this story, too: Pfersdorf's mother, Helen, a technician at the old Tucson X-Ray Laboratory. It was there that she met Caso.

"He commented to her how he would like to start a boys chorus," said Pfersdorf. "I came home one day and there he was talking to my mother and dad. Mother said, 'I want you to take singing lessons.'

"Well, you know how kids are. I would have rather been outside playing. But I said I would do it."

Twice a week, Pfersdorf obediently trudged over to Caso's apartment for voice lessons. Two other boys — Pfersdorf thinks their mothers may have known his mother — soon joined in the lessons.

By December, the group had grown to eight, enough for a Christmas Eve debut at First Congregational Church. Ten high-pitched voices filled the air that night — eight boys and two girls. It would be the first and last time girls would ever sing as part of the Tucson Boys Chorus.

Within six weeks, the group had grown to 30. Dressed in Levi's and white shirts, they sang for free at women's clubs, hospitals and the like. They also filled slack airtime on KVOA Radio, the group's first sponsor.

In 1941, the chorus made its first "tour" — all the way to Phoenix. The following year, it appeared with Ginger Rogers at a war bond concert held in the University of Arizona auditorium.

Heady stuff back then. But always there was the wooden paddle, the one Caso used to keep young egos in check. "He was a strict disciplinarian," remembered Pfersdorf. "My mother liked that."

Each passing year brought new recognition: Christmas Eve, 1944: a coast-to-coast radio broadcast from Mission San Xavier del Bac. December

1947: an extensive tour through Southern California, including an appearance with comic Jimmy Durante. August 1950: Four performances at the Chicago Fair.

In 1951, they pulled it all together: a 15-day tour of the East Coast — including an appearance on the Ed Sullivan show, a concert on the steps of the Capitol in Washington, D.C., and lengthy magazine articles in Time and The New Yorker.

But never would Caso let the boys forget their Western roots. In 1949 he organized what would become an annual event: summer camp, complete with hiking, swimming and horseback riding. Roping was added in 1952. The following year, it became part of the concerts.

"With Caso, everyone had to know how to trick-rope and everyone had to ride a horse. That's just the way he was," remembered former Tucson Police Chief Peter Ronstadt, a chorus member from 1952 to 1956.

Ronstadt found the same strict discipline — and the same treatment at the end of the paddle — that Pfersdorf had become acquainted with more than a decade earlier. "On my last tour I almost got sent home. I had punched another boy and I had a switch-blade knife in my pocket. I got a Dutch uncle talk — and seven swats."

He remembered the cross-country Greyhound bus tours lasting up to three and one-half months. He remembered high jinks in the hotel rooms. And he remembered one particular concert in St. Louis.

"It was a local show, live TV. There was a guy on the show playing a guitar. Nobody had ever heard of him. But he had this record out, so I bought it and brought it home." The unknown singer? Elvis Presley.

Tutors sometimes helped the boys keep up with schoolwork on the tours, which were usually held in early spring. Often the boys took homework assignments with them, and then mailed them back to their teachers in Tucson.

The years slipped by. Stateside tours expanded to Canada, then to Europe, Austria, New Zealand. In the fall of 1965, the chorus made plans to appear the following January on the nationally televised "Bell Telephone Hour."

And then on Nov. 10, 1965, Caso died of a heart attack, at age 65. Three days later, members of the chorus sang the last time for their director at his graveside services. Caso's first recruit, Jim Pfersdorf, was one of the pallbearers.

In early December, Jeff Haskell, a 24-year-old UA graduate student, took over as director. "I walked into a stonily silent group of closed faces," said Haskell about the group's first rehearsal without Caso.

It was a job he did not want, inherited from a man he had met one week away from death. "Caso called me on a Wednesday and we spent an hour and a half on the phone," remembered Haskell. "He had heard I had a jazz trio in town and he was looking for a new sound to back up the chorus. He asked me if I would show up that Saturday morning at rehearsals, at the Temple of Music and Art."

Haskell went, met Caso — who was, he said, already drained of color to the point of greenness — played one number at the piano and was "summarily dismissed. I never saw the man again."

Urged by the chorus parents and by his professors to take the directorship, Haskell agreed. One year, he said. He stayed for 10, shepherding the boys through a decade of recording contracts and life on the road.

"Trial by fire" is how he remembered the Jan. 2, 1966, Bell telecast. "The feeling from everyone was, 'Let's just get it done.' "

He also remembered the tours. Such as the time in Wisconsin, where it was so cold that all the locks froze on the costume trunks. And the time he carried a boy with appendicitis into a hospital — where he was refused treatment until the mother could be reached.

Then there was that business about The Paddle. "When I took over, I was going to do away with it. I said, 'This isn't the Middle Ages.' But to the kids, swats were worn as a badge of honor. They said, 'You can't mess with tradition.'

"I reluctantly agreed," said Haskell, admitting he soon warmed to the idea.

Today, the Tucson Boys Chorus continues. But one tradition, however, has bitten the dust: The Paddle is no more.

LET THE
GOOD TIMES ROLL
12

Polar Bar

SOUVENOIR MENU

ZOMBIE
$1.00
"The World's Largest Sundae"
Approximately a quart of our delicious ice cream—5 kinds of fresh fruit —crushed nuts and anything else that's handy.

SISSY ZOMBIE
.50
Twice as little for half as much. We suggest you practice on this one before trying the big one.

SANDWICHES

BELLYACHE
$1.00
"The World's Largest Sandwich"
Made of old fry cooks and other tender delicacies.

TUMMYACHE
.50
Half the pain . . . half the price.

LOTTA BULL 45
Special Steak Sandwich, jerked and stomped, on our own delicious bun.

GOLDEN BROWN PAN FRIED CHICKEN
JUNIOR, 2 pcs. .... .80
Wing and Back
MOM, 3 pcs. 1.05
Wing - Back - Neck
POP, 5 pcs. 1.35
Wing - Back - Neck
Foot - Tail

JUMBO SHRIMP
SAME GOOD DEAL AS ABOVE
Grab 'em by the tail . . . pop 'em in your mouth . . .
DELICIOUS.

THESE ARE THE ITEMS ARTHUR GODFREY GOT SUCH A KICK OUT OF ON HIS MORNING PROGRAM

Bellyaches were promised on the menu. So were Toe Ticklers and Zombies.

Is this any way to run a restaurant?

It was if you were Derald Fulton, the year was 1948 and you were trying to drum up business at your new drive-in restaurant, the Polar Bar, way out on East Speedway.

"We tried some crazy things," said Fulton, owner of the Tucson Polar Bar during its days of glory, 1945-53.

Take the Zombie, for instance: a quart of ice cream, five kinds of fresh fruit, crushed nuts and "anything else that's handy."

"For a while we told people if they could finish one, the second one was free," Fulton recalled. "A few tried, but nobody made it. One never made it out the door."

Even radio host Arthur Godfrey noticed this menu. "Someone once sent it to him and he spent 10 minutes reading it on his national program," said Fulton.

Not that it ever did much for the cash register. "National exposure didn't really help that much," said Fulton. "They weren't going to come that far."

Never mind. What counts is that they came from all over town instead — customers eager to sink their choppers into the aforementioned Zombies, Bellyaches ("World's Largest Sandwich") and Toe Ticklers (hot fudge sundae with marshmallow cream and nuts.)

Raised on a farm in the Midwest, Fulton was running a bowling alley and ice cream parlor in Indiana after the war when fate, as they say, struck.

"My partner, Paul Shaar, went to Phoenix to build a Polar Bar there," said Fulton who followed the road west with wife, Daisy, in 1947.

"The Polar Bar was right on Central Avenue," Fulton recalled. "Now that lot is covered with high rises." The strictly soda-fountain menu included such temptations as a caramel fudge pecan sundae for 30 cents, or, for a nickel more, a banana split.

"It was the best ice cream in town," said Fulton. "We made our own. Ten cents a cone, two scoops."

Within a year the business was doing well enough for Fulton to head south to Tucson, to open up another Polar Bar.

"We rolled into town down the Casa Grande Highway and stopped at a restaurant on the Miracle Mile," said Fulton. "Everyone said that was the street to build on."

But a real estate salesman pointed him eastward instead, to a tumbleweed-strewn vacant lot on Speedway, east of Country Club Road and right across the street from the old Talk O' the Town nightclub. Selling price for the lot: $16,000.

"The pavement ended at Country Club," said Fulton. "Past that, it was two little dirt lanes with a little oil sprinkled on top. At night, after we closed up, we'd go out and hot rod up and down Speedway between Country Club and Wilmot. Hardly anything was out there."

Stuck in the middle of nowhere, the Polar Bar, which cost $12,000 to build, expanded its Phoenix-based menu of ice cream delights to include sandwiches, and later, a full menu after the dining room was added.

"We figured if people were coming this far, they'd want more than ice cream," said Fulton.

Opening day, July 2, 1948, was busy, with about a dozen carhops bustling in between the cars parked on the lot out front.

In no time at all, the little restaurant was offering everything from a delight known as the Lotta Bull steak sandwich (45 cents) to a four-shrimp dinner with fries, garlic toast and soup and salad (80 cents).

"Would you believe we got the shrimp for 50 cents a pound?" asked Fulton. "We'd buy enough for a whole season and store it at the ice plant."

Incidentally, rivals for the customer's ice cream taste buds were about as scarce as a traffic jam at Speedway and Wilmot Road.

"Our only competition was the Dairy Queen down on Fourth Avenue," said Fulton. "We used to count their milk cans out back at night, to see how much they'd sold."

Business, in fact, was good enough at the Polar Bar to merit the attention of several holdup men, including two who staged a rather inept robbery at gunpoint.

"I was inside, closing up, when I heard voices outside, in back," said Fulton. "We didn't have a safe so I hid the money and went out back. Two guys were out there. One of them shot a gun in the air. I told them I was just the cook. So they asked me for my wallet. Then they jumped into the car, got about 550 feet and then the car stalled. They both ran but were later traced to the car."

Unruly teen-agers also showered the restaurant's drive-in lot with faithful attendance.

"They liked to cruise," said Fulton. "The lot would fill up and they'd drive between the rows of cars. Then it started to get rough. They'd drink beer and throw the cans. We had a couple of fights. Lots of nights I had to stay out on the lot, acting like a policeman."

The solution, Fulton decided, was takeout. Dissolving his partnership with Shaar, Fulton and his local partners at the Polar Bar, John Kinder, Donald Morris and Clyde Buzzard, started up the first of what would become a chain of Lucky Wishbone restaurants here in town.

Friday, July 10, 1953, the first one opens at 4872 S. Sixth Ave. No carhops, no dishwashers, no unruly teen-agers.

No customers either. "People would come by and park and nobody would come out to wait on them," said Fulton. "We'd tell them we'd started a new place with self-service and they'd say, 'You're not going to get people to wait on themselves.' And they were right. It took a year to get things going."

By the time the year was through, working women too busy to cook and motorists passing by on their way to the drive-in movies had turned the business around. The deep fat was frying for good.

No longer needed as a fallback business, the Polar Bar was sold. For a time, the building stood as office space for a car dealership.

Meanwhile at Lucky Wishbone, the prices are up, the hours down, and the competitors have proliferated since those days when Fulton fried chicken in the middle of nowhere out on East Speedway.

The recipe, however, remains constant. "We fixed things like we fixed them on the farm," said Fulton, by then retired from Lucky Wishbone day-to-day operations. "There's no secret recipe of herbs and spices."

One thing that has gone the way of time, however, is the old polar bear sign in the roof that once stood guard over the Zombies and Bellyaches making their way from kitchen to drive-in parking lot.

Said Fulton: "I have no idea where it is today."

LET THE
GOOD TIMES ROLL
13

Pastime Park

Pastime Park's roller rink started out as a hospital.

Murder most foul happened here. So did the healing of the sick. Later came the skaters, rolling 'round and 'round the old maple floor.

If ever a place deserved the cliché "checkered past," this would be it. From saloon to veterans hospital to roller rink — and all in the span of three decades — this was Pastime Park.

Today it's just another strip shopping center in the 3800 block of North Oracle Road. Gone are the groves of eucalyptus, the wooden cottages and mess-hall-turned-roller-rink.

Gone too is the saloon where Charles Loeb took a bullet in the brain early one morning close to nine decades ago.

A Tucson resident of 25 years, Loeb had for several years owned and operated Pastime Park's beer parlor, dance floor and picnic grounds north of town on a narrow road called Oracle.

Sunday, 2 a.m., Dec. 23, 1917. The last of the Saturday night dance crowd had straggled out, leaving its proprietor alone behind the bar.

Not long after closing time, Loeb was shot once in the chest, once in the back of the head. They found the body at dawn, along with a box of cigars on the bar — perhaps requested by the murderer. They also found a hunk of bread and cheese, thought to be the dead man's last meal.

Loeb's killers, Louis Sundeen and Barney Schiller, were eventually apprehended and sent to prison.

Two years later, 1919, Francis D. Blair, executive director of the Tucson Red Cross Chapter, was scouring the city for a likely spot for the hundreds of tubercular World War I veterans flooding Tucson hospital wards.

Remembering the old amusement park north of town, Blair, using Tucson Red Cross Chapter funds, advanced the U.S. government $4,000 to lease Pastime Park. The government eventually reimbursed the Red Cross for the loan, which had been hurriedly arranged before the amusement park's current lease expired.

On March 15, 1920, U.S. Veterans Hospital No. 51 opened. Fifty wooden cottages, each housing four men, were built behind the mess hall and clinic.

Within a year, the little hospital's 320 beds were filled to capacity and plans were made to build a more substantial veterans hospital in town.

That came true on Aug. 18, 1928, when patients and equipment were transferred to the new veterans hospital on South Sixth Avenue. On the 10-year-anniversary of that move, the Arizona Daily Star reported "the old hospital, which had received 3,583 veterans during its brief life, was turned over to the wreckers."

Not quite.

"The little wooden cabins were sold off and moved to the southeast corner of Oracle and Kelso Street, and became known as the All State Auto Court," said Lenny Dillahunty. "It was there for years and years."

He should know. For two decades, Dillahunty, his wife, Jeanette, and her parents, James and Olive Souter, operated the old Pastime Park Roller Rink — in the former Pastime Park Hospital mess hall.

Directly behind the rink stood the old adobe building where the unfortunate Mr. Loeb may have met his death. "It was old mud and straw, 2 feet thick, and there were holes in the plaster," said Dillahunty. Bullet holes, he was told by the old-timers.

When Jeanette Dillahunty's parents bought the 24 acres at Oracle and Pastime Road in 1946, the land was filled with "grass, weeds and eucalyptus trees. Oracle Road was two-lane, paved, and Pastime Road was a dirt trail," said Jeanette. Besides the former mess hall — which had already seen service as a roller rink — the property held four small apartments and one large one, where the doctors had once lived.

The Souter family all went to work — James, Olive, Jeanette and brother James.

In went a 78-space trailer park. And on again went the organ music in the barnlike building with the wooden rafters and the large windows that opened up like garage doors to let in the breeze.

"The building sides were thin and they had windows, 8-foot sections, hinged, that opened up for air circulation," said Lenny, who met Jeanette on roller skates while he was still stationed at Davis-Monthan Air Force Base.

Not long after they were married in 1950, Lenny set out to do something about the rink's air conditioning, or rather lack thereof.

"I ran a water pipe on top and put in lawn sprinklers," he said. "The water ran off the roof, down the sides and over the open windows. I think it was cooler, or maybe it was just our imaginations."

No scrimping on the hardwood maple floor, however. "Every day, Lenny cleaned the floor," said Jeanette. "He'd scatter damp sawdust, then sweep it up."

After all, nothing was too good for the customer. "If you were wealthy and had your own skates, you could skate all evening for 50 cents," remembered Lenny.

"Rentals for 25 cents," said Jeanette. "Either shoe skates or clamp-on. A skate boy put those on with a key."

Refreshments were iced-down sodas. Period. "We tried popcorn at one time," said Lenny. "But the field mice in the desert ate more than the kids."

Skating hours were five nights a week, plus Sunday matinees, with Monday and Wednesday nights reserved for special parties.

Once you were up on the steel wheels, you rolled to traditional organ music — at 78 rpm. "It was a single record changer and somebody had to stand by all the time to change the records," said Lenny.

And then the rink went big time. "One of the young men who skated there took up the organ. So he played live organ music for us," said Lenny. "That lasted about a year and a half."

After that, they went to tape recordings — but no rock 'n' roll, we'll have you know. "All of our music was strictly designed for roller skating," said Lenny.

Families, teen-agers, your grandma — they all came to Pastime Rink. "It was the place to meet all your Amphi pals on a Friday or Saturday night," remembered former "floor burner" Jane Peterson.

And in those days, Peterson added, you had plenty of adults to admire your twirls. "To run down there with a bunch of girls — forget that. Somebody's mom or grandma always went along to watch."

Luckily, no one was in the place the afternoon a lightning bolt hit the top of the roof. "The building was full of dust and splinters so I grabbed the ladder and went up on the roof to see the damage," said Lenny.

"There were so many coats of roofing on that roof that it kept the building from burning. We got the busted beams back up and at 7 o'clock that night we opened for business."

As Oracle Road changed from a narrow highway shaded by tamarisk and eucalyptus trees to a bustling thoroughfare, the family started selling off parts of the property here and there.

First went 19 acres along the eastern flank for a 66-house subdivision. The rest was sold over the years to Jack Sullivan, who developed Oracle Road Lumber Co.

On July 1, 1966, the skating rink closed down for good — 20 years to the day that the Souters first bought it. Both have since died.

"Some people have no idea what was once there," said Lenny, who retired as transportation director with the Amphitheater School District.

"But then I'm totally amazed at the people I run into who say they skated there — or their parents skated there."

LET THE
GOOD TIMES ROLL
14

Valley of the Moon

George Phar Legler, creator of the Valley of the Moon, often appeared there as the wizard.

Imagination will not let it die.

Time, vandals and a tangle of weeds have all tried, over the years, to snuff out the fairyland dreamscape of George Phar Legler, who died in 1982 at the age of 97.

And just as surely, time, volunteers and a labor of love always seem to come along to revive that jumble of rocks and caves and towers and fishponds and gardens that Legler spent more than half a lifetime creating on Tucson's near northside.

Known to three generations of kids, ages 2 to 102, as the Valley of the Moon, this 2½ acres of whimsy was conceived and executed by a wispy gnome of a man who in another, more mundane life served as a writer, a railroad man and a postal clerk. But it is what he did in his spare time — every scrap of it — that became his legacy.

"He was quite a daydreamer," said Randall Legler, George Phar Legler's son.

The railroad, which the elder Legler worked for as an electrician, first brought him to Tucson in 1916. By 1923, he had separated from his wife and gone to work as a postal clerk.

Along about that time, he also plunked down a couple of hundred dollars for a plot of caliche hillside on Allen Road.

There he sank a well and hired a man with a fear of mules to start hauling in the rocks that, more than anything else, typify Valley of the Moon.

For with pebbles and stones, cement and imagination, did George Phar Legler build his fishponds and stream beds and towers and dragons and gnomes and rock villages and caves and crooked passageways and magic stone benches.

Here also is where he carved out the two narrow cave rooms that became his home. "He denied himself any normal, ordinary luxuries of life," said Randall Legler, who as a young man helped his father fashion some of the park's miniature castles.

Valley of the Moon opened to the public in 1932. Its theme: kindness to all. Its admission price: nothing. "The Valley of the Moon is dedicated to children's happiness. The minute you charge even 10 cents at the gate, then you're selling children's happiness," was its creator's oft-quoted explanation.

In wizard garb, Legler would give magic shows and lead tours through the mysteries of his own making; the Enchanted Garden, with its gurgling waters and miniature castle; Penny Land, where everyone got a story and a shiny new penny; the great tower of Zoggog, where dwelled the Valley's imaginary protector.

"He would open up on Friday nights," remembered Randall Legler. "Some nights nobody came."

But as the stories grew about this magical place on Allen Road, so did the crowds. Scout troops, teachers and their students, parents and children, all would discover Valley of the Moon.

During the '40s, Legler introduced Bunnyland, an

11-act theater program that featured rabbits dressed — and acting out the parts — of plum roles ranging from FBI men saving a baby to "Mitsie the lady Aviatrix." Legler and his rabbits even took their show on the road, for a 1948 appearance at the Los Angeles County Fair.

With Legler by then retired from his postal job, Valley of the Moon and its tours continued through the '50s and into the '60s. But age and an automobile accident conspired against the wizard. By 1971, the man whose dream had been the subject of a four-page Life magazine spread in 1953 was a total recluse, living on vitamin pills, canned milk and apricot juice.

That is how Debbie Goodridge Bober and a handful of other Catalina High School students found him back in 1971.

Several among the group had remembered Valley of the Moon from their childhoods — visits so ethereal they had thought of them as dreams. "We didn't have too much trouble finding the place, but it was all grown over with weeds, " remembered Bober.

Roused from his cave bedroom, Legler met the teenagers with initial suspicion — which soon turned to delight when he learned that they wanted to turn the shamble of weeds and rusty milk cans back into the stuff of childhood dreams.

A core of perhaps 10 teenagers poured walls, hauled out trash, put on a new roof, weeded. In 1973, their parents organized the Valley of the Moon Restoration Association. Two years later, Valley of the Moon was placed on the Arizona List of Historical Places. By then, the teenagers, aided by Legler, were giving historical tours, in costume.

But again, time conspired against the magic. Many of the teenagers moved on, to college, marriage, jobs. And Legler grew old and frail. A broken hip finally took him out of the Valley of the Moon for good, eventually into a nursing home. Still, his former teenage helpers would come to visit. "We took turns spending the night with him," said Bober.

In 1981, the George Phar Legler Society was formed as a way to continue Valley of the Moon. Spearheading the society was Mary Anne Goodridge, whose daughter, Debbie Bober, was one of the Catalina High School students who had happened onto Legler 10 years earlier.

After Legler died, the society carried on. Tours were given. Evil was vanquished, good triumphed. And then vandals struck again, destroying gnomes and miniature stone dwellings and mirrors that for decades had reflected only wonderment.

Once again, "Kindness to All" prevailed. Volunteers stepped forward — to repair, to plant, to clean. So sweet was the result that Goodridge decided that at long last, Valley of the Moon was ready to accept Legler's ashes.

At the base of a small crooked eucalyptus tree just inside the entrance to Valley of the Moon, Goodridge would scatter the ashes of the gentle man known as George Phar Legler.

"When we planted that little tree, it was bent and crooked," said Goodridge. "As I scattered the ashes, I said 'George, this tree is unique, as were you.' "

Today, the tree grows straight and true.

LET THE
GOOD TIMES ROLL
15

Rodeo Grounds

They were all stars to us.

Bill Cheesbourg, Indian cobras, Tennessee Ernie Ford, incubating chickens, anti-craft missiles, Elvis Presley, and last but not least, Lydia — a baby elephant supposedly blessed with the vocal cords of a male rhinoceros.

These were just some of the wonders folks once came to behold at the "rodeo grounds" on South Sixth Avenue.

The rodeo grounds were it until the early '70s.

Until the early 1970s — when it was hit with the double whammy of a new downtown community center and new fairgrounds out on Houghton Road — the rodeo grounds were it in this town.

It was our community center, racetrack, exhibition hall, fairgrounds, rodeo arena, carnival midway and showcase for visiting rock stars.

But before that, it was a municipal airport — the country's first. On Nov. 20, 1919, Swede Myerhofer became the first pilot to touch down.

Next came the rodeo. At age 5, it moved in 1930 from a field near Campbell Avenue and Elm Street to the South Sixth Avenue location.

And no, cowboys didn't have to dodge the propellers. Three years earlier, the city's airport had moved to its present location.

Today, only the rodeo still comes to South Sixth Avenue, outlasting even the boxing matches, held in the Quonset huts that once echoed with the roar of the crowd.

Much of that crowd came because of the country fair, also held in the rodeo grounds.

We came by bus, by horse, by pickup truck and on foot so that we might gaze at the rutabagas and earthworms. We saw sheep sheared and pigs kissed. We watched a chicken play a piano. We listened to men with Wildroot Cream Oil on their hair tells us how to slice a potato 17 different ways.

Out on the carnival midway we rode the Tilt-A-Whirl and licked cotton candy from our fingers. We saw live cobras from India and a woman with the face of a monkey. We pitched dimes into crystal dishes. We never won.

We clambered into trailers to get out free X-rays. We learned that the atom was our friend. And we lifted our eyes into the sky, where a Navy supersonic anti-aircraft guided missile stood guard over the 1957 Pima County Fair.

Fair and rodeo weren't all that you could do at the old South Sixth Avenue grounds. In the 1950s, the same field where bulls reared and horses bucked also served as a track for what we called the jalopy races.

Two of the rodeo grounds "jockeys" — Bill Cheesbourg and Roger McCluskey — would one-day race in the Indianapolis 500. But nobody had an inkling of that back in the early '50s when "Old Leadfoot," as McCluskey was called, and "Wild Bill" Cheesbourg used to roar around the oval.

Cars were always bashing into each other. Sometimes they even piled up into the stands, usually the box seats, while coming off the north turn.

Once, for extra added racing excitement, they pitted a jalopy against a quarter horse. The car won.

It was also on this track that Tennessee Ernie Ford appeared in person, waving from the back of a convertible. Here to crown the queen of the 1958 International Livestock Ball, he also hung around for that year's livestock show, held like clockwork every spring at the rodeo grounds.

It was another Southerner, however, who would prove to be the rodeo grounds' biggest celebrity. On the night of June 10, 1956, Elvis Presley warbled and writhed his way into the hearts of some 2,000-hometown girls. "He is rather nervous and jumpy in person," wrote a reporter covering the event.

To my ever-lasting regret, I was not among the shrieking 2,000.

My chance came a few years later when Duane Eddy thumped out "Rebel Rouser" on his guitar right in the middle of the Quonset huts. No blue-ribbon jams and jellies that night.

Or peanuts. That's what earned my brother's Cub Scout troop a blue ribbon in that very same Quonset hut. Not just any peanuts, mind you, but ones gussied up to resemble miniature Cub Scouts. Thousands and thousands of 'em, each with a painted-on cap, kerchief and have-a-nice-day smile, made their mid-'50s debut at Scout-O-Rama.

Like the fair and rodeo, Scout-O-Rama was a must see. For 50 cents, you could watch the upstanding youth of Tucson build fires, erect tents, climb poles, shoot apples off the heads of willing officials, and put on first-aid demonstrations.

I'll never forget the year my dad's troop got the first-aid station — supremely coveted since you got to cover yourself with make-believe wounds, ready for bandaging.

All that gore got to be too much for one lad, however. He fainted halfway through a tourniquet.

These days, the rock stars all go downtown, or over to the Indian casinos.

The blue ribbon preserves and pigs wind up out at Houghton Road. So do the men with the amazing potato peelers.

Only the rodeo remains.

Merchants

An advance ad called the soon-to-open College Shop "a gift of vision rising from the sun-baked desert soil."

You could bank in a marble palace, sleep in a pink hotel, and buy everything from high fashion to saladitos in Tucson's shops. But no matter where you conducted business, chances were you did it with the owners themselves.

MERCHANTS
1

Dave Bloom and Sons

For years, Dave Bloom and Sons stood as a genteel haberdasher's shop on the corner of Congress Street and Sixth Avenue.

"The gentleman's corner," they called it.

Yeah, yeah, yeah.

Turns out this was also the store that sold glow-in-the-dark socks, kept live scorpions in a bottle and sponsored "Ugly Man" contests.

Well, at least the proprietors sent back the underwear made from sugar sacks.

Dave Bloom made the business a priority with his sons.

Four years after they clicked the key in the lock for the last time at Dave Bloom and Sons El Con store, brothers Herb, Dave and Ted Bloom finally dragged a few skeletons out of the closet — a closet stuffed with almost 90 years' worth of memories.

It all began with their father — and namesake of the store — David W. Bloom. In 1894, the 15-year-old left Lithuania for Boston, arriving with the proverbial 50 cents in his pocket and not one word of English in his head.

He worked his way around Boston, New York and Pennsylvania, where he became friends with J. Cress Myers.

On March 17, 1906, Bloom stepped off the train in Tucson, where he wheedled his way into a job at Steinfeld's Department Store.

Six months later, young Dave, by then joined by his friend Myers, opened Myers & Bloom at 17 N. Stone Ave.

"It was what they called a racket store, more like a five-and-dime," said son Herb. "They had things like ties and accessories, but they also sold things like dishes."

Business was good from the word go.

"They blanketed the town with fliers on the morning before the opening and sold out their entire stock in just a few days," said Herb. "It took 30 days to replace it."

In 1911, Myers & Bloom took over the old Armstrong's Dry Goods location, on the northwest corner of Congress Street and Scott Avenue.

Statehood came the following year. So did marriage, with Dave marrying schoolteacher Clara Ferrin, a native Tucsonan and one of three graduates of the University of Arizona's class of 1901.

Three sons and a daughter soon made them a family. But in 1930, Myers' ill health and the dawn of the Great Depression bore down on the store.

"They decided to liquidate the business," said Herb. Levy's Department Store, fresh up from Douglas, bought the stock and the business.

"Our father was 50 years old and out of a job," said son Ted. "He took it very hard."

But not, it turns out, for long.

Within a year, Oct. 6, 1931, Dave Bloom Men's Store was in business on the northwest corner of Congress and Sixth.

"The first thing we had to do was paper the windows with circus fliers so we could go to the circus for free," said Ted, who was then 10 years old.

From the time they could push a broom, all three boys worked in the store.

"When I was about 11, my job was to get all the bills from everybody we owed, then go door-to-door to pay them, to avoid the 3-cent stamp," said Ted.

The family business also took precedence over school.

"I was a junior at Tucson High," said Herb. "One day, Pop came up and said to me, 'I just got you out of your last class in high school. So you can report to work tomorrow at that time.' It was mechanical drawing — my favorite class."

Later, both Herb and Ted would be ordered by their father to quit their classes at the UA to work full time at the store. Both answered with an obedient "OK, Pop."

Underneath the store where these dutiful sons labored was a basement — and a pool hall not owned by the Blooms. "It had a separate entrance from the outside," said Herb. "And every once in a while, there was a police raid. There were rumors of gambling."

Meanwhile, up on the ground floor, "$35 would get you a nice coat, vest and pants," recalled son Dave.

"Some of the suits started at $15, but if you sold a $15 suit you had to pay the store a dollar," said Ted. "You were supposed to sell the $25 suit."

"And you were never to sell the suit in the window," said Dave.

"One day, a man came in who wanted a $15 suit," said Dave. "I said we didn't have any. He said he'd take the one in the window — it was a $15 suit. He tried it on; it fit. He said, 'I'll take it.' My father came back and cussed me out."

In 1940, the store incorporated, becoming Dave Bloom and Sons. Soon to follow came the war, offering both boon and headaches in the form of a burgeoning population.

"All the buses stopped right outside the store," said Ted. "The crowds would be standing there seven-deep. One day, the crush got so bad, the whole plate-glass window caved in — 14 feet of glass. My father was so upset he made the city take all the city buses off of that corner."

The war also brought plenty of shortages. "We couldn't get underwear," said Ted. "We finally called one place and told them, 'Send us everything you've got.' They sent us 50 dozen boxer shorts made out of sugar sacks. We sent them back."

New suits were also nowhere to be found by war's end, said Ted. "So we advertised: 'Bring us your suit. If we sell it, we'll keep 10 percent.' We had 200 suits hanging there that belonged to somebody else."

In 1948, the business underwent a major remodeling, expanding into the basement where billiards had once reigned supreme.

In the heady postwar boom, promotion soon became king.

"After the war, we had a souvenir sale," said Herb. "Guys were bringing in all kinds of things. We had a Nazi flag, samurai swords, tons of stuff."

Then there were the homegrown souvenirs. "We had bottled scorpions for a while," said Herb. "The UA wanted them for their venom."

Beauty also met the beast at Dave Bloom and Sons.

"Every year, we had an 'Ugly Man' contest," said Ted. "Each UA fraternity nominated an ugly man. We had their pictures on glass jars at the store. The man with the most money won a date with a Playboy Bunny.

"We had one guy who won two years in a row. He waited till everybody else's money was in, then he'd drop in a check."

The faddish '50s also saw the rise of the iridescent sock.

"People were crazy for them," said Ted. "We had 90 dozen of them. Our father came back in town and said, 'My God, cancel the order for more.' We still had 50 dozen left. We sold them down to 10 dozen, then they became hard to sell. He was right."

Active in the business his entire life, Dave W. Bloom died in 1956. His sons then entered into a three-way partnership. The name of the store, however, remained the same.

In 1963, the sons ventured east to El Con Mall. "We took the last space available," said Herb. "On the first day at El Con, we did more business than in two or three weeks downtown."

Still, they would hang on to the downtown store for another five years.

"We tried going discount downtown — one-third off everything," said Ted. "We changed the name to DBS. The first day we did three months' worth of business. The second day it was fair. On the third day, we sold $100 worth all day. It went downhill from there."

But for years, business was good at the El Con store — despite a load of Nehru jackets that arrived just as the fad was fading. "We couldn't give them away," said Herb.

By 1990, however, the peso devaluation, coupled with the closure of Steinfeld's at El Con, had taken its toll.

Also a factor, said the brothers, was a change in attitudes. "None of our five kids wanted to continue the business," said Herb. "You couldn't force them to, the way our father did us."

In early 1991, Dave Bloom and Sons held its last sale.

"We had 150 suits and sport coats, 75 tuxedos," said Ted. "All the help was gone. We closed the store, except for the three of us. Then we opened the store from 2 to 4 p.m. We had one cashier, no ads, nothing, just people walking by.

MERCHANTS
2

Valley National Bank

The building and its magnificent lobby still look much the way they did in 1929.

Newcomers can't imagine how grand downtown once looked.

The Pioneer Hotel, the Santa Rita, Steinfeld's Jácome's, Levy's. All gone — or hideously transformed.

Thank heavens, then, for that palace of marble and nostalgia hunkered down on the southeast corner of Congress and Stone — the one many of us still call Valley National Bank.

No matter that the national chain known as Bank One gobbled it up in 1993. Or that it's now known as Chase Bank.

What does matter is that for the most part the bank — and its magnificent lobby — still looks much the way it did back in 1959. Or for that matter, 1929.

Ah, yes, 1929. The year of the great stock market crash, which clanged into consciousness 10 days after Tucson's newest bank opened its doors.

One can only wonder what solace Tucson's Depression-weary public would later take in the fact that the town possessed the grandest bank between Dallas and the West Coast.

Ah, well. Depressions come and go. But marble is with us forever.

Next time you're downtown, take the time to stroll into the bank and behold:

Marvel at the 14 pink Italian marble columns marching through a lobby once billed as the most beautiful in the Southwest.

Gawk at the gold leaf ceiling and its miniature murals depicting everything from Columbus crossing the Atlantic to the coming of the conquistadors.

Admire the bronze metal railing encircling the mezzanine.

Bask beneath the two chandeliers, each costing $1,000 in their day.

Sweep down the winding marble staircase to where the massive vault — and its more than 3,000 safety deposit boxes — sits behind an ornate metal gate still engraved "Consolidated National Bank."

Already a fixture in this town since 1887, Consolidated National Bank launched "Tucson's first skyscraper" — all 10 stories of it — on Oct. 14, 1929.

Built in just over a year at a total cost of $1 million, the building boasted steel-reinforced concrete walls faced with brick and terra cotta.

The bank itself took up the basement, the main floor and the mezzanine. The remaining nine floors were rented out as offices.

In 1935, Consolidated was bought out by Valley National Bank and Trust Company, headquartered in Phoenix.

Valley Bank was still its name when Michael Hard — later Bank One executive officer for Southern Arizona — joined up in 1963.

He remembered a time when the mezzanine was filled with workers at their desks, and 15 tellers might be working the windows in the lobby below.

No one works in the mezzanine anymore, and on this particular day, two tellers are at their posts, serving the downtown workers and older patrons who make up the bulk of the bank's current customers.

In 1982, the bank had 56 employees. "Now there are 12 of us," said Carol Cloutier, then vice president and manager of the downtown office.

Centralized services, computers, direct deposit, banking by telephone — all contributed to the decrease, said Cloutier.

Still, the bank appears to be secure at that location.

Today, only a few floors are reserved for bank business. The rest are rented out to tenants.

Over the years, the bank has served as backdrop for several Hollywood productions.

In 1956, Robert Wagner tried to push a woman off the top of the building in "A Kiss Before Dying."

More recently, said Cloutier, a television crew shot a 1920s robbery scene in the lobby.

Like any old building, the bank has had its share of remodeling and modernizing over the years.

"It was an absolute nightmare when the computers came in," said Cloutier, pointing to where wiring had to be discreetly drilled through the marble.

Even so, said Hard, "We're trying to maintain the integrity of the lobby" — the kind of large, opulent lobby nobody builds anymore.

"There was a lady here this morning taking her granddaughter on a historical tour," said Hard.

"People walk in this lobby and they whisper."

MERCHANTS
3

Chinese grocers

Beans, flour, chiles and lard were the staples at Chinese grocery stores such as Joe Tang's.

In other towns, they may have scrubbed clothes. Here, they sold beans and coffee, candy and saladitos, pork chops and whiskey.

"People talk about Chinese laundries. I remember the Chinese grocery stores," said Mary Malaby.

She knows whereof she speaks.

Malaby literally grew up in the business, at a succession of grocery stores run by her father, Lee Hop.

Lee Hop was far from alone. "It wasn't unusual to see a Chinese grocery on all four corners," said Julia Benites Arriola, curator of the Sosa-Carrillo-Frémont House.

Beans, flour, chiles and lard were the staples sold at these adobe-walled stores beginning around 1900.

By the '30s, many were sporting awnings and electric signs.

While some are still around, few are operating as markets.

"None of us wanted to go into the business," said Malaby. "The hours were too long."

The oldest of nine children, Malaby's first taste came early on.

"I started using the adding machine at age 4. I couldn't reach the counter, so my father brought in a milk case for me to stand on."

It was her grandfather, Lee Goon, who started the store at 1600 S. Ninth Ave. back in the early 1900s.

When Lee Goon returned to China in 1939 to be with the wife he'd left behind, he turned the store over to his son, Lee Hop, who'd been working at his side.

"My father was born in China. He came to work here at age 18," said Malaby.

Young Lee Hop soon settled in, marrying Malaby's mother, Mary Trujillo, and raising a family. "We all lived in the back of the store," said Malaby.

Open seven days a week, the store was a draw for Indians from Sells, rolling into town on their wagons.

"We sold bales of hay, kerosene, chicken feed, 100-pound sacks of corn and beans," said Malaby. Her father cut meat, ground coffee and offered everything from Calvert whiskey to lettuce and tomatoes.

By the time she was 5, Malaby may have had the best kid's job in town.

"I was in charge of buying the candy. This salesman came in with a black suitcase and I did the sampling."

Everybody bought on credit. "When they came in and cashed their paychecks, then they'd pay the grocery bill," said Malaby.

Though lenient with his customers, Lee Hop had no patience for thieves.

When one man deliberately left without paying for a pack of gum, the proprietor shot in the direction of the man's foot. "He came back and paid his nickel," said Malaby.

In 1944, Lee Hop turned the store over to his brother and bought a bar called the Tampico.

"It was a rough bar," said Malaby. "He never allowed anyone in with a knife. It was the pachuco era. My father collected a boxful of knives."

By 1946, Lee Hop was back in the grocery store business, buying the National Market, 760 S. Stone Ave. at Five Points.

Once again, Malaby was pressed into service. "I used to hire and fire at age 12," she said.

Another bar, a drive-in liquor store and yet another grocery would follow.

Frontier Market, 3921 E. Pima St., was Lee Hop's last store. "He sold it in 1960 and I retired from the grocery business," said Malaby.

MERCHANTS
4

Carrillo's

Carrillo's Tucson Mortuary in the 1930s.

As a youngster, Leo C. Carrillo was embarrassed about what his dad did for a living.

So when the teacher asked, he announced to the class: "My father's the UA football coach."

Reckoning soon followed.

"My mom went to a PTA meeting and the teacher told her, 'I didn't know your husband was the UA football coach.'

"My mother had to have a little talk with me."

Ah, yes. Football coaches come and go.

But the undertaker, it would appear, is with us forever — especially if the last name is Carrillo.

For four generations, Carrillos have tended to the dead of Tucson from the same compound on South Stone Avenue — the one that for years also served as the family home.

No longer embarrassed, young Leo is the fourth in a long line to take up the family business — working out of the same bedroom-turned-office in which his grandfather was born.

"I can still see my grandfather at that desk, with a pencil behind his ear, calling up families and seeing if they could pay a little bit on the bill," Carrillo said. "He would carry families forever."

So would his grandfather's father, Arturo Carrillo, who started it all.

In the early 1900s, Arturo lived in Cananea, Sonora, where he sold furniture, buried the town's copper miners and served as municipal judge.

After the Mexican Revolution broke out, Arturo, according to family lore, fled town one gallop ahead of the firing squad.

By 1914, he was in Tucson — the same town where his father, Leopoldo, had made his mark as a pioneer mover and shaker.

Here, Arturo opened a funeral home with his brother-in-law, assayer Elizardo Jacobs.

Three years later, he bought Jacobs out and relocated the business to the old Ormsby home at 204 S. Stone Ave.

Soon to come were a chapel, garage and embalming room.

Through the worst of the Depression, Arturo kept the business going, taking partial payment in chickens, tortillas or firewood.

When Arturo died suddenly of a heart attack in 1937 at age 62, there was but one solution:

Yank youngest son, Leo R. Carrillo, out of college and ship him off to embalming school in California.

Meanwhile, the rest of the family muddled through by mortgaging the business.

Leo R. wound up doing business the same way his father had — burying the dead "as if they were millionaires," then getting repaid a few bucks every month.

That's the word from his son, Leo A. Carrillo, who grew up just steps away from the family business.

"I lived there until age 10, then we moved to the

University area," said Leo A., third in line to take over the business.

After college and a stint in the service, Leo A. enrolled in the same mortuary school his father attended.

During the '50s, the business expanded next door into the old Knights of Columbus Lodge.

Still, most of the old ways continued.

"We used to run visitation until midnight," said Leo C. "My grandfather used to toss the families the keys and say, 'Lock up when you leave.' "

After his grandfather died in 1984, what is now known as Carrillo's Tucson Mortuary finally updated its financial policies.

"We couldn't go with a handshake anymore," said Leo A., who's now turned over day-to-day operations to his son, Leo C.

Despite modernization, one staple remains, said Leo C.

"When families come in, a lot still say, 'I need to see a Carrillo.' "

MERCHANTS
5

Southern Arizona Bank

Hard, cold cash is what makes a bank a bank. But it's the humans inside who make its history worth telling. Now more than 100 years old, such is the case for the bank that old-timers around here still call Southern Arizona.

Over the years, it's had:

* A chief teller who went to jail for pocketing the bank's money.

* A vice president who was kidnapped for ransom.

* A chairman of the board who once served as ambassador to Great Britain.

Naturally, there was a humble beginning.

Southern Arizona Bank got its start in a remodeled feed store.

How humble? Try a remodeled feed store. First day's deposits: $2,373.75.

By the end of the second day of business, May 2, 1903, deposits at the Southern Arizona Bank and Trust Co. had more than doubled.

Capital had obviously increased somewhat by 1928. That was the year assistant bank secretary and chief teller George Gray was caught with his hand in the till — to the tune of $105,000.

With no deposit insurance and insured only with a $50,000 bond, the bank came up with the other $55,000 out of the pockets of its six directors.

One of those directors, Vice President Gordon Sawyer, would become embroiled in yet another news story four years later.

On the night of Feb. 4, 1932, Sawyer, 60, was abducted by armed men outside his own front door and held for $60,000 ransom.

Tossed down a dry well, he was found unhurt the next day by lawmen.

At week's end, John Law had its man — sometime-bootlegger Clifford Adkins, 29.

Though some maintained it was Adkins' father who dreamed the whole thing up as a prank, young Adkins would spend nine years in prison.

Time lurched onward.

In 1949, Lewis W. Douglas, U.S. ambassador to England, bought up a major holding in the bank.

By then, the bank had already opened its first branch office, featuring a little novelty known as drive-in banking.

Guarded by uniformed policemen, the bank — and its million dollars in cash — moved in 1958 into its new home office at 150 N. Stone Ave.

It was the first move in 55 years for the bank, which began a block away at 32 N. Stone Ave.

Automation — now the bane of many a bank customer — first came calling when the bank installed an automatic bookkeeping system in 1962.

That was also the year Oscar Gonzales signed on as a $550-a-month management trainee.

"Prior to computers, they had 40 bookkeepers," said Gonzales, who retired in 1991 as a senior vice president.

"They'd start working the midnight shift and work until noon down in the basement."

While banking may be considered a rather genteel profession, Gonzales remembered drive-in customers getting into fights.

"We had to call the police," he said.

Like every banker, he also rode the short-term booms and busts of this town.

"When real estate folds up, everybody has a dip."

He also made questionable loans from time to time.

"The first loss I ever had was to a priest who came in and passed an out-of-town check.

"I thought, 'Well, if you can't trust a priest, who can you trust?' "

The check bounced.

Mergeritis hit in 1975, when Southern Arizona Bank merged with First National Bank of Arizona.

The bank, later renamed First Interstate, was acquired by Wells Fargo in 1996.

Though he worked for one of the state's biggest banks, Gonzales said the future is with small banks.

"You've got to give personal service," he said.

Amen.

MERCHANTS
6

College Shop

The "obituary" was long in coming for the old College Shop on Park Avenue by the UA.

But eventually its marble and glass fell to the wrecking ball, making way for — what else? — another "office-retail complex."

So be it.

Hidden in the rubble is the lesser-known tale of those who brought the store to life.

The College Shop near the UA campus, shortly after opening in 1956.

Glickman was their name — Albert and Frances. Like so many in this town, they came for the aridity.

"My father had asthma," said daughter Marcia Roth, now living in San Diego. "They brought him out to Tucson on an ambulance plane."

That was back in '38. A year later, the couple bought Levy's University Store for women, just north of the University of Arizona Main Gate, and renamed it the College Shop.

Though Albert had been a successful clothing salesman back East, it was Frances who initially ran the Tucson shop until her husband recovered his health.

By the time she was 5, Roth was working in the store. "My father let me unpack the boxes and run the old steam pressers over the dresses."

In 1948, the College Shop opened a downtown location for a few years at 138 E. Pennington St. "We were across the street from Levy's," said Roth.

Grand plans were announced in 1955 for a new Park Avenue College Shop, just a few doors away from the original store.

An advance ad in the Star gushed on about "a gift of vision rising from the sun-baked desert soil," with "vistas of glass" and the "dusky beauty of imported Italian marble."

The architect of all that, William Wilde, was also friends with the Glickmans, said Roth.

"My father had a bookkeeper and he introduced her to Bill Wilde. After they married, they became good friends with my mother and dad."

Karen Carlson, UA dean of women, cut the ribbon for the new store in February of '56.

Boasting 14,000 square feet of store space, the shop held everything from lingerie to furs, hats to shoes, sportswear to formals.

"Their clientele was UA coeds and also a lot of middle-aged women," said Glickman granddaughter Karen Fisher Levine.

"We opened with very fine merchandise," said Roth, ticking off names like Oleg Cassini.

The store constantly courted the community, setting up coed fashion boards — but also arranging fashion shows put on by wives of Davis-Monthan Air Force Base personnel.

Levine, who also toiled in the store as a kid, remembered Saturday night fashion shows held in the store's back parking lot.

"They hired a band, played pop tunes and had sorority girls model the fashions."

All that success eventually lured burglars to the store.

"They slid in through the windows above our back steel door, stole the safe in the basement and hoisted it up on ropes through the windows," said Roth.

The robbers also stole an old Buick the proprietor kept in the parking lot. A year later, the safe, said Roth, was found "blown up next to the Old Nogales Highway."

In 1961, another College Shop opened in the brand-new El Con Mall. Four years later, Albert died.

The College Shop carried on. "Business was very, very good at El Con," said Roth.

But business turned not so good at the flagship store. The Park Avenue shop closed in 1975. By decade's end, the family had sold the El Con store.

"My mother was not feeling well," said Roth. Frances died in December of '79.

Both Roth and Levine mourned more than the demolition of a building.

"That's my legacy," said Levine, who still lives in Tucson. "My family history is disappearing."

MERCHANTS
7

Le Cave's

At Le Cave's, pineapple cake with piña colada filling is a big seller.

The place still looks the same as the day I sashayed in to order my wedding cake — three tiers, frosted roses, bells on top.

Many moons — honey and otherwise — have come and gone since then.

And still, Le Cave's bakery keeps cranking out the sweet stuff.

Still the same location at 1219 S. Sixth Ave. — right across from Santa Cruz Church. Still the same art-deco glass-block windows.

And, best of all, still the same proud proclamation above the entrance: "Home of the vegetable donut."

"On a good day, we'll sell between 200 and 300 dozen doughnuts and another 200 dozen other types of pastries," said owner Rudy Molina.

Customers, he said, flock in from as far away as the Catalina Foothills and the Tanque Verde Valley.

"They'll buy four or eight dozen at a time for meetings at work," said Molina, who's had flour under his fingernails since his teenage years.

"My dad had a bakery on Meyer Street," said Molina, who helped out in the business.

By his high school years, Molina was riding his bike over to Le Cave's. "I used to clean up around the place," he said. "It was jumping all the time."

Back then, the whole world rumbled up and down South Sixth Avenue, heading to and from a bustling downtown.

And yes, there I was, sitting in the back seat of my parents' '53 Chevy, gawking at the Le Cave's sign and wondering what in the world was a "vegetable donut."

"It's made from potato flour," said Molina, who got the recipe from Le Cave's original owner, Basil Le Cave.

In 1935, Le Cave motored west from Michigan in a Model A pickup truck. That same year, he started the bakery on South Sixth Avenue.

"He opened it up in a garage out back and kept adding on," Molina said.

After high school, college and a stint in the Marines, Molina went back to the bakery business, eventually owning part of La Boulangerie.

By 1980, he was easing out of the partnership. And by 1980, Basil Le Cave was dying.

"He called me up and told me he had cancer," Molina said. "We sat and talked, and he asked if I would take on the bakery."

Sold, for $169,000.

Working on the premise that if it ain't broke don't fix it, Molina made few changes.

Oh, there's a machine that now cuts the doughnuts 200 or 300 at a time. "In the old days we cut them by hand," Molina said.

There's also a computer and a scanner.

"People bring in a photo, we scan it and then airbrush that image onto a cake with food coloring."

Cakes are Le Cave's second-best seller. "We sell about 60 or 70 a day," said Molina, whose bakery advertises more than 20 cake flavors and fillings.

"Pineapple cake with piña colada filling is a big seller," he said.

While he still comes in every day, Molina has turned much of the day-to-day business over to his son, Rudy Jr.

The son is brimming with plans, which include selling the place and relocating.

Even so, Le Cave's — and its vegetable donut — should continue.

MERCHANTS
8

Rincon Barber Shop

University presidents got clipped here. So did the toddlers. "The worst thing was a kid getting his first haircut, crying and afraid," said Joel C. White.

"I would hold the top of the head like it was in a vise."

Chester White takes a little off the top of his lawn in the 1950s in front of his Rincon Barber Shop.

And no sucker when you were done, either. But you could skim through the comic books.

"There was a little library in one corner where kids could trade them," said White, whose father, Chester, once owned Rincon Barber Shop. "Sometimes there'd be two or three kids on the floor, reading the comics."

The shop on Sixth Street, just west of Campbell Avenue, is no more, gobbled up by road widening and University of Arizona expansion — along with other old-time merchants on the street.

"It was the last shopping area going east on Sixth Street for a long time," said White, whose father died the year after he shuttered the shop in 1966.

Hard times brought the family to Tucson during the belly of the Great Depression.

When the bottom fell out of the cotton market, Chester left his barbering job in Hope, Ark., for Tucson in the summer of '36.

"He stayed with a nephew, took his state barbering exam and got a job at Rincon Barber Shop," said White.

Then his father sent for his wife, Hettie, and sons Joel, 15, and Travis, 13.

"We came out on an old Dodge truck," said White. "There were 10 of us plus two drivers. The drivers put benches in the back of the truck and we paid $5 each to come out here.

"Each of us got to take one suitcase, one pillow, one blanket," said White, who remembered the passenger who "chewed tobacco and spit it out the slats of the truck."

They stopped in tourist camps during the night, though few could afford to rent a room.

"A friend of my mother's rented a room and she let us use the bathroom," said White. "We slept in the truck."

Once here, the boys quickly adjusted to Mansfeld Junior High School, where Joel was elected to the student council.

"I found out they liked to hear me talk 'in that funny accent.' I told them, 'It's y'all who talk funny.' "

Times got good enough for his father to buy the two-chair barbershop after its owner took to barbering passengers on the train running from L.A. to Chicago.

Back from World War II, the younger White learned barbering at a school in San Antonio, then took the second chair at his dad's shop.

Thanks to the GI Bill, he was also taking classes

at the UA, hoping to become a teacher.

"I tried to get all morning classes, worked at the shop in the afternoons and studied at night," said White, who often ran off to a class, then returned an hour later to cut hair.

"One Saturday — the busiest day — Dad was sick. I cut 30 heads of hair that day."

Customers over the years included UA presidents Alfred Atkinson and Richard Harvill, as well as UA basketball coach Fred Enke.

Sports and politics filled the air, or you could peruse the latest issue of Police Gazette.

"You let the customer do the talking," said White, who cut hair part time for three years after he went to teaching, first at Safford Junior High, then at Tucson High School.

After that, "Dad tried other barbers, but they didn't work out, so he worked by himself."

Hairstyles may have changed elsewhere, but not here. "It was still crew cuts for the young boys. For the men, it was the standard cut, clipped high above the ears," said White.

What would change, of course, was the street — and the town — past the barber pole. Changed forever, it would appear.

MERCHANTS
9

O'Rielly Motor Co.

It began with a car he couldn't stand.

The car got better. So did business. Today, the dealership that Frank C. O'Rielly started in 1924 is selling Chevys to its fourth generation of car buyers.

Good thing O'Rielly didn't get his first choice: the Studebaker.

"Studebaker was the hot car back in the early '20s, but there was already a dealer in Tucson," said O' Rielly's son, R.B. "Buck" O'Rielly.

Frank O'Rielly at the dealership he founded in 1924.

So the elder O'Rielly, who died in 1979, had to settle for Chevrolets.

"Chevy was not a big seller then," said O'Rielly. "It was almost impossible to shift gears without jumping."

Luckily, the next year's model was much improved.

"They changed the clutch. It was a lot better," said O'Rielly, who now heads the dealership.

After a stint in the Army during World War I, the elder O'Rielly joined his father in the insurance business in Phoenix.

But he quickly gravitated to the automobile — and Tucson — selling parts for Babbitt Brothers Buick and Cadillac.

"He saw that the money was in selling cars," said O'Rielly, whose father set up shop with $15,000 — all of it borrowed.

His first dealership opened in a tiny downtown storefront on Broadway. Not long after, the business rolled around the corner to North Sixth Avenue, close to where Johnny Gibson's barbershop sits today.

Back then, a 1924 Chevy roadster would set you back all of $630 — including driving lessons.

"A lot of people didn't know how to drive, so they had to give you driving lessons — how to stop, start, get it to run," said O'Rielly.

In 1929, Frank O'Rielly moved to the brand-new building he would occupy for close to four decades, at 415 N. Sixth Ave.

"When he went to get the money, the bankers said, 'What happens if you don't make it? It has to have some other use,'" said O'Rielly.

So the building was also designed to be a bowling alley. Luckily, nobody ever recorded a strike — or a gutter ball — here.

It took a while for the Great Depression to slam into Tucson.

"In February of 1932, he had his best month ever," said O'Rielly. "But in March, business dropped in half. In April, it dropped in half again."

Five lean years later, business started picking up again. Then came World War II.

Auto assembly plants soon started churning out tanks, rather than automobiles.

With no cars to sell, the elder O'Rielly played cards, took in long lunches and started to drink, said his son.

"It finally got so bad that he became one of the founders of AA (Alcoholics Anonymous) in Tucson" said O'Rielly.

"I never saw him drink after 1945," said daughter Pat Pettis.

By the mid-'50s, Buck O'Rielly was flying planes in the Air Force and his father was contemplating a move to the booming East Side.

"Dad told me he was going to sell the business if I didn't want to run it."

So the son left the Air Force and joined the family business. In 1966, O'Rielly Chevrolet opened its eastside location at Broadway and Wilmot Road.

Besides selling cars, Frank O'Rielly also gave back to this town. A small sampling:

$50,000 for the University of Arizona's new medical school.

$25,000 for kennels for the Tucson Humane Society.

$25,000 for Westcenter, a drug and alcohol rehab center.

"During his funeral, I can't tell you how many people came in and told stories about Dad and his generosity," said Pettis.

Added her brother: "I still hear from people who say, 'I knew your father.' "

MERCHANTS
10

Arizona Inn

Visitors enjoy Tucson hospitality in the same buildings where Frank Sinatra, Bette Davis and other stars did the same long ago.

Flames flicker in the fireplace, and a ceiling-high Christmas tree fills a corner of the library.

"We have to replace it once during the season," said Patty Doar, proprietor of the Arizona Inn, founded by her grandmother, Isabella Greenway.

Of course they do. Fake Christmas trees may adorn other hotels. Not the Arizona Inn.

In late 2005, Tucson's grande dame of hotels quietly celebrated its 75th anniversary.

Somehow, a glitzy splash would have seemed out of place.

"We'll be putting historic photos up in the lobby and rotating them throughout the year," said Doar's son, Will Conroy, who is now president of the inn, with Doar serving as chief executive officer.

Like Doar, Conroy has a firm grasp of the inn's storied past, which earned it a listing on the National Register of Historic Places in 1988.

"We don't have to react to market forces," said Conroy. "We have a true sense of who we are."

The same could be said for Greenway — congresswoman, philanthropist and founder of the Arizona Inn.

Widowed twice before she turned 40, Greenway moved to Tucson in the late 1920s and started up the Arizona Hut, a furniture factory for disabled World War I veterans.

First lady Eleanor Roosevelt, a close friend of Greenway's, had done something similar near President Franklin Delano Roosevelt's home at Hyde Park, N.Y., said Doar.

But when the Depression hit, people stopped buying the Hut's furniture. So Greenway opted to build a hotel in the Mediterranean-Spanish Colonial Revival style — two private homes and 86 rooms and suites spread across the 14 acres she had bought in 1927.

All of it filled with furniture from the Hut. And all of it slathered in bright pink. Doar swore the story is true that her grandmother told the painting contractor to paint the inn the same color as her forehead.

"But I think maybe paints are brighter now," Doar conceded.

Greenway also insisted that each room have a mountain view — which she assured by lying down during construction on a plank-and-sawhorses "bed" in the middle of each room.

Such attention to detail failed her at least once. After the Arizona Inn opened with a dance on the evening of Dec. 18, 1930, one of the male guests pointed out the absence of a men's room.

"The next day, my grandmother called to her Ajo miner friends, and they blasted out underneath what is now the concierge desk and made a men's room," said Doar.

Built in three months at a cost of $150,000, the inn doubled in size the following year, for an additional $125,000.

"We've never expanded," said Doar. But there has been plenty of restoration. While the Hut gradually faded away, two full-time cabinetmakers still keep busy, lovingly restoring everything from guest furniture to the check-in desk.

Once surrounded by desert, the Arizona Inn now sprawls in the heart of Tucson on Elm Street, east of a bustling Campbell Avenue. Even so, all is soothing oasis within these walls and throughout its many terraces.

After Prohibition ended, one of those terraces became a bar. And in 1937, Greenway added the swimming pool and tennis courts.

"We have photos of Gary Cooper and Clark Gable out by the pool," said Conroy.

True to tradition, he and his mother name-drop only guests who have died. Among them: Bette Davis, Frank Sinatra, Spencer Tracy and Katharine Hepburn, superstars of another age.

Every so often, someone will offer to buy the place. "I just put it in a drawer. The inn is not for sale," said Doar.

"We live in a virtual world now," she added. "You can visit the Eiffel Tower in Las Vegas. But this is real. For four generations, people have walked in here and said, 'This is Tucson.' "

MERCHANTS
11

Jacobs Assay

The Jacobses in front of family's assay office.

Sometimes dreams came true. More often they died. Died hard. Such was the message delivered day in, day out in the assay office. Still is.

"Some figured everything that sparkles is gold. But there's a lot of fool's gold out there," said Benjamin Jacobs.

For more than a century, one Jacobs or another has been telling prospectors the good news and the bad down at the assay office of the same name.

It all began in 1880, when Benjamin's grandfather, Washington, set up shop downtown, about where the parking lot of a hotel is today.

Son of a South Carolina planter and politician, young Washington roamed the West for six years, then sailed to South America, where he mined the land and married Chilean Rose Mulet. "He liked adventure," said Benjamin.

Turmoil in South America brought the couple and their three children back to America. They then traveled from San Francisco to Tucson, which Washington had passed through 30 years earlier.

"When my grandfather brought my grandmother here from San Francisco, they were building the railroad between Yuma and El Paso but it only went as far as Casa Grande," said Benjamin. "They came the rest of the way, with their three children, by stagecoach." Three more children were born in Tucson.

Washington opened for business and quickly established himself in the community. "He was a notary public, a justice of the peace," said Benjamin. "Very few people here could read and write. He could."

Washington also had a part in the discovery of copper in Ajo. He named the mine the New Cornelia, after his sister. After his death in 1899, his widow sold out to Phelps Dodge.

By then Benjamin's father, Elizardo, was running the assay business. He married Amanda Carrillo, daughter of a well-established pioneer family. "She was a catch," said Benjamin.

The family lived right next-door to the office, on property large enough to accommodate 10 children, numerous chickens, horses and a milk cow. "People would knock on the door of the house all hours of the night to leave off samples," said Benjamin.

All the children found things to do at the assay office, sweeping floors, crushing samples. Most of the customers were gold and silver prospectors, on a small scale.

The Depression brought good times to the business, said Benjamin. "For years, gold sold for $20.40 an ounce. Then President Roosevelt raised the price to $35 an ounce. That was the best thing he could have done for us, though later it hurt because the price stayed the same for years and years."

When the economic going got tough, the tough went mining. "There was nothing else they could do so they went out to the field," said Benjamin. "It didn't require much to live. Everything was cheap."

The assay office also did a land-office business during World War II, Benjamin recalled. "The country needed tungsten and molybdenum. People were trying to find it. We were assaying for long hours."

In 1936, Benjamin married Carlota Arreola, from Sonora. The young couple moved into an apartment house on West Council Street. "It had three rooms," said Benjamin, "a living room in front, then a bedroom, and a kitchen in back." When their six children started arriving, Benjamin added on two rooms.

Work at the assay office was only steps away. "I didn't need a car. Everything was close," he said.

He remembered the Tucson of his childhood and youth as if it were yesterday.

He remembered raiding the gardens of the Chinese truck farmers who used to farm along an irrigation ditch near the Santa Cruz. He remembered watching Rudolph Valentino movies at the Lyric Theater and going to dances on Saturday nights.

"Usually it would be in somebody's house. Somebody would bring along a guitar." He also remembered dances at the old Armory, on South Sixth Avenue, and window-shopping along the downtown stores; Steinfeld's at Stone and Pennington, and Jácome's and Penney's — when they used to squat on Congress Street.

It was a time of raggedy innocence. "Before Prohibition, my mother, if she was expecting company, would send us to the bar with an empty bucket, to get beer."

When Prohibition hit, thirsty Tucsonans found a way. "We would go to Barrio Anita, where the bootleg houses were," said Benjamin. "We used to say the beer tasted better there because they used the water from the irrigation ditch."

As a boy, Benjamin would often pass through the town's red-light district. "They called it Gay Alley, but it didn't mean what it means today. It just means they were all happy, all those women standing in the doorways. Nobody paid much attention. The women were well-behaved. The police officers never bothered any of them."

Everyone knew everyone else in town, said Benjamin, including the law. "We never kept a lock on the assay office. Every time we'd get a new policeman, he's check the locks, then come next-door to tell us we had the doors unlocked. We never had a lock until we moved."

Urban renewal finally leveled the business and the family home. In 1969, Jacobs Assay Office moved to 1435 S. 10th Ave. So did the equipment. In fact, some of the vials and instruments about the place look as if they may have been handled by the founder.

Today, the fourth generation, Benjamin's son, Mike, runs the shop. Their best customer remains the small miner.

Still, some things have changed. "What they mine in one day now, they wouldn't have mined in three or four years, but then it was 100 or 200 times more valuable," said Benjamin.

Comparing the prospectors and their picks to the present day mining operations complete with earthmovers, Benjamin laughed and said: "In the old days, we used to ask, 'How wide is your vein?' Now we ask, 'How big is your mountain?' "

MERCHANTS
12

Porters

The place to buy saddles, squaw dresses, bola ties and boots.

Some came from the East. Some came from Hollywood. And some came fresh from the range — with the you-know-what still sticking to their boot heels.

Cowboys and movie stars, local folks and dudes. Sooner or later they all came to Porters.

For more than half a century, here is where we bought our saddles and squaw dresses, our bola ties and boots. As for the smell of leather, the jangle of spurs, the "how-do" from the owner — heck, we got those for free.

When Tucson's first Porters hit town in the early '30s, it was already hauling the history behind it.

Saddle maker Newton Porter started it all right after the Civil War, when he set up shop in a tent outside of Abilene, Kan.

The shop was a hole in the ground. Literally. Seems the cowhands liked to use the saddler's lantern-light silhouette for nightly target practice. So the resourceful Porter simply dug himself below ground level.

What the cowhands couldn't do, a drought did. In 1888, the family pulled up stakes and moved to Washington state.

It would be a short-lived stay. "They has no idea there weren't any cowboys out there," said Eldora Porter, widow of Harold, who ran the downtown Tucson store.

By the turn of the century, the Porters were back in the saddle again, so to speak, this time in Phoenix — a town that would eventually accommodate several of the family-owned stores.

Born in Phoenix, Harold went to Pasadena at age 13 to live with relatives after the death of his mother. Hat salesman, dump-truck driver and car-wash operator were a few of the jobs he held down while attending high school and his first year at the University of Southern California.

Though he managed to get in a second year of college, Harold's education was cut short by the death of his father in 1925.

Into the family business he went, which included managing 5,000 head of sheep for the Porters livestock division. On the side, Harold also came up in 1932 with a little invention called the Ride Lite Motorcycle Seat, whose principles, said Eldora, are still used today.

"Before then motorcycle seats had no padding," she explained.

It was during the early '30s that Harold came to Tucson — and to Porters first store on East Congress Street. "It was strictly saddles back then," said Eldora — saddles others were making. "The trade ended with his grandfather," she added.

Harold's specialty, she said, was working the floor. "He enjoyed talking to people." He also introduced clothing lines in the store, stirring up some trepidation among other family members.

"His uncle was against it," said Eldora. "He said,

'If you put in clothes, the cowboys won't come in to buy the saddles.' So he made Harold put saddles every so often in front of the clothes."

Customized squaw dresses soon became one of their best sellers. "We had three or four seamstresses who made them," said Eldora. "I still have mine."

Male shoppers, meanwhile, took to wearing what Harold Porter called "gambler's pants," striped trousers similar to what the diplomats wore.

"I was married in a pair of trousers made from this cloth and after they hung from the closet for a number of years, I asked our tailor if he could make a pair of frontier pants out of them," Harold told a Star reporter in 1962. "He did and every man in town wanted a pair like 'em."

In 1938, the little saddle shop on Congress Street went uptown, all the way into the north corner of the Pioneer Hotel. "It was a wonderful location," said Eldora. And deliberately Western, from its calfskin chairs in the shoe department to its life-size fake horse — one of several to grace the store over the years.

While Harold was building up the business, Eldora, who would be his second wife, was twanging her way west as a member of a country-Western band called the Rangers.

"We came to Phoenix to play at the Biltmore," said Eldora. "The manager there wanted us to wear Western clothing so we went to Porters. One time, when we came in for a fitting, we brought our instruments with us and played in the store. Harold happened to be there that day."

An accordion did the rest. "He started playing one in our band," said Eldora. They were married in Las Vegas in 1946.

After Eldora, as well as the rest of the band, wound up working at the Tucson store, the Rangers became the Porter Band. "We played for the rodeo dances for years at the Pioneer," she added.

Cowboys, dudes staying at the Pioneer, John Wayne, Clark Gable — they all shopped at Porters. "We had no competition then," said Eldora.

And then into this garden crept a sneeze. And another. And another. "Harold had allergies and there was nothing you could do for them then," said Eldora. "A doctor recommended we go to the coast."

From 1952 to 1962, they lived in Southern California, where they opened up a small Western goods store. Meanwhile, Harold continued to keep a hand in running the Tucson Porters.

In 1962, the couple returned to Tucson. Harold sold his interest in the Phoenix Porters stores and retained sole ownership of the Tucson store. A second Porters in El Con Mall, operated by members of the family from Phoenix, also opened and closed during the '60s.

With its lease up in 1963, H. Porter's as it was known by then, moved again, this time to 828 N. Stone Ave. Still keeping the cowboys in mind, the new place featured a drive-through parking lot big enough to accommodate horse trailers.

The new store also featured such longtime employees as saddle maker Jay White, as well as window dresser Eddie Hartzell, who dressed his mannequins with the sculpted heads and hands of both the proprietor and Gary Cooper.

But the No. 1 attention-getter in the store had to be the horse with the whinny. "Harold's son Earl loved to invent things," said Eldora. "He invented the voice of a horse and put it in a little rocking horse. Kids would get on it and it would talk.

"Then we got the horse that would whinny when someone opened the door." The final horse with a whinny was sculpted by Frank Polk. Still, something was missing.

"Harold told him, 'I need a man on the horse to show off the clothes.' So he sculpted Richard Merchant, a rancher near Green Valley."

All through the '70s, the store prospered. In the end it was illness, not lack of customers that closed this Tucson institution for good in 1983.

"Harold developed emphysema," said Eldora. "He couldn't get down to the store. Finally he was on oxygen. And the lease was up. We found a company that specialized in going out of business.

"We had to have our last day of business by April 1. We sold out of everything by March 26. It all went — stuff that I wouldn't have believed.

Five years later, Harold Porter died at age 84.

The horse with the whinny and its rider went to the Cowboy Hall of Fame in Oklahoma City. Eldora kept the sculpted heads and hands of her husband and of Gary Cooper, as well as other mementos of the store, including the inevitable fake horse head or two.

"Yes, it was very hard to sell," she said about the store. "It took a lot of thought. I still see people who say, 'Oh, I wish you hadn't closed.'

"It looks awfully quiet now on Stone Avenue."

MERCHANTS
13

Ted Walker Trailers

They slapped them together out of tin and canvas, and sold them like crazy to a town on the verge of boom.

Back then, everyone called them trailers. Or worse.

It's 1940. Tucson is about to be jolted awake by a swarm of defense workers and the military — all needing a place to live.

Ted Walker did a brisk business selling 6-by-15-foot trailers on South Sixth.

About that same time, a young man sells his auto parts business in St. Louis, herds his ailing wife, Daisy, and two younger daughters into a car and heads west.

Behind them rolls their home, an 18-foot trailer. "The Tucson Chamber of Commerce told us, 'If you're coming, bring your own house,' " said Ted Walker, who didn't take long to see the light.

By 1943, the man who would wind up selling trailers longer than anyone else in the country was doing a brisk business at his South Sixth Avenue location. "There was one other dealer in town," he remembered.

And no one got in a snit if you called the product a trailer, either. In fact, that was probably the kindest thing you could say about a 6-by-15-foot domicile that boasted a gasoline cooking stove, wood- or coal-burning heater, and icebox. No indoor plumbing, no holding tank.

The roofs were canvas, the walls tin and plywood, the insulation non-existent. "We had what they called spun glass," said Walker. "I went back to the factories in Michigan and saw the women working. They'd put up the outside wall, they'd coat the side of the wall with flour-and-water paste, and then stick spun glass to it."

"Leatherette," a covering similar to Naugahyde, provided the finishing exterior touch. "They didn't go to aluminum until the early '50s," said Walker.

With those first Tucson trailers came the courts to accommodate them, including one Walker owned on South Fourth Avenue. "There were maybe a half-dozen trailer courts when we came to town," he remembered. Fees at his court were $10 a month, excluding utilities. "We had a shower room, yes of course. None of the trailers had bathrooms."

A large "court" for workers at Davis-Monthan Air Force Base also sprang up on South Tucson Boulevard. "For $27 a month, you got a trailer, a lot and utilities," said Walker, who bought up some of the trailers after the park was disbanded at war's end.

"After the war, that's when business really took off," said Walker, who had to convince the banks that trailers were not a passing fad made necessary by the war. "They didn't want to finance or insure them. They'd say, 'Why, those things have wheels on them.' "

The returning servicemen and the retirees and the folks who liked the affordability of trailers just kept on coming. Eventually, the banks relented.

By the spring of 1949, a certain trailer-park lifestyle seemed to be emerging in Tucson, as witnessed by this account in the local press:

"Becky Prichard, of the Desert Haven Trailer Court, 3332 Romero Road, was last night crowned the Tucson trailer court queen before an estimated 2,000 trailerites and other interested spectators who jammed the Desert Haven court.

"C.V. Parker, publisher of the weekly Tucson Trailer Times, said last night that the event was, to the best of his knowledge, the first of its kind on such a large scale in the United States.

"Mrs. Prichard, in addition to the 1949 title, walked off with the first place prize money of $200 and a gold trophy.

"In second place was Lola Fay Cassidy, of the Ace-hi trailer court, 3253 E. Speedway. Third was Doris Reisinger, of the Shari-I-Don court, 356 E. Roger Road."

Contest judges were Jerry Martin, sheriff of Pima County; Julian B. Tuthill of the Tucson Chamber of Commerce; and Jesse Ferguson, governor of the Loyal Order of Moose.

In October of that year, Gov. Dan E. Garvey and Tucson Mayor E.T. "Happy" Houston formally opened a two-day "Western trailer Round-Up" at the old Tucson Sports Center. Festivities included not only a display of the industry's latest models, but also a western jamboree, "highlighted by the wedding of Lolita Parker and Al Rawlinford."

While all the "trailerites" were out kicking up their heels, the industry itself was undergoing massive changes. In came aluminum, out went the walls. "The width went to 8 feet, then 10," said Walker, who retired in 1979 "You couldn't haul a 10-wide around so easily."

Modern refrigeration, plumbing and air conditioning also went in. Meanwhile, the sometimes-seedy trailer court found itself replaced as well by a landscaped park, complete with pool and sometimes even a recreation center.

As the '50s came to a close, the industry was reported to have spent more than $1 million to replace the dreaded "T" word with the term "mobile home."

"By the mid-'60s, we were selling double-wides that went from $35,000 to $50,000," said Walker, still remembering his biggest sale: a 65-by-28-foot behemoth that went for $50,000 in the early '70s.

The inevitable bust in the local industry occurred not long after. In 1973, there were more than 60 mobile home sales lots in the city. Two years later, that number had been halved, as inflation and high interest rates took their toll.

So did the high price tags. "We went through an era where we got bigger and better and more expensive, but we forgot about the person who couldn't afford a double-wide," said Eugene "Sonny" Rickles, executive director of the Arizona Manufactured Housing Association.

Good times or bad, said Walker, there's always one advantage to mobile home living that hasn't changed much in Tucson: "It tends to cut down visiting friends and relatives staying too long. Trailers tend to steer people toward hotels."

(Ted Walker died in 1993)

MERCHANTS
14

Roh's

"If all the TV dramas are as simple as the Charles Ruggles show televised from 8 until 8:30 p.m., radio has nothing to fear after the video novelty wears off." — the Arizona Daily Star, Dec. 5, 1949.

Radios and phonographs were the early mainstays, then Roh's joined the television age.

The crowds alone should have been the tip-off to the hapless reporter who wrote those words to eat by.

Late afternoon of the day before. Already, men, women and children have filled every chair inside the old Tucson Radio Service store downtown. By 10 p.m., they're jammed up on the sidewalks out front.

All here to share in wonder at a snowy image pulled in with boosters and 60-foot antennas all the way from Phoenix, where that town's first television station has just gone on the air.

Another three years and two months will pass before Tucson's first television station comes on line. Time enough to tinker and test — and maybe even sell a few television sets to a public that can hardly wait.

Neither can Tucson television pioneer Ed Roh. Years before Phoenix went on the air, Roh was picking up occasional transmission "skips" all the way from Houston.

"Yes, it was snowy. But you could still make out the figures and call letters," said Libby Roh, who motored as a young bride from Nebraska to Tucson with her husband, Ed, in 1939.

Object: open up their radio/phonographic store, which they did the following year. "We rented the front room of a filling station. I did the business end and Ed did the technical end," said Libby Roh, describing the life's work of her husband, who died in 1977.

From the gas station, Roh's Radio Co. soon moved to a former dry cleaners. "We lived right behind the store," Libby recalled. "My husband worked half the night."

Radios and phonographs were the mainstay then. But in 1947, Roh had several experimental television antennas bristling from the roof of his shop.

When Channel 5 — and its hours-long test pattern — went on the air in Phoenix, the shop kept its set on several hours a day so its service people could adjust the sets to the signal. The fine-tuning knob, said Libby, was "used frequently."

Being the first on your block to have a television back then required two things: enough bucks to afford as much as $600 for a new set, and to be living in an area with good reception.

"It depended on line of sight from Phoenix," said Libby. "You could get good reception in Marana. But in some places in Tucson the mountains got in the way."

Ed Roh soon figured out a way for potential buyers to see what kind of picture they'd receive at home.

"He and Armando Rodriguez, who worked for us for 42 years, would take a 40-foot collapsible antenna to the home and hook it up to a TV set and they could see exactly what to expect," said Libby.

"We popped it up right from back of the truck," remembered Rodriguez. "Then we'd run an extension cord into the customer's home and plug it into an outlet."

While searching for the best reception, the two might move an antenna completely around a customer's house. "One time, I forgot to drop the antenna when we went around the back of the house," said Rodriguez. "I drove straight into the power lines."

Neither man was injured, though electricity was out for several hours in that part of town, Libby reported.

Good reception, said Rodriguez, often had little to do with the size of the pocketbook. "It could be frustrating. The customers had the money and wanted it, but they were just in the wrong areas."

Frustrated viewers, however, could always hang around the store — and its flickering screens. "During the World Series baseball games, so many customers would drop in that we finally had to rent 30 or 40 folding chairs for them to sit in," said Libby.

"We brought in lots of ashtrays and there was lots of smoke and cheering. Some of the businessmen from downtown brought their lunches to eat while they watched the games. The only thing lacking was the beer."

During the 1952 presidential conventions, the Rohs also took their powerful antenna system — and four television sets — to the old Tucson Gardens, former site of many a boxing and wrestling match.

"We had the sets — Magnavoxes — right up in the ring where they did the sparring," said Libby. "Each set faced a different direction."

The morning after Adlai Stevenson won the Democratic nomination, the Star had this to say about the political telecast beamed from Phoenix: "The reception was clear and the crowd had an excellent ringside view."

Libby and Ed Roh's viewing audiences also spilled into their living room. "We had a good signal at our home on Silver Street," said Libby. "Our children were young and their friends were at the door every evening to watch television. It didn't matter what was on."

Mealtime disruptions soon led to limiting the video visits to one night a week. "Their favorite programs were Morey Amsterdam and Milton Berle," said Libby. Viewing the dim screen, of course, was done in the dark.

All during the program the outside door to the room would open and close, said Libby. "Our children's friends would bring their parents, and the parents would bring their friends, too. When the lights came on at 9:30 we'd find a room full of strangers."

Finally, the great day dawned: Feb. 1, 1953: KOPO-Tucson (now KOLD) went on the air. Thousands crowded the studio to watch Mayor Fred Emery snip a blue ribbon. Cameras caught the town's first video kiss — between a sponsor and his wife.

Appliance stores all over town broadcast the momentous occasion, live. "Free transportation!" "Free coffee and doughnuts!" "See yourself live on TV!"

The papers were full of ads: "Win a 1953 Hoffman." "21-inch blonde." "Nothing finer than a Stromberg Carlson."

Other noteworthy ads also started popping up with some frequency: "Learn TV repair." "Hundreds Needed." "Top Pay." "Lifetime opportunity."

Customers accepted the need for frequent service calls, said Libby, pointing out that heat generated by 15 to 20 tubes caused many failures.

So sensitive were the early sets to interference, said Libby, that an employee from the power company was kept busy tracking down the noise.

"He was armed with a meter and a Zenith Trans-oceanic radio to locate the leaky transformer, neon sign or whatever was causing the trouble. Sometimes it was a butter keeper in the refrigerator."

Often, said Libby, her husband tagged along. "After all, it was his customers who were complaining."

Recalling those early images that used to "skip" across the screen years before Tucson's first television station came to town, Libby said: "We would stop work and watch the wonder of it all. I often wonder how people can take such a miracle for granted."

MERCHANTS
15

Baum & Adamson

The roads were rutted and the rubber still came from trees. Which was bad news for American drivers and their tires.

On the other hand, it was great news for the tire salesman. Case in point: two young men who took a chance on a business and each other back in 1923. Their names, of course, were Harold Adamson and J. Clayton Baum.

Baum & Adamson was one of the first privately owned gas stations.

If you bought a tire in this town anytime from the '20s through the '60s, chances are good it came from Adamson and Baum.

Better make that Baum and Adamson. And in case you were wondering, our ears were the only reason why Baum came first.

"It just sounded better that way," said Hal Adamson Jr., son of Harold.

Madge Baum, widow of J. Clayton, agreed. "It was more melodious that way. It just sang out."

Cincinnati is where the men first knew each other. Adamson, the older of the two, came West first, back in 1917. "Asthma," said Hal Jr. "The doctors told him he wouldn't live if he stayed."

It was in Clarkdale where he landed his first job in Arizona, selling Standard Oil products. The company soon had him selling all over the state — Flagstaff, Phoenix, Nogales, Bisbee. Tucson is where he landed last.

Meanwhile, Baum, also a Standard Oil man, arrived here during the early '20s.

By 1923 both knew what they wanted to do with their lives — and it wasn't working for other men. About that time the L.T. Shank Tire Co. put up its "for sale" sign on the corner of Stone Avenue and Pennington Street. A few years later a somewhat grander edifice, known as the Pioneer Hotel, would rise on the very spot. But back in '23, tires were the name of the game on that corner. The would-be partners went looking for capital.

Still in their 20s, the two men got a $5,000 loan from the old Consolidated Bank. The rest of the money they came up with themselves.

Their first business said Hal Jr., was just a storefront. "They did all the work out front, on the curb." The bulk of the business, he added, was changing skinny, high-pressure tires found on early automobiles to the thicker "balloon" tires then coming into style.

"Tires in those days only lasted 3,000 miles," said Hal Jr. "The roads were poor and cars all carried two spares. In 1925 my dad went to California. He replaced seven tires on the trip."

While business has been known to ruin many a friendship, this one continued to thrive. "They were good friends all their lives," said Hal Jr. "And so were their wives, right up until my mother died in 1981."

In 1927, Harold Adamson married schoolteacher Manie Robertson. By then, Clayton and Madge Baum had been married five years.

"We were living on 15th Street and had a three-bedroom house," said Madge Baum. "They were building a house, but it wasn't ready. So they came and lived with us."

In 1925, the business moved up the street. "Stone and Pennington had become too crowded and they had a chance to sell the land at a good price," said Hal Jr.

"They sold it for enough to move way out of town — all the way to the railroad tracks," Stone and Toole avenues, to be exact. "They were strongly criticized for going so far out of town."

More than tires would be sold at this new location, said Hal Jr. "It was one of the first privately owned gas stations in Tucson. Remember, this was still the era when Andy Martin was selling gasoline out of his drugstores."

Tuneups, wheel alignments and balancing all followed. So did a second store, which by 1929 was doing a booming business on the corner of Speedway and Park Avenue. By then, Baum & Adamson had also changed its tire line from Michelin to B.F. Goodrich.

Six days a week the store was open. Baum took care of the books and the inventory, while Adamson worked the sales floor, said Hal Jr.

Madge Baum disagreed. "Clayton was out on the floor just as much. They had different temperaments. Some people liked Harold better, others liked Clayton.

"They both had a great trust and faith," said Hal Jr. "There were a lot of handshake deals."

During the '30s, Adamson briefly dabbled in politics after winning a Democratic seat in the 13th Arizona Legislature. He served only one term. "When he found out that everyone wanted to scratch each other's backs, he bowed out," said Hal Jr.

Gas stamps and rationing were the order of the day during the war years. "One stamp was worth four gallons of gas," said Hal Jr. "And if you needed tires, you had to plead your case with the Office of Price Administration. Then you had to turn in your old tire when you got your new one."

But the worst effect of the war on business, said Hal Jr., was keeping the help. "They were all in the Army." As a result, he started working in the retread shop while still in junior high school, back in '44.

"The following year, I started pumping gas at Park and Speedway. I pumped gas all through college — 17 cents a gallon."

Boom years after the war, as Baum & Adamson added one branch after another. By the mid-'50s, the next generation of sons was on board: Hal Jr. and Jim Baum.

Not that the original owners did much slowing down. "My father was there every day, including Saturday afternoons," said Hal Jr.

"Oh, they couldn't keep their noses out of it," said Madge Baum. "They just loved it."

By 1968, Baum & Adamson had six locations and 70 employees. "It was the biggest Goodrich dealer in the country in terms of dollar sales," said Hal Jr. "The mine tire sales were big-ticket items."

That was also the year that Adamson, 74, sold his half of the business. "It was like leaving old friends," said Hal Jr., who started up Mobat Adamson Tire Co., doing business with the mining industry.

Harold Sr. got a real estate license. "My father always had an eye for real estate," said Hal Jr. "Baum had often told him, 'If I'd listened to you about real estate, we'd be rich.' "

In 1971, Clayton Baum died at age 76. Three years later, his old friend and former business partner followed the same path.

The company they founded carried on for only a few more years. By 1986, it was all gone. B.F. Goodrich had stopped producing Baum & Adamson's mainstay: the giant off-road tires used by the mines and contractors.

Looking backward one last time at the men who started it all, Hal Jr. reflected: "They were young, they were hardworking, they took a chance."

MERCHANTS
16

Cele Peterson

Tucson was a town of 33,000 souls the day Cele Peterson greeted her first customer.

Some 75 years later in a town almost a million people larger, she was still at it.

Dressed all in black, save for a turquoise top, she sat behind an ornate desk at the front of her Midtown store.

Everyone who came in the store swiveled her way. They knew she would be there.

"Hello, hello," she responded to their greetings. Little matter that she saw only a blur of shapeless forms.

Cele Peterson, grande dame of Tucson fashion .

Irony is there if you want to find it. The woman who brought so much visual grace and beauty to Tucson had been blinded by macular degeneration. Had been for some time.

And yet, here she was, as always, working in the store that still carried her name.

"I never worked a day in my life," she said. "It's enjoyment, a challenge."

The Great Depression, World War II, a fire that injured 16 of her employees — Peterson weathered it all, operating a succession of stores across Tucson, including her landmark store downtown on East Pennington Street.

"We pioneered the street," said Peterson. "There were three little houses there and Reilly Funeral Home."

In time, it became known as "Fashionable Pennington Street." No need to ask the major contributor to that moniker.

She was the last to leave downtown — after Levy's, after Steinfeld's, after Myerson's, after, yea, verily, even Jácome's.

Her downtown shop, said Peterson, "was the prettiest store in the Southwest. There was nothing else like it in Arizona."

So well-known was its proprietor that more than once she'd get a letter simply addressed to: "Cele Peterson, Arizona."

Lady Astor shopped at Cele Peterson's. So did Debbie Reynolds and Elizabeth Taylor, together — before Liz stole Debbie's husband, that is.

Even Gen. John J. Pershing stopped by for a chat.

"He came into the shop with his sister, May," said Peterson. "He sat and talked to me while his sister tried on things."

Once more, history had intertwined with her life — a life that began early in the 20th century. Exactly when, she wouldn't say.

Reared in Bisbee, she watched from its hills as the Mexican Revolution unfolded.

"We would play hooky from school and climb the mountain and watch what was going on. We saw the pitched tents and, way off in the distance, a puff of smoke."

She watched as striking workers in the copper mines were shuttled into cattle boxcars and deported.

And she saw the Chinese herded into Bisbee jails. None, she said, "was allowed to let the sun go down on his back in Bisbee. I don't know why."

After a year at the University of Arizona, Peterson enrolled at Sullins College in Bristol, Va., earning a degree in political science.

She also studied at George Washington University, where she would meet her future husband, Tom Peterson.

Hankering to work on Capitol Hill, Peterson went to see Sen. Carl Hayden. "He asked me what I could do, and I said I did not know."

So the Arizona senator sent her to the manuscript division of the Library of Congress, where she wound up translating Spanish manuscripts.

In the summer of '31, she was sent to Mexico City to work in the archives. It was in Mexico where she met a couple of women from Tucson.

"They wanted me to come up and open up a shop in Tucson," said Peterson. "I thought it sounded like fun."

When she told her friends in Washington what she had planned, they bet her it wouldn't last a year. "They lost that bet. Here I am 75 years later."

In October of '31, she opened her first store on Stone Avenue, between Congress and Pennington streets. "My folks helped me get started. It was a very tiny shop."

Business was good. So good that within a year, she moved the Co-Ed Shop, as it was then called, to larger digs at the southeast corner of Stone Avenue and Pennington Street.

It was during that time, 1934, that she married Tom, in Bisbee. "He took over the finances of the store," said Peterson, who continued to do the buying and merchandising.

When her five-year lease was up, Peterson moved to a little house on Pennington Street, even though her request for a $5,000 loan had been denied.

"It was in the middle of the Depression. We just had to make it unique."

And so she did, stocking the store over the years with everything from $600 ball gowns — equivalent to $6,000 today — to Station Wagon Togs, Peterson's own line of clothing made from denim and corduroy.

Winter visitors, customers from Mexico, the wives of Fortunate 500 executives — all flocked to the store, which now bore her name.

"The most clothes I sold in my entire career, and it still holds today, was 52 dresses to one woman," said Peterson. "She was from New York City."

It was after the war when Peterson noticed a change in fashion. "It was a different attitude, much more casual. During the war, a lot of women wore pants."

Asked then whether slacks would stay in style, she answered, "Not a chance."

Later, said Peterson, "I ate those words."

In 1956, she was working on moving into a larger location next door when a workman's torch caught her existing store on fire. Sixteen employees suffered smoke inhalation, she said.

Until her new store could be completed, she moved temporarily into a spot near East Broadway and South Country Club Road.

While the downtown store remained her flagship for the next quarter-century, she ventured out to the burbs, including El Con Mall, Casas Adobes Shopping Center and Foothills Mall.

In the early '80s, she closed the downtown store for good. El Con Mall and downtown parking problems did it in, she maintained.

"There were a couple of police who loved to give tickets," she said. "We had park-and-shop, but you were not supposed to give a ticket without a purchase. We gave them anyway."

Later, she would hold forth from her lone store at the Crossroads Festival shopping center, at East Grant and North Swan roads.

One of her five children, daughter Quinta Peterson, runs the store. Helping out are several longtime employees.

"I have three employees who have been with me 30 years," said Peterson, who lost her husband in 1989.

For decades Peterson hosted a local five-minute radio show five days a week called "Star of the Day."

"That gave me connections to the world," she said. Those connections also led to her involvement with many worthy community causes, including the founding of Casa de los Niños.

When Casa founder Sister Kathleen Clark came to Peterson with her idea of starting a refuge for abused children, Peterson offered her a building she owned on East Speedway at North Fourth Avenue. In 1973, it became the first Casa de los Niños.

Looking back on a lifetime of achievement, Peterson said, "Nobody does it alone. I had the most wonderful people helping me."

Not to mention all those loyal customers.

"I just had a customer come in who told me I sold her her wedding dress 50 years ago," said Peterson. "Now she's coming in to buy a dress for her 50th anniversary."

Bear Down, Arizona

Shirlee Bertolini struts her stuff in the UA cactus garden in '54.

Polo teams and cavalry training were once part of the University of Arizona experience. So were musty old libraries and burgers bought in a place called Louie's.

BEAR DOWN,
ARIZONA
1

An Oasis with cactus and snakes

The campus may change, but there will always be Old Main.

Even those of us who once pondered there tend to think of it as "The Brickyard."

No longer a cluster of quaint old buildings, the University of Arizona has gorged on entire neighborhoods.

Along the way, it's also taken on the rather soulless look of an industrial complex.

Bud Simons remembered another UA — one that gave him trees to climb, cavalry drills to gawk at and a boyhood about as bucolic as they come.

"Not many people know the campus as I did," said Simons, who grew up in a two-bedroom house south of Speedway at 1071 N. Warren Ave.

Years ago, the long-vacant house was torn down for the widening of Speedway.

When his parents moved there in '28, it was still creosote country — few neighbors, little in the way of trees, and a patch or two of grass.

No wonder that the handful of kids in the neighborhood all gravitated to the UA — "an oasis in the desert with its huge lawns and gigantic shade trees," wrote Simons in his memoirs, "A Neighborhood No More."

Officials allowed the children to gambol on university lawns and fields, and prowl about its buildings.

"A lot of the buildings had exhibits in the basement," said Simons, who took them all in.

He and his friends also swatted balls on UA tennis courts, swam summers in the UA pool and watched athletic teams work out on the grassy fields.

Soon, students were allowing them to shag balls, carry equipment and troop right into their fraternity and sorority houses.

"We helped them decorate their floats and their houses," said Simons.

Still, even attention from sorority girls couldn't compete with the dusty spectacle of the ROTC cavalry unit — the country's second largest — clip-clopping twice a day past his house.

Stabled where the mall — "all cactus and snakes" — crosses Cherry Avenue, the horses and their riders would cross Speedway each morning, heading for the drill and polo fields that now lie beneath University Medical Center.

After drills, the men and their horses returned to the stables.

As Simons got older, he and his brother were allowed to cross Speedway — since traffic was so sparse — to watch the drills.

"That's where we learned to swear," said Simons, who only once said the words in front of his mother.

Here again, ROTC students "adopted" the kids, allowing them to take practice swings while perched on stationary wooden mounts used by the polo team.

The university's boundaries back then went east to west from Cherry to Park Avenue, and north to south from Second to Fourth Street.

Simons was there when the streets in his neighborhood were paved — and when WPA workers built the stone wall on the northern edge of the campus east of Mountain Avenue.

The Great Depression sent both neighbors and students to struggling.

Many rented out rooms, back porches, even sheds to students — $5 a week.

"It was a terrible time," said Simons.

But in 1936, things started turning around — which he partly credited to the advent of the swamp cooler.

In 1941, his parents sold the house. Three years later, Simons enrolled as a student at the university he knew so well.

He went on to earn a medical degree at Stanford University and practiced general surgery in Tucson until retiring in 1987.

Though Simons said he preferred to live in the present, his book is a tender look back at a university — and a childhood — that no longer exists.

A copy is available at the Arizona Historical Society, 949 E. Second St.

BEAR DOWN,
ARIZONA
2

Polo Team

Polo brought national attention to the UA.

Some were rich men's sons. Others had fathers who plowed the land for a living. But all had one thing in common.

"We were a bunch of kids who grew up on horses," said Bill Dent, a farmer's son who wound up swinging a mallet for the University of Arizona polo team.

Yes, polo — as in jodhpurs and English saddles.

For 19 short years, this — not football, basketball or baseball — was the sport that brought honor and national recognition to the Tucson campus. All without a dime of collegiate funding.

Hey, who needed it? Not when you had Will Rogers stumping for the team, Calvin Coolidge shaking its hand, and Benny Goodman blowing mellow during fund-raising stomps down at the old Santa Rita.

The first ponies thundered across the caliche in the spring of '22, on what is now Arizona Stadium grass. Once the stadium started going up, polo moved to another field — one long ago swallowed up by University Medical Center.

Not that UA polo was the only game in town.

In 1924, wealthy industrialist Leighton Kramer moved to Tucson and promptly set about putting in a polo field on his property.

Dude ranches and private schools also did their part to swell the ranks of mallet swingers here in the Old Pueblo.

"When I came here in 1941, there were eight polo fields — in a town of 30,000," said George Masek, who played polo at the old Southern Arizona School for Boys. Opponents, said Masek, ranged from other prep students to "ranch kids."

Masek later played polo in the Geebung Seniors Polo Club, an offshoot of the Pima County Polo Club. So did Jack Goodman, who went from swinging a mallet at the old Evans School back in '37 to playing polo for Yale. Yale's mounts, he added, belonged to the school.

Here at the UA, the horses belonged to the government — more specifically, the U.S. Cavalry, which conducted ROTC drills on campus right up to World War II.

"I guess they were training for another Charge of the Light Brigade. We used to have charges in the desert with our sabers drawn," said John Donaldson, captain of the team on the day the UA played its last polo match ever: Dec. 7, 1941.

"That was our last game on remount horses," said Donaldson, also a member of the Geebung Club.

Three years after a cavalry unit was established on campus, the polo team got off the ground, thanks to Lt. Col. Ralph M. Parker, professor of military science and tactics. Parker would serve as the team's first coach.

"All our coaches were military men," said Dent, whose prowess with a mallet would lead to his induction into the UA Hall of Fame.

"It was a varsity sport," said Donaldson, a teammate of Dent's. "You could earn a major letter, just like football, basketball and baseball."

But unlike other sports on campus, polo was self-supporting. Hence, the fund-raiser. In 1924, a gymkhana was held to "help finance sending the polo squad to the East to accept the challenge of Yale and the winner of the Eastern Tournament."

Events included a cavalry drill, pony race for ladies and something called a "Cigarette and Needle Race."

Some $3,000 was raised, enough to send the team and 24 horses to the East, where it lost to Princeton in the national intercollegiate championship.

Never mind. The 1924 team went on to take Manhattan by storm, commanded the prose of Damon Runyon and even presented a cowboy hat to a rather dour-looking Calvin Coolidge.

Enter the '30s, and whom do we have hustling up the money for the polo team? Why, none other than Will Rogers, who blew into town in the spring of '31, played polo with the boys in his "rolled-up Levi's," then roped, grinned and aw-shucked to a full house down at the Fox Theatre.

Proceeds were used to send the team back East on yet another round of tournament play.

Unlike the well-to-do Eastern teams who took their ponies with them, the UA usually traveled horseless, depending on borrowed mounts along the way.

Not that the local horses were much better. Of the 40 horses available for play when Donaldson was on the team, "16 were reasonably decent and four were outstanding."

As the '30s slipped into the '40s, the team was still depending on the kindness of strangers to get it to the games on time.

"When William Holden and Jean Arthur were in town making 'Arizona,' we had them as guests at a horse show," said Dent, captain of the 1940 team.

He also remembered a dance at the Santa Rita Hotel, with music courtesy of the Benny Goodman Orchestra. "We took all the furniture out to make room. And all the proceeds went to the team."

Much of the money went straight into the gas tanks of the cars carrying the team across country to play in the 1940 National Intercollegiates in Boston.

"We played military teams and colleges with ROTC all across the country," said Donaldson, who donated his Ford convertible to the transportation cause.

Accommodations ranged from fraternity houses to basements with cockroaches, remembered Dent, captain of that year's team.

Though the team lost in the first round of the intercollegiates, it made an impression wherever it went — from sports columns to drawing rooms. "They had great receptions for us back East, and a fancy party in Boston," said Dent, who now lives in Phoenix.

Polo season usually ran from October through April, with local games played on Saturdays and Sundays. "They had bleachers and box seats, or you could drive up and watch from your car," said Dent. "We had good crowds."

Still, there was always a little bit of an image problem associated with polo, especially for Westerners: Wasn't that just an effete sport for the wealthy?

"When I got out of high school in 1935, I tried to get a scholarship to the UA," said Dent, who first watched the UA team play the locals in Yuma. "They said, 'Polo players don't need scholarships.' I said, 'This one does.' "

Instead, he worked for a year before enrolling at the UA in the fall of '36. When the call for potential polo players went out, he was there. "They took us all out to the stables and gave us a horse and mallet," said Dent. "I hit a screaming back shot."

He was in, second team. The next year, he made first team.

The UA supplied the riding equipment — all English. Players supplied their own boots. "My boots were Western, for the arch support," said Dent, who rode his last horse in 1975.

On Sunday afternoon, Dec. 7, 1941, the UA polo team rode to an 8-5 victory over the Southern Arizona Polo Club. Its captain, Donaldson, scored two of the goals.

The next two series of games were canceled, one due to weather, the other "due to war conditions." And that, as they say, was that.

Before long, most of the team members were in uniform. Not until May 27, 1944, however, did the last of the UA's ROTC Cavalry horses go up for public auction. Ranchers, mostly from Southern Arizona, paid a total of $4,225 for 64 horses.

Polo in the Old Pueblo, however, would not become a thing of the past. In the late 1940s, the Pima County Polo Club was formed. Jack Goodman and John Donaldson were among its first members.

BEAR DOWN, ARIZONA
3

Varsity Inn

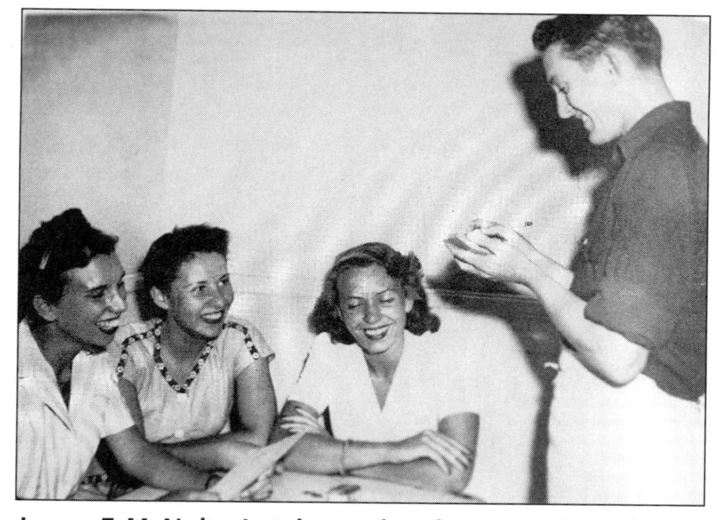
James F. McNulty Jr. takes orders from co-eds at the V.I.

"Stardust" on the jukebox, customers pounding on the piano and a future congressman taking orders. This was the Varsity Inn — "Where college celebrities loiter."

Never mind that the hamburger steaks sometimes approached shoe-leather status, or that the air hung heavy with cigarette smoke — Chesterfields, mainly.

What counted was that in those pre-Student Union decades of the '20s, '30s and '40s, this was indeed the college hangout for those who chose to matriculate at good ol' U of A.

Reportedly the first building to go up among the shops now clustered along University Boulevard west of the main gate, the V.I., as everyone and his professor called it, was owned by a succession of proprietors over the years.

Ask anyone who ever sipped a cherry Coke there from the mid-'20s to the mid-'40s, however, and he'll remember just one name: Stella Moore.

She and her husband, Ed, bought the business in 1924. "For contact with real collegians and the balmy atmosphere of fellowship, drop into the V.I. Ed Moore, proprietor," ran an ad in the 1930 "Desert" yearbook.

But it was Stella who kept the V.I. going — both before and after her husband's death in 1939.

A thin, auburn-haired woman, Stella Moore not only fed a generation of college kids, she gave many of them a helping hand.

"After she retired, she got a letter from some banker who'd made it big," remembered Moore's daughter-in-law, Ede Moore. "He sent her a letter, and $500. The letter said, 'I never could have made it without your help.' "

Besides a menu featuring everything from burgers to homemade ice cream, the Varsity Inn boasted a counter that sold 41 kinds of candy, not to mention just about every brand of cigarette. ("Chesterfields outsell all other brands," declared a 1936 article in The Wildcat campus newspaper.)

The clientele ranged from jocks and big men on campus to sorority sisters and professors dropping by between classes.

"There were lots of fraternity and sorority kids, but it wasn't too snooty," said John Barringer, a frequent V.I. customer during the mid-'30s.

It was there at the V.I. where he frequently met his future wife, Frances, between classes. "They had a delicious lime-freeze drink. We'd chip in our money. They also made a terrific sloppy Joe barbecue."

The place had colonial pillars and a porch out front, wooden floors and booths inside, said Barringer. "There were booths around three walls, and a counter big enough for eight or 10 stools along the other wall."

Pennants from the various intramural athletic teams the V.I. sponsored over the years also decorated its walls.

"I swam with a swimming team sponsored by the V.I.," said Barringer. Also on the team: Will Rogers Jr. "He swam with us in '33," said Barringer.

In 1935, UA tackle William Roberts bought the Varsity Inn, but it appears to have been a rather brief ownership. For by 1937, Stella Moore had bought the restaurant back.

Through it all, a jukebox belted out popular tunes of the day. So did the customers — this time on an old carved-up piano. "I think some of them played for meals," said Barringer.

And maybe slung a little hash as well.

"Yes, it's true. I was the fleet-footed waiter of the V.I.," said former Democratic Congressman James F. McNulty Jr., owning up to an old 1946 "Desert" yearbook ad that showed him scribbling down orders from three grinning coeds.

By then, Stella Moore, whose local restaurant credits also included the Pirates Cove and the Dutch Mill, had again sold the Varsity Inn — this time for good.

But the tradition of hiring cash-poor college students still seemed to hold sway.

"I went to work at the V.I. 72 hours after I got to town," said McNulty, who credited the cashier with getting him the job. "He took mercy on a fellow Bostonian."

McNulty arrived on the train in January of '46, determined to get a college education on the GI Bill. "Spartan" best described his lifestyle.

"I don't remember a salary, and tips were few and far between. But I did get a free meal for every shift I worked," said McNulty, who usually worked the lunch and dinner hours.

As for paying customers: "For $1.10, you got a full meal — soup or juice, the entree, vegetable, dessert and two slices of bread."

Knowing what — and how — to order often gave this waiter an edge over the customers.

"The cook would fry up a bunch of hamburger steaks in the morning, then heat them up on the stove all day long. By the end of the day, they were like a charred shoe. God almighty, they were blackened ruins. But he sold them all day long and sometimes into the next day.

"Well, sometimes I wanted one of those steaks. I knew they never had a name on the order, so I'd put on the order for a hamburger steak, rare, no gravy. The cook would take down the order, say, 'Sonuvabitch!,' stomp over to the refrigerator, get the red meat, give it one minute on each side, then send it out.

"I'd bring it back and say, 'The customer said it was too rare.' That's why I always said 'no gravy' — because otherwise he wouldn't cook it any more. He'd curse some more, but he'd have to cook it."

McNulty stuck it out as a waiter at the V.I. for two years. Then in '48, he tried a different approach. "For two years, I rented the place from 6:30 to 9 p.m. and made milkshakes," he said.

In 1951, McNulty, armed with a brand-new law degree, joined up with two Bisbee attorneys, brothers Martin and James Gentry. Incidentally, the Gentrys also put themselves through law school by working at the V.I. during the '20s.

1951 was also the year the University of Arizona dedicated its Student Union Memorial Building — an event that some think may have led to the eventual demise of the V.I. "People weren't going down to 'The Square' as much," said Barringer.

Nevertheless, the V.I. persevered under a succession of owners during the '50s. But by the 1960s, the burgers and shakes were gone forever. Somehow, the Varsity Inn had evolved into a men's clothing store. Later, bicycles were sold on the site.

Meanwhile, Stella Moore went on to other ventures, including working for several years in the UA's mail bureau.

But it was her days at the Varsity Inn that most would remember. When she died in 1972 at age 80, the Arizona Daily Star paid tribute in an editorial.

Though not officially connected with the university, Stella Moore, noted the editorial, "held a place in the friendships and an influence over the traditions of a whole generation of University of Arizona students."

BEAR DOWN, ARIZONA

4

Arizona State Museum

Birds' skins and elephant teeth were among its early "treasures." So was its curator, a part-timer who drew an annual salary of $100.

Clearly, much has changed since territorial Gov. Nathan O. Murphy took pen in hand well over 100 years ago and signed into creation what we all know today as the Arizona State Museum.

The ever-popular buffalo, in its finer days.

Located in Old Main (along with just about everything else back then), the Territorial Museum was staffed for more than 15 years by lone employee Herbert Brown.

Described as "a typical Victorian amateur scientist," Brown, during his 20-year career with the museum, also owned the Tucson Citizen, served as warden of the territorial penitentiary at Yuma and became the first vice president of the Arizona Humane Society. Whew.

"He was an example of men in the late 19th century who were interested in many things," said Raymond Thompson, former museum director.

Under Brown's direction, the museum acquired everything from arrowheads and minerals to Brown's own collection of native birds' nests.

Brown was still in charge in 1905 when the museum, along with the UA library, moved into the brand-new edifice now known as the A.E. Douglass Building.

But after Brown's death in 1913, the museum's collections were packed in crates and put into storage.

Two years later, the museum got back on track after UA President Rufus Bernhard von KleinSmid hired Byron Cummings as both museum director and head of the new department of archaeology.

A classical languages professor and organizer of the University of Utah's first football team, Cummings was also enthralled with the archaeology of the Southwest.

But even he must have blanched when he first set eyes on his new "museum."

Said Thompson: "The story was that von KleinSmid took Cummings to where everything was still stored in boxes and said, 'Here's your museum. Go to it.' "

That he did. By the end of 1915, the Arizona State Museum was ensconced on the third floor of the new Agriculture Building. One room held Brown's bird collection; another displayed various artifacts.

"That was typical of the times, to show everything," said Thompson. "They put it all on tables or hung it on the walls."

In his first year on the job, Cummings was paid a grand total of $1,400, said Thompson, mostly for professorial duties. "The pay for museum director was still around $200 as year."

However, Cummings quickly climbed the ladder of academia, serving as dean of the UA College of Letters, Arts and Sciences, as well as dean of men. In 1927, he ascended to the presidency.

But within the year he gave up the post to return to his first love: the classroom. His, however, was a classroom scratched in ancient soils.

"One of his greatest contributions was teaching young people the thrill of archaeology," said Thompson, who met Cummings in the early '50s. "To go to a site with Dean Cummings and eat canned beans was something people would talk about for years.

"It was a time when all the continents had been explored, all the oceans. Geology and archaeology were the two fields left that provided young people with an adventure."

Cummings' field expeditions included collecting Anasazi materials in Navajo and Tsegi canyons. In addition to his work in the field, he oversaw two moves during his tenure.

In 1930, the museum moved into the underbelly of the new football stadium. Sure, the roof leaked and the street out front was unpaved. But the new quarters did provide room for some rather ingenious displays, such as the dozens of Indian baskets attached to the underside of the stadium seating.

And greeting visitors at its new location was the museum's latest "treasure," that stuffed and somewhat seedy buffalo that would later hold court for years on the current museum's second floor.

In 1935, the museum finally moved into a home of its own. Designed by noted Tucson architect Roy Place, the building went up for $88,000, funded by the Depression-era Works Progress Administration.

"It was the middle of the Depression, the state was dying, and professors were being paid in scrip. But Dean Cummings got the building," said Thompson.

Three years later, Cummings retired. His replacement: Emil Haury, one of those former wide-eyed students who had studied at Cummings' knee.

"Cummings showed up in Kansas to lecture at Haury's college," said Thompson. "Haury was interested in paleontology and natural history. So Cummings invited him to go to an excavation in Cuicuilco, Mexico."

Haury stayed on in the Southwest, completing his undergraduate and graduate degrees at the UA. In 1934, he received his doctorate in anthropology from Harvard.

But five years earlier, Haury's reputation was already made. For 1929 was the year researcher Andrew Douglass' tree-ring research led to the ability to accurately date ancient ruins. And Haury was there, helping to collect the ancient woods that finally led to the discovery.

Little wonder that a giant redwood section that details tree-ring dating has for years been a focal point of the museum's displays.

"Haury got into places early in the game and laid the foundations," Thompson said about the man who researched such sites as Ventana Cave and Snaketown, both treasures of Hohokam artifacts.

But archaeology was changing, both at the dig and in the museum.

"Under Cummings, the emphasis was on how much stuff you had, not what," said Thompson. "Under Haury, exhibits interpreted the life of a people."

BEAR DOWN, ARIZONA
5

Cavalry training

The UA cavalry thrived for 24 years.

An officer and a gentleman. That's what each would be — with sabers drawn and horses charging.

It would be a world of white gloves and military balls, gleaming spurs and smart-stepping boots.

And then came World War II.

"The Russians and the Poles had horses; the Germans had the tanks. After 1939, that changed everything," said Sky Lininger, a member of the last Reserve Officers' Training Corps cavalry unit ever to train at the University of Arizona.

"The Fighting 56," they called themselves — these college juniors who left in June of '43 to sign up for war — a war that no longer depended on the horse to carry soldiers into battle.

When the last of the UA cavalry rode off into the proverbial sunset, so did a somewhat brief history stretching back 24 years.

In 1919, a cavalry unit was established at the UA in the department of military science and tactics. Within a year, the department had acquired 60 mounts, plus jumping paddock, tack and stables. A crack polo team and women's riding classes soon followed.

"The Army provided all the horses, all the staff," said Maury Speer, a 1938 UA grad who went through cavalry training.

The first stables were at North Cherry Avenue and East Third Street. In 1936, the stables were moved north of Speedway.

Back then, ROTC was mandatory for all first- and second-year male students. Those who stayed with the program during their junior and senior years did so on horseback.

"There were no advanced units that weren't cavalry," said Speer. Their reward for staying in the saddle: "After graduation, you got a commission as a junior lieutenant."

Before the war, every cavalry unit undertook six weeks of active duty after its junior year. "We rode our horses down to Fort Huachuca, cross country," said Speer. "We bivouacked every night. There must have been 50 or 60 guys."

By the fall of '42, Speer was back at the UA, this time as cavalry instructor. But there would be no summer encampment to look forward to for the unit that trained under him.

"We signed up in the fall of '42 for 17 weeks of basic training," said Lininger. It would begin as soon as the unit's junior year was over.

In the meantime, there were still drills to practice, high-topped boots to struggle into and horses to mount. Or not.

"Some guys were scared to death of horses," said Babe Hawke, one of the "Fighting 56."

Tom Black, another member of the group, agreed. "Some never could ride. They kept falling off the horses. But I don't recall anybody getting washed out." After all, added Black, the unit also had its share of crack horsemen.

Somewhere in the middle were the rest — often young men who'd grown up on farms and ranches around Tucson and learned to ride at an early age.

Those not quite so at ease in the saddle could always pay special heed to the Army training films used in the course — including the all-important "how to mount and dismount" instructions.

Besides engaging in mounted drills on campus, the ROTC cavalry often headed for the nearby foothills and desert.

"Four of us used to volunteer to be scouts on maneuvers," said Black. "We'd go out to the old Venice Gardens bar and restaurant, park our horses in the shade of the tamarisk trees and drink beer while the others went through their charges."

Not that it was all lounging about under the tamarisk trees. Sometimes there were injuries during drills — both to man and horse. "The most common injury was getting stepped on by your horse," said Hawke.

Then there were the jumping exercises. "Sometimes the horse would come to a jump and stop and you'd keep going," said Lininger.

Horses, too, were occasionally at risk. "We had mounted pistols," said Hawke. "You'd shoot at targets to your right, then across to the other side. A lot of times the horse would jump when you shot. Those were automatics we used, which means you could kill your horse."

Hawke was on the firing range when he witnessed just such an occurrence. "The instructor would get your name, and the name of your horse and say, 'You just paid for the horse.' "

Cost: $21. "That was a whole month's pay."

Despite the occasional mishap, however, this was no bungling F-Troop. "It was an honor to be in the cavalry," said Hawke. "There was a real feeling of esprit de corps."

Speer agreed. "No question, the horse cavalry was the epitome of what a guy tried to get in if he could. Pershing, Patton — all the elite generals came from the cavalry."

But change, the men acknowledged, was coming. Said Hawke: "Most of us realized we were not going to fight in this war if we stayed in the cavalry."

In February of '43, Speer left the UA cavalry unit to join the U.S. Army Air Forces, as it was then called.

Esprit de corps finally met up with reality for the rest of the men later that spring as the last cavalry unit headed for induction into the U.S. Army. "That time, we left our horses behind," said Lininger.

Many wound up at Fort Riley, Kan., headquarters for the Army cavalry. "There were 100,000 horses there. But men were being dispersed to the different services," said Lininger. "You could sign up for one of two regiments. One was horse; one was mechanized."

Trouble was, said Lininger, "after basic training, they didn't know what to do with us. The cavalry OCS (Officer Candidate School) had closed down. So they shipped us back to the U of A in the fall of '43."

There, the men bunked in a former equipment room at the football stadium and took classes in everything from psychology to the anatomy of a horse while awaiting acceptance into various officer candidate schools.

"Some went to armor, some to infantry," said Lininger, who would return to Fort Riley as instructor of the same 17-week basic training course he'd just undergone.

Black went into infantry officer training, while Hawke took aviation cadet training. "We showed up at the base in Santa Ana (Calif.) in boots and spurs, to go into the Air Force," he said.

One of their number would die during the war. Ten would make a career of military service. After the war, many returned to the UA to resume their studies. So did Speer, who was reassigned to the university — this time to teach Air Force ROTC.

Despite several petitions to bring it back, the cavalry never returned to the UA campus.

BEAR DOWN,
ARIZONA
6

Basketball

Morris K. Udall rose from "bench-rider" to first-string forward — despite his glass eye.

They've had a coach who ran off to Hollywood, a one-eyed player who made a run for the presidency and a "court" that just ran, period — at least when it rained.

"Humble beginnings" doesn't begin to describe the birth of basketball on the University of Arizona campus.

It all began here in Arizona Territory back in 1897, when a few UA students chose up sides on a dirt court and played a little game of hoop. As in singular. Final score: 3-1.

The following year there was a rematch — though the ball collapsed by game's end.

Things got better in 1903 when Herring Hall, the school's first gymnasium, opened. The team's most frequent rivals: Tucson High School and the YMCA.

It would take the legendary J.F. "Pop" McKale to bring UA basketball into the collegiate arena. Barely.

During his 1914-21 tenure as head basketball coach, McKale saw the team through a 49-12 record — though just 18 of those victories were against college teams.

In 1921, McKale handed his hoops duties over to James H. Pierce. Pierce would guide the team through two seasons before leaving Tucson for Hollywood, where he would marry Tarzan creator Edgar Rice Burroughs' daughter Joan and become the final silent-film era Lord of the Jungle.

In Pierce's second season here another sort of star emerged in Harold Tovrea, who amassed UA scoring records that would stand for almost 25 years.

Pierce had several noteworthy achievements himself, including a 27-5 record for an .844 winning percentage. His teams also recorded the first Arizona victories over USC and UCLA.

In 1925, McKale — who had been promoted to athletic director — hired Fred Enke as basketball coach, ushering in an era that would last for more than 35 years.

By then the team had all but abandoned a too-small Herring Hall in favor of other environs.

"We played at the old Armory and at Tucson High School," said former Tucson High coach and administrator Rollin T. Gridley, who wore a Wildcat basketball uniform through three seasons back in the mid-'20s.

Gridley still remembered beating Tempe Teachers College (now Arizona State University) in the brand-new Bear Down Gymnasium on opening night, Jan. 21, 1927.

He also remembered what it took to play on that new hardwood floor. "The basketball team painted the floor. Three coats. We did it for nothing."

Billed as Tucson's first indoor facility for both athletic events and "social affairs," Bear Down Gym saw plenty of action as a student dance hall.

"They'd wax the floor, which was terrible for a basketball court," said Gridley. "And our shoes had suction cups on the bottoms that would accumulate the wax. We'd have to go to the sidelines, get a towel and wipe the wax off."

If the shoes were a mess, so was the ball.

"The basketball wasn't a perfect sphere the way it is now," said Gridley. "Coaches would sometimes put just a little air in them, or else blow them up to the bladder mark."

Solo officiating was also the norm, said Gridley. "Of course it got kind of rough when the referee turned his back."

Team scores rarely went past 30 points, thanks to the rule that called for a jump ball after every basket. "The clock was running all the time," said Gridley. "If your team could score 30 points, you usually won."

There were no tutors, said Gridley. And not much attention paid by the press. But the agony of defeat was the same then as now.

"I remember my last year we came within one point of beating USC," said Gridley, memory stretching across a time chasm of more than 65 years. "I was the guy who lost the game. I missed the free throw."

Though Gridley remembered going by train to out-of-town games in Texas and California, the 1933-34 team wound up playing a tour of the Midwest by bus — or by thumb.

Twice, the team wound up at the side of the road — once after the bus broke down between St. Louis and Tulsa — and again after a second bus caught fire between Tulsa and Oklahoma City.

"We just scrambled out of the bus, got our bags out and helped put the fire out," Coach Enke would tell Abe Chanin, in Chanin's book, "They Fought Like Wildcats."

Better times were around the corner.

Beginning with the '45-46 season, Enke's teams launched a six-year reign that would take six straight Border Conference titles, run up 81 straight home game wins, and travel to six postseason playoffs or tournaments — including the 1946, 1950 and 1951 National Invitation Tournaments held in New York City's Madison Square Garden.

"I remember it very vividly," said Marvin Borodkin, who was captain of the 1946 team making its inaugural visit to the Garden, to play in what was then basketball's most prestigious tournament.

"There were 23,000 people at the Garden and every one of them was smoking a big cigar — or so it seemed. We ended up choking, though Kentucky didn't seem to be bothered."

Indeed. Kentucky won 77-53. "They also won the national championship that year," said Borodkin.

After the loss, the team headed straight home on the train, said Borodkin. "A group of people met us at the SP railroad yard."

Like Borodkin, several on that 1946 team were returning vets — both from World War II and from prewar UA basketball teams. Among them: future Secretary of the Interior Stewart Udall, who played for two seasons prior to the war, then rejoined the team in '46.

The following year, Stewart Udall's younger brother, Mo, joined the team, rising from "bench-rider" to first-string forward — despite the fact that he played with a glass eye.

In what would become a much-savored, oft-quoted tale, the future congressman and presidential contender would recall his last game against New Mexico, where he scored 24 points and left the game to a standing ovation with two minutes remaining.

"A sportswriter called out, 'Udall, you're a liar. No one shoots like that with a glass eye.' I plucked out the slippery orb and gave it to him, saying, 'Mister, I haven't been able to see much out of this one. You try it.' "

Most of the players were homegrown. "There was no recruiting," said Borodkin.

No weight training either. And no dunking. "The coach wouldn't allow it," said Borodkin, who following graduation became an assistant to Enke for a few months.

During his 25th year as head basketball coach, Enke would weave his most magical year. The '50-51 team finished the season 24-6 and would play in both the NIT and NCAA tournaments.

Ranked 12th nationally in the final Associated Press poll, the team lost in the first round of both tournaments.

On Dec. 8, 1951, the 81-game home-win streak came to an end at Bear Down with a loss to Kansas State. That same season saw the debut of Hadie Redd, the UA's first black basketball player.

But by the late '50s, the team was no longer a powerhouse in the West. Failure to recruit, said many.

Enke retired after the '60-61 season. His successor was Bruce Larson, a former UA player and Enke's assistant coach.

Among his challenges: keeping the Cats competitive in the more demanding Western Athletic Conference. Among his standouts: point guard Warren Rustand, who was UA student body president and Academic All-American.

By the late '60s and early '70s, however, Larson's teams were posting more losses than wins. Their gym was also falling apart.

In the fall of 1970, construction began on McKale Center. The following year, the team played all of its non-conference home games at the Tucson Community Center.

But the Cats seemed to miss their cozy old gym, losing five of those seven games and finishing last in the WAC in the '71-72 season.

Not long after, Dave Strack, the UA's new athletic director, named Fred Snowden as head UA basketball coach.

Snowden's first season was also the last for basketball at Bear Down Gym. On Jan. 18, 1973, the Wildcats closed down the venerable old gym with their seventh straight home victory, beating the University of California at Santa Barbara 79-77.

In just three seasons, Snowden — the first black man to be hired as head coach of a major sport at any NCAA Division I university — would put his team in postseason play.

Meanwhile, names such as Coniel Norman, Eric Money, Bob Elliott and Herman Harris were becoming household words — both in Tucson and elsewhere.

It was Snowden's '75-76 Cats that would make it to the big dance — their first NCAA Tournament since 1951. Only a loss to heavily favored UCLA in the round of eight kept them from the Final Four.

But in the final half of his 10-year tenure at Arizona, "The Fox" would seemingly lose his touch, with three consecutive losing seasons. On Jan. 8, 1982, Snowden announced his resignation.

Less than three months later, Ben Lindsey was hired. He lasted one year — after leading the team to its worst showing in school history. The season ended with a dismal 4-24 record, including eight straight home losses.

New athletic director Cedric Dempsey quickly hired Lute Olson away from Iowa. The rebuilding had begun.

Former players such as Gridley and Borodkin could only marvel at the changes in the UA's basketball program.

"It's big business now," said Borodkin. "Whether that's all for the best is questionable."

BEAR DOWN,
ARIZONA
7

Bob Svob, a true-blue Wildcat

Yeah, yeah, yeah. You just think you bleed red and blue. When it comes to being a true-blue Wildcat, few can trump the circulatory system of Bob Svob.

Svob became a Wildcat in 1937 when he rolled in from Jerome to play football under J.F. "Pop" McKale.

When World War II erupted, Svob, by then a husband and father, trained at Bear Down Gym before shipping out.

Not long after the war was over, the guy was back at the UA, earning a master's in administration to go with his degree in physical education.

Bob Svob went go on to become the UA's dean of students.

By then, he was in charge of the UA's intermural sports program. By 1966, he wore the title of dean of men. In 1972 he became dean of students, a post he held until he retired in 1983.

Add it all up and it amounts to more than 44 years on campus, interrupted only by two years in the Navy.

As dean of men, and later dean of students, Svob weathered everything from anti-war protesters to panty raids.

"I was responsible for booting off my own fraternity, Sigma Chi," he said. "Twice."

Even tougher duty reared its head from time to time.

"The worst was when a student was killed," said Svob, a father of four. "I had to call the parents in the middle of the night."

Born in Jerome to immigrant parents, Svob made all-state in football. He also made Ripley's "Believe It or Not" after place-kicking a football 300 yards in October of 1936.

"Remember, Jerome is built on a hill," said Svob. "The ball just kept rolling."

McKale soon put this all-star in his place.

"On our first day of practice, we were all lined up. Pop said, 'All you fellows who made all-state, step out two paces.' We did. Then he said: 'Get back in line. See, you're not better than anyone else.' "

Even so, it was the beginning of a lifelong friendship, said Svob, with McKale even lending him money for his first house.

In September of 1939, Svob secretly married his high school sweetheart, Shirley, who would go on to attend what was then called Tempe State Teachers College.

"We were going to keep it quiet, but then she got pregnant," said Svob, who was suspended from school after he told the dean. "You could be married, but it couldn't be a secret."

Out of school for the spring 1940 semester, Svob worked at a stationery store, and the newlyweds settled into an apartment near the university.

After regaining his eligibility in summer school, Svob played for two more seasons, graduating in 1942.

Two years later, he was the school's freshman football coach — and training for war at Bear Down Gym, which had been turned into a naval indoctrination school. By '46, he was back as a grad student.

Years later as dean of students, his office in Old Main would be taken over during a student protest. "They almost set it on fire," said Svob. "Almost every day, there was some sort of commotion on campus."

During his time, he saw the withering of curfews and dress codes and the advent of unisex dorms.

He also had to deal with booze and marijuana. "We'd call them in, say, 'If you break the rules again, you're gone.' Sometimes they did. They were gone."

As a widower in later years, Svob would devote his time to woodworking and community causes such as the YMCA, serving as a volunteer for more than 45 years. At least once a year, he returned to Jerome. But come football season, he would be back in the stands, rooting for the Wildcats.

As for the old UA campus he strolled onto back in '37, "it's not there anymore," said Svob. "Most of what I remember is now asphalt and sidewalks."

BEAR DOWN, ARIZONA
8

Shirlee Bertolini, twirler

Flaming batons, as it turns out, can be a real pain.

Oh, not because all that tumbling and twirling could singe some skin or set someone's hair on fire.

No, it's because the batons have to be set aflame in mere seconds. Can't miss a beat with the band, after all.

Wilbur Wildcat was five years in the future in 1954 — the year future twirling coach Shirlee Bertolini came to town as the UA's first female twirler.

Half a century later found her still on the field.

Shirlee Bertolini twirls fire in '55.

After earning a degree in psychology in 1958, Bertolini became the UA twirling coach, guiding two generations of women in the ways of the baton.

About 75 of those women — some of them grandmothers, no doubt — came back for their first reunion ever in 2004 as the UA feted Bertolini during three days' worth of activities over homecoming weekend.

"Never in a million years did I imagine this," said Bertolini, who turned every dime of her coaching salary over to the Shirlee Bertolini twirler scholarship fund, which she founded early on.

"My husband has always supported me," added Bertolini, whose husband, Donald, had a dental practice for 35 years before earning his medical degree.

Besides coaching the UA twirlers, Bertolini judged twirling contests across the United States. Many of her recruits came from those contests.

"I get 25 or 30 tapes a year, and we accept maybe three or four girls, depending on the open spaces," said Bertolini, who sometimes picked twirler hopefuls up at the airport and squired them around campus.

"She treats everybody like her daughter," said former UA twirler Denise Baldwin, who organized the twirler reunion. "During school breaks, she'd even let us store things at her house."

In 1999, Bertolini — who taught twirling in 17 countries and 20 states — quit offering private lessons. But she still twirled at homecoming.

"I haven't missed a homecoming in 50 years," said Bertolini, who worked with eight band directors, from Jack Lee on.

"She's seen a lot of band directors come and go, and yet she's never had the attitude someone in her position could have, that, 'Oh, I'll be here after you leave, Sonny,' " said Jay Rees, UA band director.

"Shirlee is wonderfully professional."

It all began with a stick.

At 10, Bertolini, then Shirlee Demchak from Detroit, wanted to twirl in the worst way.

For the first six months, she practiced with a broomstick and did odd jobs to pay for lessons.

By high school, she was winning major competitions and twirling as head majorette — as they were then called.

In 1952, she worked up a drum major routine for a baton-lessons classmate, Bill Lester, who was recruited by Lee to come to Arizona.

Lester got Bertolini to come to the UA as soon as she was done with high school, along with Ken Teel, another drum major.

"The campus was beautiful," said Bertolini. "I had never seen a palm tree. I called them pineapples."

Wearing what appeared to be a giant Q-tip on her head, Bertolini twirled mainly to martial music back then. "It was John Philip Sousa."

Times changed. Later teams would twirl to the Talking Heads, including their song "Burning Down the House."

Flaming batons, of course, were a given. So was Shirlee Bertolini.

"What else would I be doing right now?" she asked.

What indeed.

BEAR DOWN,
ARIZONA
9

The Big Game

It happens every year, just before the season of peace on Earth, good will toward men. In an arena reeking of fear and loathing, the multitudes meet, face to face, with a great gnashing of teeth and beating of breasts.

And some call it sport.

Fans know otherwise. For them, nothing else matters except that their team down there on the field — be it the Wildcats or be it the Sun Devils — annihilates the other team.

The 1973 game continued a rivalry that started in 1899.

Lose your job, your wife, your hair — just don't lose this game.

Few would have guessed back in 1899, when the two schools first met at Carrillo's Gardens in Tucson, of the great rivalry that would arise out of this annual pigskin contest between the University of Arizona and what is now Arizona State University.

Tempe Normal school is what they called ASU back then. But before you snicker too loudly, know that the UA's coach — brother of a chemistry professor at the school — volunteered for the job. Know also that the UA lost, 11-2, to the Normals, as they were then dubbed.

And all were perfect gentleman. In his book, "They Fought Like Wildcats," Abe Chanin quoted the UA student newspaper's account of the meeting: "The Normal boys were met at the train and were given a hearty welcome by the football boys and many students. They were then brought out to the University where on arriving the students gave them three hearty cheers."

The two schools would next meet in 1902. The UA won that one, 12-0. In fact, all nine contests entered by the two schools between 1902 and 1931 were played on Tucson turf — and all were hometown wins.

In 1931, the Wildcats tasted their first defeat, 6-0, by the Bulldogs — which is what the Normals had become. The game also marked the first time the two teams squared off in Tempe.

But it would take a dozen more meetings — and a game that jarred Tempe boosters to the bone — before Arizona State College, as it was then known, would hand the Wildcats another defeat.

Varsity Stadium, Tucson, September 1946, is a time and place forever seared into the memory cells of some diehard Tempe fans. That was the night the Wildcats clobbered the Bulldogs 67-0 in front of 12,000 fans. Total offense for the UA: 438 yards. Total offense for Arizona State College: 41 yards.

At the end of the season, first-year ASU coach Steve Coutchie was fired, the Sun Angel Foundation was begun and the team underwent the metamorphosis from Bulldogs to Sun Devils.

Into this frying pan jumped Boston College assistant football coach Ed Doherty, who was hired with one goal in mind. "About three weeks after I was hired there was a meeting in the college president's office, with me, the president and a couple of Sun Angel members," recalled Doherty, who would later become athletic director at Salpointe Catholic High School.

"They told me they had beaten the U of A only twice since 1899. So the Sun Angels had agreed to back us for three years. If at the end of three years we had still not beaten the U of A, they would throw their support to Phoenix College."

The push to beat the Wildcats, said Doherty, started on the season's first day of practice. "The thing I remember about the whole series is unbelievable pressure on the coaches and the players."

It took three seasons, but the Sun Devils under Doherty finally got their Wildcat scalps, 34-7, in 1949. "Everybody was throwing everybody in the showers," said Doherty.

The following year he repeated the victory, in enemy territory — the first time Phoenix had beaten the Wildcats in Tucson since their initial meeting in 1899. But Doherty resigned at the end of the season, unhappy at what he saw as recruiting violations at Tempe.

A few years later, Doherty made history when he became the only man to coach both Arizona football teams.

When he took on the job as head football coach for the Wildcats in 1957, Doherty found the same withering pressure to win the big game that he had felt in Tempe. But by this time, Tucson was facing a machine. "Dan Devine was their coach that first year, Frank Kush the second year," said Doherty who was fired after suffering losses to Tempe — 47-7 in 1957, 47-0 in 1958.

Not that the '50s were all bad times for the Wildcats. For three straight years, 1953-55, Arizona racked up victories against the Sun Devils. This was the era of halfback Art Luppino, who led the nation in rushing yardage in 1954 and 1955.

It was Luppino who scored the Wildcats' lone touchdown in 1955 to beat the Sun Devils, 7-6. But the game, Luppino would later tell Chanin, was grueling: "I took a hell of a beating that night, I got mauled."

Wanting to beat Tempe so bad it hurt was nothing new to the Wildcats. A young back by the name of Charlie Gilleland played against the Bulldogs in 1925 with a broken cheekbone.

As the rivalry between the players increased, so did the intensity of the fans. Within just a few scant years of those first gentlemanly "hurrahs" for each other's teams, fans were regularly painting — and sometimes burning — their school emblems into each other's mountains and buildings. And more than one campus fountain has bubbled from time to time with the hated colors of its archrival.

Besides bragging rights, the victor got a hulking bronze trophy that some have likened to "the rabbit ears for a 1949 Muntz TV."

Shifted back and forth between the winning schools since 1979, the 7-foot trophy — titled "The Big Game" — was created by ASU art professor Ben Goo. Said Goo on the occasion of the unveiling: "The significance of the sculpture comes about in an abstract, non-objective way."

Uh-huh. Try telling that to thousands of screaming fans for both universities. Or to Ed Doherty, who felt the hot breath on the back of his neck on both sidelines.

"They told me at both schools, 'You can lose every game. As long as you win the last game, you're all right.' "

BEAR DOWN,
ARIZONA
10

Polo Village

A war brought it to life. Medical science brought it down.

In between, it served more than two generations of the matriculating married at the University of Arizona. Polo Village they called it, though it never actually sprawled over the same ground the ponies once trod.

Home in a Quonset hut with a white picket fence. That was Polo Village, created in 1946 to house returning veterans, come to get an education on the GI Bill.

The huts, located in two complexes just east and west of the old polo field on Vine Avenue north of Speedway, started coming down in 1966 to make room for the vast University Medical Center complex.

Miriam Pattison and her mom, Frances, at the pool Karl Pattison dug.

The last of the steel-ribbed structures — all that remained from the original 114 huts and five temporary dwellings — were torn down in the summer of '84. Nineteen families got their eviction notices the January before.

Quite a comedown from the glory years, when Polo Village had a co-op store, a "washateria," a study hall, a newspaper, and a duly-elected mayor and council, who wrestled with such problems as dusty streets, lidless garbage cans, lack of clothesline space, roaming dogs and — always — how to make a hut a home.

"It took you a while to get used to living in a curved house. And the walls were paper-thin. You spoke very softly unless you wanted the neighbors to hear," said Mary Lacagnina, who with her husband, Michael, spent the years 1952-57 in Polo Village.

Only 20 when they moved in, the Lacagninas both left with college degrees — and two children, born in the village.

By the mid-'50s, population figures in the village were topping 800. As soon as they graduated, villagers had to leave to make room for someone else on the waiting list. But while they were there, this was home. For as little as $18 a month, including utilities.

That's what the first 49 student families paid back then in September of '46. They also cooked on hot plates, cooled with iceboxes and sweated without swamp coolers. Those who coughed up an extra $6 a month could rent the hut furnished.

Each of the huts, 24 feet by 48 feet, housed two one- or two-bedroom units. Residents were encouraged to spruce up their tiny front yards with picket fences and flowers. "There was a manager who got after you if you didn't mow your yard or keep your picket fence painted," said Lacagnina.

Those with a flair for decorating got their huts featured in a regular column that appeared in Quonset Quotes. Most of the paper, however, dealt more with the prosaic, such as the classified ads. Sample: "Haircuts — 35 cents" or "Wanted: potty chair."

Living it up meant college and cake at the neighbors' — bring the kids, of course. "If you were having a big party, you'd go to Nogales — in those days you could bring back a gallon of rum or tequila," said Lacagnina. "We'd throw it together in the most horrible, horrible punches."

The first village council, called the Veterans Committee, was elected in the summer of '47. Not long after, it became the Polo Village Council. Despite the lopping off of its military title, however, it would be another 16 years before the village would open up its picket fences to non-veteran married students.

Taxes — $2 a year per family by the mid-'50s — went toward such civic endeavors as Christmas parties, dances, homecoming floats and wiener roasts.

And while other UA students might get worked up over, say, the Big Game with Arizona State College (as it was called back then), Polo Village had its own gridiron showdown on Turkey Day.

The Diaper Bowl. A classic confrontation, held on the polo field. East Village vs. West Village. Eight men to a team. Spectators were the players' offspring, usually found wandering about the field. Nobody kept score.

In 1956, the co-op store, beset by competition from a newly opened Consumers' Market, closed after six years in operation. Apparently veal chops at 80 cents a pound and orange juice at 19 cents a can were not enough.

Vacant, the store became a study and meeting hall. Now the council no longer had to meet in the nursery school.

The times, they were a-changin'. In 1959, the washateria, installed during the 1949-50 school year, also closed for lack of use. It soon reopened, however, as the women's meeting hall.

When word came down in 1963 that the village would be making way for a new medical school, the Arizona Wildcat polled those affected by the move.

Although most villagers staunchly defended their digs, one replied, "It's the closest thing to a slum I've ever lived in." Said another: "Who in his right mind would like to live in a Quonset hut?"

Yet when the last huts were really going, going, gone in 1984 to make room for still another addition to the medical complex, the remaining villagers protested the loss of their cheap quarters, by then running $76.50 a month for a two-bedroom hut.

Inmates from Southern Arizona Correctional Release Center tore down the final huts, storing the salvage wood, metal covers and ribs. Plans were made to make them huts again — this time for prisoners.

"We made friends for life in the village," said Mary Lacagnina. "There's no way we could have made it through school without it. But those huts were ready to come down when we left."

BEAR DOWN, ARIZONA
11

The Library

Librarians locked up the books they thought students would steal.

All it took was a step or two.

And suddenly you were transported from a dusty, palm-lined university to an ivy-encrusted citadel of higher learning. Harvard perhaps. Or even Oxford.

Especially if your studies took you, via marble stairway, to the upper-floor reading room of the University of Arizona Library.

"No other single influence on the campus will do more to elevate the taste and desires of the students than to study and dream in this quiet, beautiful room," wrote a student in the 1927 "Desert" yearbook.

That room, as well as the rest of the 2-year-old building that surrounded it, would last another half-century before the inevitable replacement.

Today, the UA library system holds millions of volumes — much of that on computer, microfilm, or tape. Its full-time employees number in the hundreds.

What a difference a hundred years or so can make.

When the University of Arizona officially opened for classes on Oct. 1, 1891, its library was one shelf in Old Main, filled with mining, engineering and agriculture books. Its staff was one professor. His card catalog system was a shoe box.

It's been growth, growth, growth ever since.

By the turn of the century, UA President Millard Parker and Professor Howard Judson Hall — he of the shoe-box-card-catalog system — were lobbying the territorial Legislature for a real library.

In 1904 they got it, in the form of a building that would house for a time not only the library but also the Territorial Museum, president's office and a few classrooms. Price tag: $26,000.

Yes, of course it was a tremendous sum. But then, as one legislative committee noted, here was a library that would serve the needs of the university "for all time to come."

Into this edifice went 8,000 volumes, 70 sets of periodicals and one Estelle Lutrell, who would serve as librarian for the next 28 years.

She was still on board in 1925 when the library "for all time to come" was replaced with a larger building near the main gate.

Inside these walls many a 20th-century scholar would ponder and peruse, present company included.

Built for just under a half-million dollars, this library began its life with 56,000 books and a staff of seven.

Designed by architects John B. Lyman and Roy Place, the three-story red-brick building featured Mexican amapa woodwork, marbled lobby and an Italian Renaissance interior. On a more utilitarian note, steel stacks held potential spacing for close to a quarter-million books.

"It was the newest building on campus," said Pat Paylore, who enrolled at the UA in 1925 and went to work in the library while still a student, 35 cents an hour.

In 1930, Lutrell offered her a full-time job. She hemmed and hawed. Finally an exasperated Lutrell told her, "Well, it's not like taking the veil."

It was, however, the same as deciding upon a career. Paylore would work there for the next 34 years, often as acting university librarian.

A decade later, UA student Phyllis Ball would take the same tack. She too, made 35 cents an hour. After graduation, Ball also hired on full time at the library in 1944 — a move Paylore counseled against.

"She looked so indecisive; I didn't think she'd stay," said Paylore, who later shared a home with Ball.

"I stayed longer than anyone else," said Ball, who stepped down as manuscripts librarian in 1986.

That same year, Ball would publish her labor of love, "A Photographic History of the University of Arizona 1885-1985." Many of its pages are devoted to the history of the UA Library.

Like most former students, she too had fond memories of that grand old reading room and its dramatic bank of almost floor-to-ceiling windows.

"The drapes were pale gray, and not cleaned very often. Finally, they were in shreds," said Ball. A Tucson company was hired to make new drapes.

"They said they would hem them after they were hung. They brought in the sewing machines and there were no outlets. We had a hell of a time getting extension cords."

The same problem would rear its head again, on a more-than-balmy day. "They decided to have summer school registration in that room," said Ball. "One of the professors came in and said: 'We're dying of heat. We've got to get some electric fans in here.' But we couldn't, of course."

The room eventually was modernized with some rather ugly fluorescent lighting, which replaced the elegant drop ceiling lamps. "Those light fixtures wound up in the basement," said Ball. "I kept trying to find them."

When it came to operating hours, here was a library that believed in a civilized closing hour. "We always closed at 10 p.m.," said Ball. "None of that all-night business, for heaven's sake."

No sleeping over your Shakespeare either. "We had tables and chairs that were purposefully hard," said Ball, though she and Paylore did remember a certain janitor who would "stretch out and go to sleep on the reading room tables."

By the 1940s, the stacks were so crowded with books that they lined the floors in every aisle. In 1951, a large stack addition to the rear of the building solved the problem — for a time.

"The stacks were originally all closed," said Ball. "You went to this beautiful marble counter and the books were paged for you. As the UA grew, of course, this became a staggering job."

In 1962, the stacks were finally opened up to library patrons. "I was opposed to it violently," said Ball. "I said, 'They're going to walk off with everything.' "

To prevent that, the library installed its first security system. "We had a checkout in the lobby," said Ball. "People did not want to open their bags. Even the professors had a fit."

Not until the '50s was air conditioning installed. "We were used to the heat," said Ball, who confessed to wading through the waters whenever the lawns out front were flooded.

With the building already in upheaval over the air-conditioning installation, employees knew that the time was right to lobby for a new paint job inside.

"The walls had never been painted since the building opened," said Ball, who likened the original color to a drab shade of "elephant's breath."

"We were all sick to death of it," said Ball. After much consultation and discussion, the new color went up. "Same old elephant's breath."

Rare books and manuscripts were kept in locked cages, said Ball, who became head of the library's first special collections department in 1958.

"I remember when the 'Kinsey Report' came out. Boy, was that locked up," said Ball. But not because of censorship, you understand.

"It was so popular — all the sex books were. We were afraid people would take them."

Despite various additions over the years, the library eventually ran out of room. In 1973, ground was broken for a brand-new library next door to venerable Bear Down gym. Price tag: $12.1 million.

Moving time came during the Christmas break between the 1975-76 academic year. "We all worked, from the highest to the lowest, over the break," said Ball.

During the move, a bonanza of books was discovered behind the shelves in the open stacks. "We found all sorts of things that had fallen through the cracks."

Today, both that building and the one preceding it still stand on campus.

After it was vacated back in '25, the original library building assumed a rather checkered past, going from Law College to College of Education to Psychology Building to the inevitable "Old Psych Building."

It's now known as the A.E. Douglass Building, named for a long-term UA professor and former acting president.

As for the building that many of us still think of as the library, it's now part of the Arizona State Museum. Happily, that glorious reading room still looks much the same.

BEAR DOWN, ARIZONA
12

Louie's Lower Level

Louie's opened in '57 as an "ultra-modern cafeteria lounge."

If anything on campus shouted, "Hey, kid, you're not in high school anymore," this was the place.

Not a window anywhere, hamburgers sizzling all hours of the day and night, and half the diners with a cigarette in their hands.

This was Louie's Lower Level — at least in the days before smoking was banned.

When the popular eatery in the basement of the University of Arizona's Student Union closed after a grease fire in 2000, Louie's was still dishing the chow.

But even before the fire, its days were numbered. Ah well, Louie's had already made an indelible mark in the memories — not to mention the cholesterol counts — of thousands of Wildcats.

When the Student Union opened in 1951, there was no Louie's — only a basement area with dirt floor and unfinished ceiling.

A year or so later, students turned it into a meeting and party place, complete with sawdust over the dirt and portable lighting.

So who, everyone wants to know, was Louie?

"It came from a kid on the student activities board," said Bill Varney, Student Union director from 1958 to 1984.

"He said, 'This is just like a place in Chicago where you went down the stairs and there was sawdust on the floor. It was called Louie's Lower Level.' "

The name stuck, said Varney, who came by that story from his predecessor, the late Marvin "Swede" Johnson.

In November of '57, Louie's opened as an "ultra-modern cafeteria lounge," complete with card-playing section, television and pastel-colored booths.

Jack Redhair, then student body president, was among the first to partake of Louie's menu, which included everything from pizza to salads.

He remembered burgers for breakfast and a jukebox that cranked out the hits, three for a quarter.

"The place was jumpin' seven days a week," said Varney. "Kids studied there, read their mail there, met their future wives there."

Perhaps the grandest entrance anyone ever made at Louie's belonged to Redhair's wife, the former Diane Vance.

Back then, a UA publication called Arizona Kitty-Kat had a little feature called "Kitten of the Month."

In March of '58, Diane Vance won the "honor." The publication also sponsored "A date with Diane," which turned into several dates, including one at Louie's.

"They flew me in a helicopter, and I landed on the girls' athletic field," said Diane Redhair, who then proceeded to Louie's.

The times they kept on a-changin'.

Nov. 22, 1963, the day President Kennedy was shot: "Service cancelled in Louie's as crowd huddles before TV," read the headline in that day's Wildcat.

Kids were still watching TV at Louie's a decade later.

In fact, when the grill caught fire in 1973, some had to be pulled away from their favorite soaps.

In 1993, there was a brief push to shut down Louie's in favor of name-brand franchises.

Never happened. Costs were too high.

But eventually, it all came to an end.

Thanks for a great run, Louie — whoever you are.

Hometown Notables

Johnny Gibson's was a downtown beacon where everyone had something to say.

One gave us haircuts, the other the opera. Then there was the boxer, the iceman and the TV cartoonist. All made sure we would never forget them.

HOMETOWN NOTABLES
1

Newsies

He's a fixture of the Great Depression, burned into our collective memory as surely as the bread lines, John Dillinger and "Brother Can You Spare a Dime?"

Walk past any downtown corner of the 1930s and there he was, all pluck and perseverance.

"Paper, Mister?" he'd call out, offering you the world as of press time, nickel a day.

Newsies gather outside the Citizen building at Stone and Jackson.

"We called ourselves 'newsies,' " said Armando Membrila, who sold both the Star and the Citizen during the '30s. "We had to stand on the corner and holler out the headlines."

Afternoon corner sales were strictly for the Citizen, of course. "After school, you bought your papers at the Citizen building on Stone and Jackson," said Membrila. "We paid 2 or 3 cents a paper and sold them for a penny over."

Any boy could do it, said Membrila, long as you were "tough enough to be on the street."

The trick, he said, was finding a good corner, such as Stone Avenue and Congress Street, then holding onto it.

"You'd have certain customers who bought from you. If kids stole your customers, there would be a knock-down, drag-out fight."

Six days a week he did this, for just about a year. "I don't think I ever missed a day."

Then he graduated to a paper route, first for the Citizen, then for the Star.

"You had to maintain good grades to deliver for the Star," said Membrila. "Gilbert Acosta (then assistant circulation manager) used to check our report cards."

Delivering papers to his 160 customers began at 2 a.m., down in the basement of the old Star building on West Congress Street.

"I'd fold the papers, put them in duffel bags over my bike and head out."

The westside was his route — Menlo Park, St. Mary's. "It was all coyotes and dirt roads," said Membrila, who was usually slinging the papers by 3 a.m.

"You had to be done by 6 a.m. They had a guy, Buster Durazo, who'd ride around the routes after 6. He carried old newspapers in his car. If you were still delivering after 6, he'd throw them at you."

Ah, but the wages were worth it, $7 or $8 a week.

"It helped put me through high school," said Membrila, who graduated in '41. After the war, he stopped by the office of his old boss, Acosta, who by then was circulation manager of what had become Tucson Newspapers Inc.

All those years of submitting report cards must have paid off. Membrila was offered a job in the mailroom. In 1989, he retired from the Star's business office.

Hot off the presses is the way Cress Lander sold 'em for the Star back in the early '30s.

"My brother James and I would get the papers

when they came out, around 1 a.m., then we'd go to the places where people were just leaving — the Pioneer, the Santa Rita, a couple of restaurants — and we'd sell them. This was on the weekends, early Saturday and Sunday mornings."

Afterward, said Lander, "We'd go back down to the Star and go to sleep in the distribution room."

By 5 a.m., they were back on the streets, this time selling papers to a world just waking up.

"We'd sell to the different motels and trailer courts along South Sixth Avenue, all the way to the vets hospital," said Lander, who also sold out-of-town papers from Los Angeles, Chicago and New York City.

For 10 years, they did this, all through the Depression.

"Sometimes we were making only pennies," said Lander, former director of community services for the city of Tucson. "In those days, grown men made a dollar a day. If you made 25 cents or 50 cents, you were doing all right."

Rain or shine, you hawked those headlines. "I sold the Dillinger story. I sold the Huey Long stories," said Lander, who indeed did shout from time to time: "Extra! Extra! Read all about it!"

So did Mike Levkowitz, another Depression-era paperboy who sold both the Star and the Citizen.

"At the time, we had sensational headlines," said Levkowitz, who held down the corner of Congress Street and Church Avenue, best as he could. "Everybody muscled in on the territory," he said.

The profit wasn't bad, sometimes amounting to as much as 80 cents a day. "It was either that or work for my father for free," said Levkowitz, whose family owned the Chicago Store.

Within a year, he was also selling the Sunday Star door-to-door on Speedway, as far east as Park Avenue.

"I had a bicycle with a little red wagon behind it," said Levkowitz. "Those Sunday papers were heavy."

If ever there was an elite cadre of newspaper boys, it had to be those who flung out the headlines via motorcycle.

"There were four or five routes at that time. We covered roughly 30 miles," said Charley Thornton, whose newspaper career with the Arizona Daily Star began in 1928, first by bicycle, and later by motorbike.

His first motorcycle route ran from Grant Road to the Rillito River, between Stone and Campbell avenues.

"It was all a series of chicken farms," said Thornton, who counted a bootlegger among his customers. "When it rained, you could smell his place a quarter-mile away."

Eighty cents a month is what he collected from his customers. "If we collected 100 percent, Mr. Gay (Edward), the circulation manager, took us all out for a picnic."

Most on the collection route paid in coins. "Occasionally, we'd get a $5 or $10 gold piece," said Thornton, who would go on to coach wrestling teams at the Arizona State Schools for the Deaf and the Blind.

Delivering the Star was all pre-dawn work, of course. "In the wintertime, it would be so cold all us guys on motorcycles would stop and build a fire out in the boondocks beyond Drachman Street."

Not that everyone appreciated the early-to-rise approach.

"I used to live on Corral Street, by the Masonic Temple," said Thornton. "There was a row of shacks behind us where the old-timers lived. When I'd start my motorcycle at 3 or 4 in the morning, this one old guy would come roaring out, shotgun in hand.

"After that, I'd push my motorcycle into this little alleyway, jump on it, get it in gear and I was gone."

Besides his 200 Star subscribers, Thornton also delivered the Citizen for a time along East Broadway. "That was a good one, because it included the El Conquistador Hotel. They gave every guest a free newspaper."

Dogs snapping at his heels, fire ants in his face, mud splaying around his feet, brushes with errant automobiles. Those were the hazards of the trade.

"I was collecting up by El Con when a car ran me off the road, knocked me off in a ditch," said Thornton. "I was knocked out for four or five minutes."

But the money almost made up for it, sometimes as much as $75 a month. "At times, I was making more money than my dad," said Thornton, who also delivered out-of-town newspapers, picking them up from the morning train.

"There were no jobs then — except carrying newspapers."

HOMETOWN NOTABLES 2

Duke Dillas

Cut the cards one way, he was William Dillas, husband, father and small-town businessman.

Cut the cards the other way, he was Duke Dillas, gambler and proprietor of the old Varsity Smoke Shop — where the pool balls clacked and the phones always jangled with the sure thing.

Duke Dillas' Varsity Smoke Shop.

Place your bets, ladies and gentleman. Place your bets with Duke. And many did, until the odds — and the law — went against him one time too many.

"He was like a Damon Runyon character. He never knew a stranger and everyone called him Duke — except my mother," said Kathy Brown, Duke Dillas' oldest daughter.

In 1955, Dillas left town for good, after paying a $1,000 fine on a gambling charge. By then, his glory days were as faded as an old racing form.

"He had higher gambling stakes than Las Vegas," said George Gekas, a former partner of Dillas' who helped turn the Varsity into a café back in the late '40s.

"I'd come down with the doughnuts in the morning and guys with a piece of the action would be sleeping on the pool tables, waiting for the games to be over," said Gekas. "There'd be $60,000 to divide."

Card games, horse racing, football games — they bet on them all. "They had a ticker machine for the games and races. Duke had his own office in the back. That's where he took in the bets. He had two phones," said Gekas, adding that he steered clear of gambling.

Though small change by comparison, the café out front also managed to turn in a tiny profit. "It did the biggest business in town," said Gekas. "We'd do $400 for breakfast — and that's when hot cakes were 15 cents."

Only 32 customers could squeeze in at a time, sitting at stools 'round a horseshoe counter. "People used to line up outside," said Gekas.

But never on Sundays, when it was closed for the day. "My father used to take us down there on Sundays, and my sister and I would make sundaes at the fountain," said Brown, who carried memories both fond and hurtful of her father.

Born in Chicago in 1909, Duke Dillas was a first-generation American son of Greek immigrants. Times were dismal. "He had to quit school in the third grade. He helped the street vendors," said Brown.

The experience, she added, may have marked him for life. "He was embarrassed that he only had a third-grade education. But he had a knack for remembering people's names — and he had a wonderful mind for numbers."

In 1925, he caught a westbound train heading for Arizona. Dillas wound up in Bisbee, where he went to work in a store owned by the Levy family. He also fell in love with one Mabel Frost. They married in Bisbee.

In 1936, the couple and their two young daughters moved to Tucson, where Dillas went to work in the men's department of Levy's department store.

"He was a very sweet guy, very handsome," said Oscar Montaño, longtime Levy's employee. "But he was addicted to gambling."

Hard times continued to dog the family. Mabel sold homemade lunches to Brown's classmates at University Heights Elementary school. She also taught for a while at the old Arizona Sunshine School.

And then sometime in the mid-'40s, the family's fortune began to change, said Brown. "I don't know if he got the money through betting, but all of a sudden, my dad had bought the Varsity, and we were living in this nice home on Ninth Street."

Located at 34 S. Stone Ave., the business during the early '30s had been a pool hall known as Dooley's Varsity shop, Dooley Bookman, proprietor.

After Bookman died in 1935, it became Tommy's Varsity shop up until the mid-'40s.

Brown, of course, remembered it as a café — with a few pool tables in back. "My dad taught my sister and me how to play pool."

Their mother did not approve. "My mother hated gambling and cards. My father taught me how to play gin rummy when I was 4 — out of necessity, I guess."

Her parents had other differences as well. "They were complete opposites," said Brown. "Mother taught Sunday school and was the choir director at Grace Episcopal Church. She was blond, quiet, gentle.

"My father was swarthy, and open and friendly, like Zorba the Greek. He always wore a suit. He was so handsome. He walked down the streets of Tucson and everyone knew him."

But the way Duke Dillas made a living would drive a wedge into the family. "Our home life was not like everyone else's," said Brown. "My father slept late in the morning, then went to the Varsity, where he stayed till late at night."

Years later, her father would tell her, "I didn't hurt anybody. A stockbroker does much worse."

But young Kathy was hurt — especially when her father was arrested while she was still in junior high school.

"It was front page news. I didn't want to go to school. My mother took me to see Kenneth Anderson, the principal at Mansfeld Junior High. And that kindly, wonderful man convinced me I could go back. No one ever said a word to me about it."

After the arrest, her parents' marriage, said Brown, turned "icy." Still, they stayed together. "My mother took care of the family. She also took care of my father's mother, who moved in with us."

Not that there weren't some good times sprinkled here and there. Brown remembered picnics in the park, attended by Tucson's close-knit Greek community.

And she remembered how her parents once loved to go dancing. "He was a good dancer. So was she. They used to go to La Jolla nightclub."

In 1950, a young attorney by the name of Robert Morrison was elected county attorney. His first order of business: clean up the gambling in Pima County.

Duke Dillas was one of the first casualties. "That's when things started getting hot around here," said Brown. That same year, her parents divorced.

On Nov. 15, 1954, Dillas, along with two other Tucsonans, was arrested once more during a gambling raid at three separate homes. All three pleaded guilty.

On Jan. 24, 1955, Dillas was fined $1,000 in federal court. "My father never did time, but he must have been threatened with going to prison," said Brown. "That may be why he went to California and never came back."

Long before then, George Gekas had taken sole ownership of the Varsity Coffee Shop, as it was then called. "Duke sold out to me for $7,000," said Gekas. "I sold the pool tables to some people down the street and put booths in there."

But by 1956, Gekas had sold the Varsity as well. Meanwhile, Duke was working in a men's clothing store in California. "He was there for a while. And then the lure of the easy money got to him," said Brown. "He was doing bookmaking in Long Beach."

Though Brown and her father eventually reconciled, her parents never did. "Mother died in 1968. The day after she died, my father called me, sobbing. He said, 'Your mother was the best person I ever knew.' "

In 1984, Duke Dillas came back to Tucson for good. "He was very ill," said Brown. "He came back here and he died here. There was no place else for him to go."

HOMETOWN NOTABLES
3

Bill Richey

They don't make childhoods like this anymore — at least not in Tucson.

"My mother would drop us off at Sabino Canyon and we would stay two or three weeks at a time, swimming and fishing in the creek — drank out of it, too.

"There were four or five of us. We took canned goods and hunted frogs and rattlesnakes. We were like Tom Sawyer."

Oh, to be a kid in Tucson back in the '30s — at least a kid named Bill Richey.

Adulthood would prove to be equally interesting.

A Golden Gloves champ, Richey put himself through law school for a time by serving as bouncer at a local honky-tonk.

Bill Richey hit the books by day and a few jaws by night.

"I would go to law school with big bites in my fists. Those cowboys on the southside were something else."

Born at home in a house that still stands at 624 N. Seventh Ave., Richey roamed all over downtown, from movie houses to candy stores.

Though his father was prominent Tucson attorney Tom Richey, not all was carefree childhood for Bill and his four siblings — not with the Great Depression bearing down.

"Dad had a beautiful fig tree. My sisters and I would pick the figs and take them to Steinfeld's market. We got paid 10 cents a pound."

Sometimes he shot doves to augment the family table. "Dad used to say, 'Thank God for the Chinese grocery stores.' They would keep us on the tab until Dad got a check."

The Depression ground on. "Dad lost the house, and we moved out to 20 acres he owned at Prince Road and Mountain. The coyotes would come in the yard and eat the watermelon.

"It had been a chicken ranch, all adobe. It had a real good well on it. My mother took the old walls of the chicken ranch and the house and had it rebuilt."

Times turned a little better by 1940, when Richey enrolled at the University of Arizona.

There, Richey veered from animal husbandry to engineering to liberal arts. What he did like was boxing class. "It taught me the fundamentals."

I'll say. In 1941, Richey took the light-heavyweight Golden Gloves title for Arizona. By day he hit the books. By night he hit, well, a few jaws, boxing at the old Canvas Castle, which became the Tucson Sports Center.

"I won my first 19 fights; 17 were knockouts," said Richey.

He was a Marine by late 1942, slogging through the Pacific. After the war he went back to college, this time on the GI Bill.

Awarded an athletic scholarship, Richey attended Michigan State for a year, then transferred back to the UA.

Even during law school, he fought an occasional bout or two. Never mind that some occurred in the middle of the parking lot of the old Chanticleer nightclub, where Richey served as bouncer for a time.

"I was broke and the job paid $2 an hour."

Once he set up his law practice in 1952, Richey hung up his gloves for good.

For the next 31 years, he would practice law in this town. He also served a term in the Legislature and became the husband of a U.S. District judge — Mary Anne Richey.

After Mary Anne died in 1983, Richey retired and moved to the White Mountains. In 1991, he married the former Judy Ziehler.

Now back in Tucson, Richey still finds much to like.

"I don't know so many people anymore. It's diluted with all those who are moving in. But I like Tucson. It was a nice town back then. It's great now."

Even if you can't drink water from the creek anymore.

HOMETOWN
NOTABLES
4

Sandy Duckett

Not many women commuted by motorcycle, let alone raced them back in the '50s.

This woman did.

"Usually I was the only woman, but not always," said Sandy Duckett, who vaguely remembered another female racing from time to time.

Races were held weekend mornings on an old World War II auxiliary runway — about where the Marana Northwest Regional Airport would later go.

It was one-on-one drag racing, no money, no prizes. "There were 20 or 30 of us. We'd just all get together."

So did the men ever give her a hard time? Nah, said Duckett. Well, maybe just once.

"I did hear about one guy I beat who supposedly went back to Phoenix and sold his machine."

Though Duckett only raced for a year, she did jump back behind the handlebars a decade later when the "Route 66" TV series filmed in Tucson.

"Somebody called up from the production company. I got my dad to baby-sit the kids and I did the stunt riding for Julie Newmar," said Duckett.

Her role was to roar up the Sixth Avenue underpass, nearly colliding with the TV show's trademark Corvette.

Duckett also rode down a mountain near San Xavier with a double for Martin Milner, one of the stars of the show.

Credit the Korean War with Duckett's brush with fame.

In 1951, her then-husband, Lee, who was the proud owner of a Harley-Davidson, was sent to Korea.

"He told me, 'If you can start it, you can ride it,'" said Duckett. "It was harder than hell to start. I would get home from work and practically pass out trying."

Finally, she got the engine to turn over. "I rode it every day to Grand Central, where I was working."

That sort of grit and gumption came early.

Born in Ohio in 1925, Duckett, along with her parents, wound up in Las Vegas after the Depression left her dad jobless.

When her father's hopes of getting a job building the Hoover Dam fell through, he found work as a tenant farmer in the area. "I think it's maybe where the Strip is now," said Duckett.

A year later, they moved near Prescott, where relatives lived.

Here, Duckett went to school, working at Walgreens in her senior year of high school to earn money for flying lessons.

When the flight school in Holbrook where she worked after high school moved to Tucson, she moved with it.

During the war, she also did riveting work one summer in Long Beach, and lubricated the tail units of planes out at Ryan Field.

But what she really wanted to do was go to college. Armed with a tuition break from a sympathetic dean, and a $100 loan from her flight-instructor boyfriend, Duckett graduated from the University of Arizona in 1949.

It was in college where she also got involved with car racing, thanks to a friend whose husband raced cars.

Soon, she was selling tickets for races held in a former cornfield across from Gilpin Airlines, on Tucson's northside. She also worked the ticket booth for the jalopy races held at the Tucson Rodeo Grounds.

Here, she even drove a car during a qualifying heat for a powder-puff race. "By the time I got around the track, the race was over," she said.

From 1957 to 1974, Duckett worked as an administrative assistant for the Tucson Airport Authority.

Still, she seemingly never lost her taste for adventure.

In 1974, she went to work for a dozen years as a secretary for the U.S. Foreign Service in such locales as Mozambique, Swaziland, Yemen and El Salvador.

"It was lots of fun," said Duckett.

Maybe almost as much fun as racing motorcycles.

HOMETOWN
NOTABLES
5

Madeline Berger

The Saturday Morning Musical Club in Safford in '22.

We had the mountains, we had the cacti, we had the wide-open spaces. About all we were lacking, eight or nine decades ago, was a little culture.

"One time we had an opera with a death scene in the middle. After the death scene was over, everybody in the audience got up and went home." That's the tale Tucson pioneer Roy Drachman loved to tell.

Into this cultural wasteland ventured Madeline Dreyfus Heinman Berger, bringing with her an appreciation for the arts that culminated in 1927 with the creation of the Temple of Music and Art.

Over the years, the rococo building down on South Scott Street would host everyone from Jascha Heifetz playing the violin to Tallulah Bankhead emoting.

Besides visiting artists, the building during its days also sheltered a number of permanent tenants, including the Tucson Little Theatre; studios for dance, voice and violin; a tearoom; and something known as the Rishi-Krishnanandi and Para-Vida Center.

The temple also served as permanent home to its founding force, the Saturday Morning Musical Club. Not surprisingly, this too was begun by Madeline Berger, as she was known in her later years.

Just who was this woman of refinement and how did she become such a force in Tucson's fledging art scene?

"She was born in Nevada City, Calif., in 1875," said her nephew, John Dreyfuss. (The Dreyfuss family spells the last name at least five ways, he said — hence Madeline's dropping the final "s.")

After her father died, her mother ran the family bakery and brewery for a short time, then sold it and moved to Los Angeles. There, Madeline met and married Simon Heineman, who among other things, ran a liquor distributorship out of Tucson.

Here the couple settled about the turn of the century. Schooled in voice and piano, Madeline Heineman soon began seeking out women in the community with similar arts leanings.

In 1907, a few of these women gathered in Madeline Heineman's Victorian parlor for the first meeting of the Saturday Morning Musical Club. Naturally, Mrs. Heineman was the club's first president.

At the end of its first session, the club had grown to 50 members who met in each other's homes and presented classical recitals by homegrown talent. In 1910, the group sponsored its first visiting artist, well-known singer Frieda Langendorff.

By 1914, the group was hiring an auditorium for its meetings and looking for a permanent home. A decade later, with membership rolls swelling, the club was still looking.

That year, 1924, Simon Heineman died. But Madeline's dream of a permanent home for the arts did not. Two years later, she persuaded wealthy winter resident Alexander Berger — soon to be her brother-in-law — to donate $100,000 toward the building fund.

"The family gossip was that she originally set her sights on Alex, but he told her he was too old for her and sicced her on his brother Harry," said John Dreyfuss. Madeline married Harry Berger, a Tucson investment broker, in 1928.

Dreyfuss also contended that Madeline and Alexander Berger struck a deal. "He told her he would donate the money to the temple if she could raise $50,000 from Tucson merchants. She was very persuasive."

November 1926. Metropolitan Opera coloratura soprano Amelita Galli-Curci turns the first spadeful of dirt. The Temple of Music and Art goes from dream to reality.

A year later, Oct. 21, 1927, thousands turned out to hear a "Spanish orchestra in costume" play in the patio, and to gawk at the red carpets, the pipe organ, the velvet curtains and the oil paintings — including one of Madeline — which would grace the lobby of the temple for more than four decades.

The following week, Jascha Heifetz became the first of many visiting artists who would play the temple. Among the others: Paderewski and Rachmanioff, Nelson Eddy and the Ballet Russe de Monte Carlo.

"My aunt seemed to draw famous people and gather them around her," said John Dreyfuss, who, as a boy, often visited his aunt in her home at 1 Paseo Redondo.

But even the charms of Madeline Berger could not shield the temple from the Depression. After losing its tax-exempt status the year after it opened, the temple for a time became a motion picture theater. Audiences who a few months earlier had thrilled to Heifetz were now watching Dolores Del Rio in "Ramona."

In 1932, the Saturday Morning Musical Club offered the temple — and its $65,000 mortgage — to the city of Tucson. The city declined.

Somehow, the temple persevered. In 1940, Madeline Berger stepped down as president of the Saturday Morning Musical Club, after 30 seasons as its president. When she died in 1943, her funeral was held at the temple.

"Everybody in the world was there," said Justina Keller, whose mother, Elizabeth Healy, was an early member of the club. For 35 years her mother also worked at the temple, booking the acts.

In the spring of '42, you could catch performances by Heifetz, pianists José and Amparo Iturbi and tenor Jan Keipura. A ticket to see the Iturbis, for example, would set you back $1.10, including tax.

"Almost everyone you could think of played at the temple," said Keller. "Tucson was the stop between El Paso and Los Angeles, so we got almost anybody you would expect."

Audiences, turned out in best bib and tucker, were escorted to their seats by a dozen or so high school girls, recruited as usherettes.

"We wore evening gowns and long white gloves," remembered ex-usherette Louise Stover, sister to John Dreyfuss and niece of Madeline Berger. "After the performance started, we would all sit in the balcony and sneak cigarettes."

Besides backing performances at the temple, the Saturday Morning Musical Club supported a number of musical clubs for Tucson youngsters. It also sponsored twice-weekly radio programs, broadcast over KVOA. Sample programs from 1942: "The Importance of Civil War Defense" and "The New Art of Radio Writing."

During summers, the un-air-conditioned temple — like much of the town — shut down. "All the dance schools held their spring recitals at the temple," said Keller. "They used to open the doors and pray that it would be cool that day."

In 1972 — the same year the community center was built — the temple was sold and turned into a Mexican movie theater.

Today, after a succession of former owners and a $2.9 million restoration in 1989, the ornate Spanish building is home to the Arizona Theatre Company, its thespians reciting their lines on its venerable stage.

HOMETOWN
NOTABLES
6

Boilermaker Dick

You just never know sometimes how a story's going to arrive.

A while back I wrote a column that cited an old newspaper ad about a 1925 boxing match here in Tucson, featuring a man by the name of Boilermaker Dick. Didn't know a thing about the guy, just liked the sound of his name.

Next day I got a call from a woman with a message about as direct as they come: "I'm Boilermaker Dick's daughter."

Yes, she was.

Boilermaker Dick liked to put up his dukes.

"I think my father fought professionally for about 10 years," said Beatrice Amado Kissinger, whose father's given name was Ricardo Amado — part of a pioneer family that settled in Patagonia.

Even out of the ring, Boilermaker Dick liked to put up his dukes, said Kissinger.

"He just liked to fight. We used to go to dances and after every dance, my dad was always in a brawl."

Her father and mother were childhood sweethearts who grew up in Patagonia but married in Globe, where her father went to work in the mines.

"When the mines shut down, they came to Tucson about 1918 and he got a job with the Southern Pacific in the roundhouse," said Kissinger.

She figured that's where her dad picked up his nickname.

It was a name that would stick with him long after he left the ring — and the roundhouse, said Kissinger.

"People in Nogales called him Boilermaker Dick for years. Only my mother called him Ricardo."

Born in the barrio in 1922, Kissinger hardly remembered her father's fights in Tucson, such as the eight-rounder he pulled back in '25 against Bob Mandell at the Tucson Garage — where ladies were "cordially invited."

"I used to hear a lot of conversations," said Kissinger. "My dad did a lot of street fighting in Barrio Anita."

In 1928 her father was laid off from the roundhouse, and the family, by then numbering five kids, moved back to Patagonia.

She had vague memories of attending fights inside canvas tents, and being afraid someone would hurt her dad.

"I remember crying, 'Don't hurt him. Don't hit him.' "

Alas, someone did deliver a punch serious enough to send her father to the hospital one time with a ruptured spleen, said Kissinger.

Along the way, Boilermaker Dick hung up his gloves, at least professionally. Amateur hour was another matter.

"Every Saturday night, a dance was held in Patagonia," said Kissinger.

"It was a big social event, with a band. At midnight there would be a supper with tamales and coffee. And after every dance my dad was in a fight."

By the early '30s, the family had moved to Ruby, where Kissinger's dad and her older brother went to work at the mine.

"We had such a good time in Ruby," said Kissinger. And every Saturday night the family went to the dances, this time in Arivaca.

You guessed it.

"Afterwards, my dad would be in a fight," said

Kissinger. "It was kind of a sport with him."

Her parents left Ruby in the late '30s and the family resettled in Patagonia. "My dad worked some of the little mining claims, mostly silver." What's more, he was still throwing punches.

"There was a little guy from Nogales who was always picking a fight with my dad," said Kissinger.

After high school, she became a Navy nurse, married and had six children. Her mother lived to be 98. Her father died at age 66.

"He played hard," said the daughter of Boilermaker Dick. "He just beat himself to death."

HOMETOWN
NOTABLES
7

Johnny Gibson

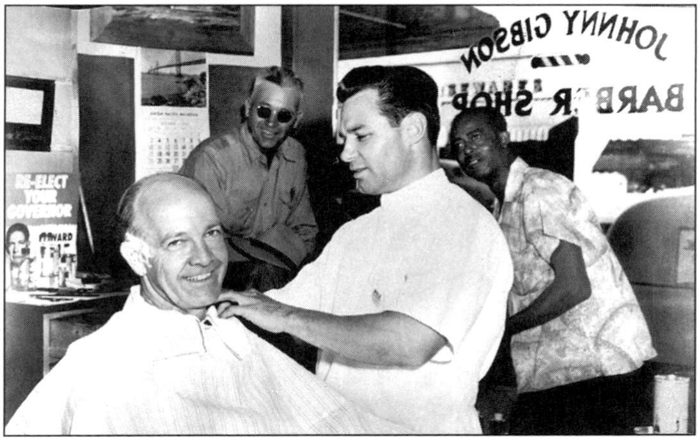

Johnny Gibson cuts Gov. Howard Pyle's hair in '54.

Buildings came and buildings went, as the wrecker's ball flitted 'round and 'round downtown Tucson.

Still, some things endured. Notably, the buffalo head, the grainy photographs of men flexing their muscles, the smell of hair tonic, and the small, dark-haired fellow who presided over what may have been downtown Tucson's last barbershop.

"When I started, there were lots of barbershops downtown," said Johnny Gibson, who for more than 60 years cut hair and shaved whiskers at the same North Sixth Avenue location.

Here is where our fathers and brothers went for their haircuts while our mothers shopped at the nearby Sears Roebuck and Co., just down the street.

"Go see if your father's done," my own mother would tell me. And so I would tiptoe into that male domain, cluttered with Police Gazette magazines and the gentle banter of men arguing baseball statistics, or whether Ike would beat out Adlai Stevenson for a second term.

Politics, sports, the state of downtown — they still talk that talk here at what was once Johnny Gibson's Barber Shop, sitting in the same yellow chairs in front of the same time-spattered mirrors.

"Everyone talks about downtown construction. When I first started, they were just building the new Levy's," said Gibson.

"We were just kids," said Gibson with a laugh, remembering that day spent with his best buddy, Art Ezell. "I was 17 and he was 16. We got out my mother's old hair tools. We whittled on one another, and then his mother judged us. She said 'John, it looks like you got the worst of the deal.' "

Encouraged by that faint praise, Gibson started "whittling" on the heads of his friends and fellow paperboys.

Originally from Humboldt, S.D., a 14-year-old Gibson and his mother moved to Tucson so that she could nurse a brother ailing with tuberculosis back to health.

"I was most impressed with Tucson," Gibson recalled. "I wrote home. 'They have two skyscrapers here.' And they did — the Pioneer (hotel) and the Valley National Bank."

The little family settled into a rented house on a chicken ranch that would one day become what was known for years as Cliff Valley Golf Course.

"It was six miles from town, and there were no buses," said Gibson. "I walked 2½ miles to Amphi Junior High."

During Gibson's junior year at Tucson High School, his mother, who was nursing a woman with TB, came down with the disease. To help make ends meet, Gibson signed up with the Civilian Conservation Corps and was sent to a camp on the Mogollon Rim.

"I made $30 a month and sent $22 home," he said. And then fate, as it often does, sashayed right on in.

"There were 200 guys at camp, plus the leaders, and four guys cutting hair," said Gibson.

"But every six months they had a turnover. All the guys cutting hair left."

With the camp bereft of barbers, Gibson got to thinking. "I sent off $3.50 to Sears Roebuck for a set of barber tools, including the electric clippers."

The first customer's clips came gratis. The next one cost 20 cents. Gibson recalled: "He said, 'You're not bad.' " I cut hair for the next eight months, 20 cents apiece, at night after the regular day's work was done. Then I raised the price to a quarter."

About the same time Gibson's two-year stint with the CCC was ending, his mother died. So Gibson took the $300 he had saved from skimming over the scalps of his campmates and took the bus to the nearest barber's college in Los Angeles.

After graduating in May of '42, Gibson motored to Phoenix to take his state exams. Perusing the local pool halls, he found a likely head of hair on which to demonstrate his barbering prowess.

"I promised him $5 to do a shave, haircut, and massage, but the next day he didn't show." Desperate, Gibson ran out into the street and collared the first transient he found. "I told him if he'd let me shave him and cut his hair, I'd pay him $5 and buy breakfast for him and for his buddy."

Tucson's best-known barber thus became one by working on a man whose "hair stuck out like Dagwood," with a "beard made of iron."

Back in Tucson, Gibson scouted up his first barbering job at the old Santa Rita Hotel, making $28 a week.

Soon after, World War II intervened. Volunteering as a paratrooper in the 101st Airborne, Gibson jumped into the Normandy invasion, was taken prisoner, worked in a German makeshift evacuation hospital, escaped, was found at Bastogne and eventually was shipped back to the United States.

"After I recuperated, I went right back to the Santa Rita," said Gibson. Glory days those, with Nick Hall running the hotel. "The cattlemen and the cowboys all came in for their shaves, and they all mingled with the winter visitors." And all for 65 cents for a haircut, 35 cents for a shave.

But Gibson, who had married Pearle Klamm after the war, wanted his own business. He found it at the old Palace Barber Shop. For sale: $3,000.

"The rent's still the same as it was 40 years ago," said Gibson. So are the sinks, the tortoise-shell mirror and the mop bucket he inherited.

During the late '40s and the early '50s, Gibson was building his body as well as his business, earning the titles of "Mr. Arizona" in 1950 and "Mr. Tucson" in 1951.

"My real interest was in competitive weight lifting," said Gibson, who still competes in senior events. Times were good in the days when men and boys wore their hair short, and everyone found occasion to come downtown.

And then came the '60s. One by one, Tucson's stalwarts of the retail trade either shut down or moved to the suburbs. Meanwhile, hairstyles were creeping over ears and past collars.

"Long hair was hard on the barber," said Gibson, who cut his five-chair operation back to two chairs. "Barbershops were closing up right and left, right up to the '70s."

But not the long, narrow shop at 53 N. Sixth Ave. Somehow it persevered long enough to see things come full circle.

"We're now inundated with University of Arizona boys," said Gibson. The rancheros and the cowboys still come in, too, as well as a slew of government workers, he said. "They hit us hard at lunch hour."

And yes, you can still get a decent shave. "We use strop razors with Schick injections in them," Gibson said. "You can't hone and strop a razor that sharp."

What you won't get here is a hair "styling." There are no blow dryers, no curling irons, no mousse. "We use crème oil," said Gibson, firmly.

"Very few are going to barber college anymore," he said with a sigh. "Now a guy can go in a beauty shop and get a haircut."

Somewhere else, that is. "I like it here," said Gibson, taking in the row of hair tonics, the sporting magazines, the worn linoleum. "I plan to stay here till the undertaker picks me up from right under my chair."

(Johnny Gibson sold his shop, now called Curley's Downtown Barbershop, in 2001. As of publication, he still cut hair there every Tuesday.)

HOMETOWN
NOTABLES
8

Charley Thornton

When you write about times that preceded your own, you'd better have some good sources.

One of the best was Charley Thornton, who told me what it was like to sell newspapers during the Depression, and how it felt to wrestle men down to the mat.

A Tucsonan from the late '20s on, Thornton was best known for the wrestling programs he coached at the Arizona State Schools for the Deaf and the Blind during the '40s and '50s.

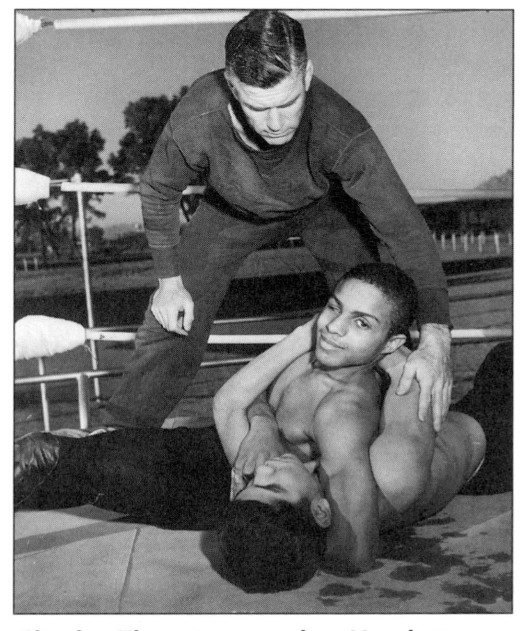

Charley Thornton coaches Howlett Smith and Frank Elias, bottom, in the '50s.

Not only did Thornton coach the students, but he took them on Rim-to-Rim hikes of the Grand Canyon. Bear in mind, we are talking visually impaired here.

"I had worn-out shoes, but it was an experience that couldn't be beat," said Frank Elias, a champion wrestler and 1954 ASDB graduate.

Thornton, said Elias, also taught him how to water ski.

As for his coaching skills, "Charley had a way about him," said Elias. "He didn't have to yell or demand. He made the rules, and we abided by them."

In June 1993, Thornton, then 80, went hiking in the Santa Catalina Mountains and never returned. Searchers found his body at the bottom of a 40-foot dry waterfall.

To this day, Thornton's death is a mystery. Still, one certainty remains: "He was doing what he loved to do," said son Bill Thornton.

One thing Charley never lived to see was his induction into the Pima County Sports Hall of Fame, which happened in 2004.

"I had never heard of it," said Bill, who about a year earlier had wandered into the hall's downtown location, at 110 S. Church Ave., in La Placita Village.

Before long, he was nominating his father. "The reaction from everyone was that it was long overdue," said Bill.

Born in Nogales, Ariz., Charley was farmed out to various relatives from the age of 5 on, after his mother died.

Tucson became home by the time he was a teenager.

Here, he threw out newspapers, first by bicycle and later by motorbike, on routes that stretched across 30 miles.

It was at the old Congress Street YMCA where Charley learned to wrestle. Before long, he was earning anywhere from $3 to $15 a night, grunting and groaning in small towns such as Mammoth or Casa Grande.

He also did his share of refereeing in places including the old Armory and the Labor Temple.

"That's where I saw a lady come down to the ropes and start hitting one of the wrestlers in the head with her shoe," Charley once told me.

In 1947, Charley volunteered to help start a wrestling program at ASDB.

Two years later, the school put him on the payroll, "though he sure didn't do it for the money," said Bill.

With help from the Lions Clubs of Southern Arizona, Charley put in a railed running track for his wrestlers, so they could work out.

"He was a big believer in running," said Bill, who as a kid often accompanied the wrestlers on weekend hikes, as well as on treks through the Grand Canyon.

In fact, the group's first Canyon hike in 1956 so inspired then-Sen. Barry Goldwater that he penned a personal letter to Charley, praising the boys for their accomplishment and Charley for his leadership.

"Charley said we could do it, no matter what," said Elias.

For that kind of inspiration, the Hall of Fame also created the Charley Thornton Award, to be given annually to a young person or team who has overcome adversity.

Tucson High basketball player and stroke survivor Joe Kay was its first recipient.

HOMETOWN
NOTABLES
9

Georges DeMeester

"Music Under the Stars" in 1976.

Dead palm fronds formed the band shell, and on occasion the audience wound up in the drink.

Such were the early days of the Tucson Pops Orchestra.

Sometimes they played in motel patios, sometimes in the park. But always, it was "Music Under the Stars." And always in those early years, it was just one man at the podium — Georges DeMeester, founder and first director of the pops.

The man who brought Debussy and Gershwin to the lawn chair crowd was born to an Old World family, heavy on musical talent.

"My whole family was musical," said DeMeester, born in 1896 in Belgium. His father was the leader of a band that performed while teetering on bicycles.

"They rode their bicycles in formation, the way college bands do," DeMeester told me back in 1991, in a booming, heavily accented voice.

Days for the young DeMeester were filled with schoolwork, along with early-morning and late-afternoon study at the music conservatory.

By 1913, he was playing in an orchestra. When World War I broke out the following year, the 18-year-old DeMeester fled the enemy, but only briefly.

"The Germans got my name from a list of members of the musicians union. They said, "Do you want to play for us or do you want to go to the concentration camps?' We played."

In 1927, DeMeester came to America on a ship bound for New York City. "I played violin with the ship's orchestra," he said. But when the ship returned to Belgium, so did its violinist.

As soon as the paperwork was in order, however, DeMeester returned to the States, this time for good.

"I arrived in New York on Labor Day," said DeMeester. "On Wednesday I went back to work at the Strand Theatre on Broadway."

In 1930, DeMeester won an audition for a four-month gig out West, at a new hotel called the Pioneer, in a town called Tucson.

It would be a four-month adventure, nothing more — until fate, Beethoven and Enriqueta Martinez intervened.

"The Tucson Symphony was going to have a concert," said Enriqueta, who played violin in the orchestra. "We asked Georges to help. It was Beethoven's Fifth.

"I had never seen so many notes in my life. I was struggling. Then I looked up and there he was, playing the darn thing by heart."

The flustered Enriqueta forgot her place. "I had to pretend I was playing."

"Of course I knew," said DeMeester, who would marry this daughter of a pioneer Tucson family in 1935.

Once his hotel gig was up, DeMeester had to scare up other work. He and his violin went just about everywhere — from giving music lessons at private schools to playing at the old Blue Moon and Wetmore's dance halls. "When Prohibition ended, we played in the streets when the beer came in."

Even the government was good for a gig in those dark Depression days. In 1936, DeMeester took over as technical director and teacher of the Old Pueblo Mexican Orchestra, whose musicians drew their pay from the Works Progress Administration.

"They had to pass a proficiency exam to be paid," said DeMeester, who conducted rehearsals at Davis School. "I couldn't speak Spanish and they didn't like me. But I kept on and they all loved me, finally. I got them all to pass."

When the first pops concert was held is debatable. DeMeester remembered one benefit concert played in the early '50s at El Conquistador. "But there was a dollar donation."

In 1953, he conducted several concerts on the grounds of the vets hospital. "I got my friends from the symphony," said DeMeester. "There were 22 at the beginning."

"We had patients looking out the window," said Enriqueta, who accompanied her husband to every pops performance.

Just about everyone agrees, however, that the first free, under-the-stars Tucson Pops concert was held April 23, 1961, between the swimming pool and children's play area of the Hiway House motel on North Oracle Road.

The 40-piece orchestra tackled the "William Tell Overture," "Tales From the Vienna Woods" and a hellacious wind that finally forced DeMeester to roll up his score and use it as a conductor's wand.

"Only experienced musicians could have managed so well, battling with the wind and having to read music in semidarkness," read the next day's newspaper account.

The following spring, the pops had a new home, this time at the Ramada Inn. Again, they played near the pool. Live radio began covering the concerts, over stations KTUC and KFMM-FM.

Podiums for the conductor were impromptu and varied. Once, it was a French Provincial nightstand, complete with drawer.

"I was afraid he was going to fall off that thing," said Enriqueta, "but he never did."

Less lucky were some younger members of the audience, who had gathered around the pool. "The kids were in the wading pool with their clothes on," said Enriqueta. "Their mothers were so mad, they stripped the clothes off the kids right there and they all went home with nothing on."

After three seasons at the Ramada, the Tucson Pops moved to what is now known as Reid Park. DeMeester turned to Gene Reid, then Tucson parks director, for help.

"When we started it was pretty pitiful," said Reid. He began by lashing 25 or 30 wooden serving tables together to form a stage for the musicians.

Then came the band shell. "We nailed some two-by-fours along the back, strung some wire, and hung some palm fronds," said Reid.

Thankfully, the palm-frond band shell soon gave way to one made of canvas, stretched between 3-inch pipes.

"I had friends at D-M (Davis-Monthan Air Force Base)," said Reid. "I told them we needed canvas. God, you couldn't believe the amount of canvas they brought back."

More than enough to form a canopy. Trouble was, said Reid, it flapped around whenever there was wind. "So we got up this light aluminum roof."

The metal roof, by the way, may have added a new dimension to the percussion section. "The kids used to throw rocks on top of the band shell," said Enriqueta. "They'd make a 'bang!' "

Money to pay the participating musicians came from a variety of sources over the years, including the Saturday Morning Musical Club. Major funding, however, came through the Music Performance Trust Funds, distributed by the national office of the American Federation of Musicians.

From the beginning, the concerts were a hit. Soon, crowds in excess of 3,000 were sprawling across the grass on warm Sunday evenings.

One Star critic described it in this way: "Even the Metropolitan Opera couldn't have produced a more enchanting setting than Mother Nature did last night for the Tucson Pops Orchestra. The deep salmon sunset yielded to the full moon. The players looked attractive, the ladies in white, the men in white jackets."

In 1973, DeMeester stepped down, handing over his conducting duties to Charles "Bucky" Steele. Thirteen years later, a newly renovated band shell would be renamed the Reid Park Outdoor Performance Center.

One year later, the band shell was again renamed, this time for the man who first gave us "Music Under the Stars" more than 40 years ago.

Once more, DeMeester took up his stance at the podium, leading the orchestra through a medley of old familiar numbers.

"In all the years, we were never rained out," said DeMeester, remembering all those Sunday concerts on all those starlit nights. "And the last song, the people always stood up and clapped."

HOMETOWN
NOTABLES
10

Maria Urquides

Lincoln was still a practicing attorney and Tucson had just shifted from Mexican to American soil in 1854, the year her father was born.

Now that's a claim few could make in this town.

One who could was Maria Urquides, educator, community leader and something of a pioneer herself — both in the field of bilingual education and in the fact that she arrived in town squalling and kicking in 1908, four full years before statehood.

Maria Urquides was a pioneer in bilingual education.

Born in the barrio, she listened as a child to her father's tales of a Tucson still under siege.

Orphaned at age 11, Urquides' father, Hilario, lived with a family named Lee. "They had a flour mill near 'A' Mountain. I can remember my dad saying they used to have him climb to the top of the mountain to check for dust on the horizon. Apaches."

Hilario's wife, Mariana Legarra, born in Tucson in 1871, also sprang from roots long set down here.

Their youngest child, Maria, grew up in a town teeming with different cultures — Chinese, Mexican, Indian and Anglo. "That was the beauty of Tucson back then," said Urquides, who preferred to call herself Mexican-American. "We all needed each other."

Her earliest school days were spent at what was then called Safford Elementary. "It was a very happy experience," said Urquides.

Curiosity, however, may have prompted the family's move away from the barrio while Urquides was still a child.

"When they legalized prostitution in Gay Alley, it was right in back of our property," she remembered.

"My dad quietly built a fence, but my curiosity was aroused and I loosened the boards and pushed in. Someone hollered 'Hi, honey. Come on over.'

"So I got acquainted with the girls. I was running errands for them, getting good tips. That's the first time I ever had strawberries and cream with pink sugar. Well, my dad discovered what I was doing and so we moved."

Her father never went to school a day in his life, and her mother had to quit school in the third grade. But their youngest child would graduate from college — the first in the family to do so.

"For a Mexican-American girl to go to college was very unusual," said Urquides. "My older brother pitched a fit, my mother cried. But I went."

She credited three teachers at Tucson High School with setting her sights upon a higher education: Mary Balch, Madge Utterback and Lillian Cavett.

"Miss Balch, who as my homeroom teacher was also my counselor, asked me what I was going to do when I got out of school," said Urquides. "I told her I was going to work at Steinfeld's.

"She said: 'Oh no you're not. You're going to be an elementary school teacher.' I said, 'I am?' "

Quick as a wink, Balch switched Urquides' junior-year subjects into a more academic mode. "Before, I was just coasting along," said Urquides. "I just about failed algebra."

The transformation continued. "One day, Miss Balch heard me sing. So she took me to Madge Utterback (then Tucson High's chorus director) and had me sing. I had a pretty good voice.

"Then they took me to Lillian Cavett (then the school's drama director). They had me walk across the stage. I walked across it just like I was on the baseball field.

"Well, they took me in." And how. From a Gypsy in an operetta, she then went on to play the title role in "Belle of Barcelona."

Toast of the stage though she may have been, Urquides still felt the sting of discrimination in 1920s Tucson.

"In my junior and senior years, when I was into music, I began to notice that although I was friends with Anglo girls, I was never asked to go to their homes for parties." Worse still, "The Mexican-American girls decided I was being a gringacita."

The state teachers' college at Tempe is where she headed after high school. Again, her old homeroom teacher came through, this time by arranging a job at the college, cleaning the bathrooms in her dormitory.

Urquides supplemented that by singing Mexican tunes at a Tempe restaurant.

Both parents were at her graduation. "My father had tears streaming down from his eyes." Not long after, Hilario Urquides died.

By then, his daughter, armed with a two-year teaching certificate, had just begun to teach at Davis Elementary School. She would remain there for the next two decades.

"I'm sure I got the job because I spoke Spanish," said Urquides. "It was 1928, just before the Depression. The school was 98 percent Mexican-American, along with a few Indians and two Anglo families."

She taught everything from ancient history to woodworking, music and art to physical education. "It was the largest elementary school in Tucson, 720 kids."

Summertimes, she worked toward earning her bachelor's and master's degrees from the University of Arizona.

One of her fondest memories of those years at Davis is helping to create Oury Park out of an abandoned tourist camp.

"Oury Park was originally the city farms, where they kept the horses and horse-drawn vehicles servicing the city streets," said Urquides. "After the city moved all of it to Silverbell Road, it became a tourist camp for a while."

She, along with volunteers from the YMCA and a new parents' organization known as Club Adelante, went to the Pima County Board of Supervisors, asking for use of the abandoned property.

"We cleaned the bathrooms, cleared the fields, and built a library and a baseball diamond. Two years later, we got a pool. Then to my distress they closed it to black children, except on the day before it was cleaned."

Those were also the years when Spanish-speaking children were automatically shunted into 1-C, which totally immersed them in the English language. Only when the children were deemed English-proficient — which took anywhere from a few months to two years — were they allowed to attend regular classes.

Urquides went along with the program. "If I ever go to hell, it will be because of the kids I punished for speaking Spanish," she would later say.

After two decades at Davis School, Urquides was suddenly transferred to Sam Hughes, three days before the start of the school year.

"For 20 years I'd taught Mexican-American kids and Indians. Sam Hughes was all Anglo, affluent. I had to find out why I was being transferred."

Sam Hughes needed more experienced teachers was the only official reason Urquides was given. She was also told that perhaps she was too interested in the lives of her pupils outside of the classroom.

"If you're teaching at Davis, you can't divorce their school life from their personal life. I had visited the homes of every one of those kids."

But she stayed at Sam Hughes. "And I wound up visiting the homes of a lot of those kids too." She also wound up broadening horizons — hers as well as those of her pupils.

"I thought, 'How can I teach these kids something they don't know?' So I decided, 'OK, I'll teach them how to make adobes.' We made a little adobe hut.

"As it turned out, Sam Hughes was the best thing that ever happened to me. It enriched my professional and cultural life. Before, all I was interested in was the Mexican-American child. Now I learned about the Anglo child."

When Pueblo High School was formed in the mid-'50s, its new principal, Elbert Brooks, asked Urquides to come aboard.

It was there that she, along with fellow teachers

Henry Oyama and Adalberto Guerrero, began sowing seeds that would blossom into the bilingual education movement.

First, they came up with the Spanish-speaking students. Then they, along with other educators, surveyed 35 school districts in five Southwestern states.

The report from that trip, "The Invisible Minority," was published by the National Education Association. In 1968, the Bilingual Education Act was passed.

Though proud of that accomplishment, Urquides would later say: "Bilingual education is not what I hoped it would be — because we didn't teach the monolingual child, the Anglo child, to speak Spanish."

In 1978, she retired from the same district where 50 years earlier she had greeted her first class of eager 6-year-olds at Davis School.

Looking back on a lifetime of memories, she reflected: "Of all the years I taught, there's not a moment I regret."

(Maria Urquides died in 1994.)

HOMETOWN NOTABLES
11

The Iceman cometh

Oh for a chunk of it — cold, clear, shivers-down-your-spine ice.

That's all it took to send everyone from madams to urchins out in the street, heeding the call of the men with the gunnysacks slung from their shoulders — sacks filled with ice.

Arizona Ice and Cold Storage Co. circa 1932.

"Little kids would jump on the back of the truck. They all wanted a piece of ice. They'd call me 'Pina' — pineapple. I always gave them a piece," said Constant "Connie" Weinzapfel, who as a teenager hauled ice for two companies here in town.

No doubt about it. From beer halls to bordellos, private homes to restaurants, the iceman was a much-anticipated caller.

The town's first iceman was Paul Marooney, owner of the first Cosmopolitan Hotel, who started it all sometime back in the 1870s.

Sixteen mules hauled the precious machinery for Marooney's plant all the way from Colton, Calif.

Other ice plants soon sprang up — and folded — during the decades.

In 1923, yet another one — Arizona Ice and Cold Storage — came to town. This one stuck around. Founded by Jack B. Martin Sr., the plant later churned out the cold stuff for years under the name Crystal Ice and Cold Storage.

Arizona Ice was the company Weinzapfel worked for during a couple of summers back in the late '20s. "I helped a man who had a franchise to sell ice along one of the routes."

It was not a job for sleepyheads. "I'd get up about 4:45 in the morning, go down to the ice dock." The dock would be swarming with trucks, waiting to be loaded with ice. "While we were waiting, we'd sharpen our ice picks."

When it was their turn, Weinzapfel and the man he worked for would load the ice — cut from 300-pound blocks into 25- to 100- pound sizes — into the back of the truck.

By 5:15, they were on their way, down a route that included both the barrio and the red-light district. Though customers had cards they put on their windows when they needed ice, many forgot, said Weinzapfel.

"When we got about a block away, we'd start blowing the whistle. It was connected to the exhaust pipe. It went whooo-whooo, just like a train whistle. Everybody was asleep, we woke them up."

If the practice created any irate customers, Weinzapfel was unaware of it. "They always wanted ice early in the morning, before it melted."

The big blocks went to restaurants, the smaller blocks, down to 25 pounds, went into home iceboxes. Some, however, could only afford the 12½-pound sizes, said Weinzapfel. Those sold for a dime. Slivers went to the kids, for free.

Among the steadiest customers were the working women of Gay Alley, then the town's red-light district. "They wanted ice every day, sometimes twice a day," said Weinzapfel. "They used it for drinking water."

Twice a day, seven days a week, men worked the ice routes. "We ran all the way. We delivered as high as 60 300-pound blocks a day, go back and get some more."

When the man he worked for lost the route, Weinzapfel started hauling the cold stuff for Home Ice Co., which operated in Tucson during the '30s and '40s.

In 1936, Weinzapfel went to work for the railroad and permanently retired his ice tongs, if not his memories.

By the time Opha Probasco started work at Arizona Ice in 1935, the blocks were selling for a penny or two a pound.

As a 16-year-old kid in the middle of the Depression, Probasco was paid a quarter an hour for a full day's work.

"I used to ride in the backside of the truck, hanging on to the grab bars," said Probasco, who years later still had his ice tongs, pick and scabbard.

The route he worked served what was then considered the northwest side of town, all the way up to Grant Road.

"Businesses we went to every day — the restaurants, the beer joints," said Probasco. "With houses we'd hit both sides of the street at the same time. Sometimes they saw us; sometimes we'd have to holler out, 'Iceman!'

"In some part of town, we'd yell 'hielo' — 'ice' in Spanish."

During the years Probasco hefted the ice around on his shoulders, a price war hit town.

Union Ice, a small company on South Sixth Avenue, started it, he said.

"They were selling ice a nickel for 25 pounds. But you had to buy it at the plant. Arizona Ice dropped its prices too, but not as cheap as Union. It was quite an ice war. It was so cheap, people were giving their dogs ice water."

Travelers also bought ice, said Probasco, and not only for their water jugs. "People would put it in buckets and pans and put it in their cars."

Eventually, Arizona Ice swallowed up both the Union and Home companies. "We had Union Ice by the late '40s, Home Ice by 1951," said Jack Martin Jr., son of the founder.

The best years of the company, he said, were during the war. "All those troop trains were coming through. We ran truckload after truckload of ice to the train station, night and day."

In the days before the railroads air-conditioned their passenger cars, it was ice, said Martin, that served as a substitute. "Each car had a bunker underneath where you loaded the ice. Then a fan was run over the ice and through a ductwork system."

Peacetime and refrigeration started the slowdown. By the mid-'50s, Arizona Ice routes had dwindled from 32 to eight.

"When the ice routes diminished to the point that a man couldn't make a living, we put in little vending machines," said Martin. "We sold block, cubed or crushed ice out of the machines. It was my job to go around and collect the money."

Goodbye to the gunnysacks. This ice came in paper bags, said Martin, similar to what charcoal comes in today. "Later on, we went to plastic."

In 1951, Arizona Ice added a big freezer for storage, said Dina Panos Kwiatek, who was hired by the company that same year.

Into the cold went everything from shrimp to kosher pickles to Christmas trees. "We'd get the trees about a month before Christmas and store them," she said.

In the '50s, Martin Sr. sold the business but stayed on as manager until his retirement in 1959. He died in 1977.

To him may go the honor of owning the last in-use icebox in town.

"He insisted that ice was still the best coolant," said the son. "My mom had a fit. She had a refrigerator and a freezer.

"But he kept the icebox. And they always delivered to him."

HOMETOWN NOTABLES
12

Chuck Waggin

Chuck Waggin doodled his way into the hearts of thousands of children.

He gave us color in a black-and-white world.

Though his given name was Charles Amesbury, every kid in town knew him as Chuck Waggin, the zany host of "Cartoon Corral."

"He was even listed in the telephone book as Chuck Waggin," said his widow, Carol Amesbury.

Back in the days when weekday afternoons belonged to the kids and nobody had heard of Oprah, Waggin ruled the Tucson airwaves.

From the mid-1950s to 1963, he rode those waves at KVOA, doodling his way into the hearts of thousands of Tucson youngsters.

"He would do a cartoon, the children would copy it at home and send them in," said Carol. "He would get oodles and oodles of them and bring them home."

Her job was to pick a winner. "Many of them were perfect, very artistic. So I would often pick other names of kids you didn't see over and over."

She also made his studio props, such as the three female dummies Waggin occasionally danced with on the air.

"He'd come home for lunch and say, 'Well, what am I going to do today?' One day I had a wool sweater that I'd washed and shrunk. He took that and said, 'I'll be a bullfighter today.' "

Waggin was also known for the cartoon panels he drew that ran with the Arizona-Sonora Desert Museum's column by George L. Mountainlion.

The cartoons and the column were published every Sunday in the Arizona Daily Star during the 1960s.

Waggin also came out with two books of his own, "A Light-Hearted Look at the Desert" and "A Light-Hearted Look at the Roadrunner." He did the drawings, Carol supplied the prose and the poetry.

The northwest-side home where she and Waggin moved to more than 40 years ago would soon be filled with his artwork. "He just loved art," said Carol.

He also loved her. "We knew each other since junior high," said Carol, who, like her husband, grew up in Berkeley, Calif.

By the time he was 6, he was winning art contests. But when Waggin graduated from high school in 1933, it was the belly of the Great Depression.

So he went to work driving a truck. When he hit the watershed mark of $50 a week in 1938, they married and raised a son.

During the war, Waggin found work in the California shipyards. After the war, he went to work for Sears, unloading freight.

In 1952, he moved to Phoenix at the urging of his brother-in-law.

There, said Carol, he was told, " 'You know,

there's a new thing here, a television station.' "

Soon he was churning out drawings for commercials and station breaks at the state's first television station.

A year later he came to Tucson and went to work for brand-new KVOA, Channel 4.

"The station's staff consisted of me and the man who was building the station," Waggin told the Star in 1982.

"Cartoon Corral" headed for its last roundup in 1963 after "The Huntley-Brinkley Report" took its time slot, said Carol.

But her husband stayed on as the station's art director.

In 1982, Waggin retired. But he continued to photograph and make slide shows of desert critters scurrying through his yard.

"He called it, 'An Acre of Nature,' " said Carol.

Bone cancer took his life in 1993.

"He was such an amusing man," said Carol, shaking her head. "I had a laugh a day with that man."

Didn't we all.

War and Disasters

A gas leak caused Supreme Cleaners to explode, killing four.

We danced on the eve of Pearl Harbor,
then marched off to war. Closer to
home — a plane crash, an explosion
and the death of a president.

WAR AND DISASTERS
1

Train wreck of 1903

The aftermath of the Esmond train wreck.

What a fearsome sound it must have made, roiling out across the desert.

On Jan. 28, 1903, two passenger trains collided head-on east of Tucson, in the heart of what we now call Rita Ranch.

Fourteen people died on the spot, their bodies mangled and burned almost beyond recognition.

So great was the force of the 2:55 a.m. collision that the Pullman car at the rear of the eastbound train was jarred loose, rolling 14 miles down the track into the Tucson train yard it had left just minutes before.

Its sole passenger, a Pullman porter, emerged shocked but unscathed, bearing witness to the horrors ahead on the track.

About the same time, a brakeman on that same eastbound train managed to hike several miles from the wreck to the Vail station to wire for help.

Doctors on board a relief train from Tucson rushed to the scene.

The undertakers and reporters soon followed.

"Undertakers Parker and Reilly have fourteen bodies," reported the next day's Star, which described the condition of the bodies in gruesome detail.

The wreck itself, reported the Star, "Presented a scene never to be forgotten: the two monster engines were literally torn to pieces and the cars piled on top of each other, enveloped in sheets of flames and clouds of smoke."

The injured, at least 18 in number, were hauled back to town for treatment.

Meanwhile, coffins lined the wreckage, waiting to be filled.

Among the reported dead: the engineers from both trains, a fireman and several passengers, including a "millionaire capitalist."

Three of the dead were listed as "hobos," including one, reported the Tucson Citizen, "who was riding the brakes and was pinioned by the collision. He was burned to a cinder."

It was one of the deadliest train wrecks in Arizona — and certainly the worst involving the Southern Pacific line in Southern Arizona, said Tucson historian and writer William Kalt, author of "Tucson Was a Railroad Town."

Naturally, it was attributed to human error, with most fingers pointed toward E.F. Clough, night operator at Vail.

At 2:40 a.m., just minutes before the crash, a westbound passenger train, with engineer Jack Bruce at the throttle, pulled into the Vail station.

There, Clough was supposed to pass off two written orders to train conductor G.W. Parker.

One of the orders, sent minutes earlier from Tucson, was to sidetrack the train at the Esmond siding, four miles down the track, until an eastbound train passed through.

Parker testified that he never got that order. Though initial reports cast some blame on the conductor, subsequent coroner's juries exonerated Parker and found Clough at fault.

Just before the crash, Clough, realizing the crucial order may not have been received, wired the Tucson office.

But it was too late. Five minutes later, Clough wired back that, "There was a large sheet of flame ahead on the track."

By the time of the inquests, Clough had disappeared. Parker was later fired by SP but found work at another railroad, said Kalt.

While the train tracks were eventually moved to the west, the ruins of the Esmond station — built close to that fateful siding — would stand for another century.

On Nov. 27, 2003, the station burned to the ground.

But you can still see remnants of the old train bed running near the busy intersection of Rita and Houghton roads.

On the intersection's northwest corner, a Fry's grocery store sprawls right over the crash site.

WAR AND DISASTERS
2

Armistice Day

There will be a parade on Veterans Day, perhaps a concert or two. Schools and government offices will be closed.

And don't forget that huge two-for-one sale of one kind or another down at the mall.

Veterans Day wasn't always done that way — let alone named that way.

Armistice Day was what we once called it, marking the end of the war that engulfed Europe in 1914 and three years later, America.

It all ended on Nov. 11, 1918. The war to end all wars — or so we thought.

Southern Arizona sent its first men to that war on Sept. 9, 1917, seen off by 2,000 flag-waving well-wishers.

Thirteen months later, Tucsonans were giddily awaiting the end of the war.

Not knowing exactly when the armistice would be signed, city movers and shakers, reported the Star, agreed that "the celebration would and could only be spontaneous."

Some advertisers lost no time in jumping on the peace bandwagon. "Germany is coming to her senses," crowed an ad for the New York Store on West Congress Street.

Yet others had failed to get the message. "Use more eggs to save meat," ran an ad for, of all things, Lucky Strike cigarettes.

"World freed of Hun menace" was bannered across the next day's paper, along with stories of "wild scenes of joy" across America.

If Tucson experienced "wild scenes of joy," it was not to be found in the Star.

What was reported was that food prices were still expected to remain artificially high.

But there was good news as well: The draft was canceled. Even better, baseball would return to a full schedule the following spring.

Still, much remained to be done. An editorial in the Star exhorted Tucsonans to "remember the countries that are looking to America to be fed and clothed."

The Star also got behind a "Back to School" campaign sponsored by the U.S. Department of Labor.

The drive was to counteract the "wage dazzle" that had lured boys and girls away from school during the war and into jobs with little promise.

A year later, President Woodrow Wilson proclaimed Nov. 11 as Armistice Day.

New Yorkers, it was reported, celebrated with "Prohibition Booze," made from hair tonic and prune juice.

Meanwhile, merrymakers in Tucson lived it up at an Armistice dance at the Armory.

The University of Arizona held a "rousing patriotic assembly" in the auditorium.

After the faculty declared the rest of the day a holiday, students, the UA band, assorted veterans and "a squad of young ladies who carried the flag" marched from the campus to Downtown.

It might also be noted that several merchants, including Myers & Bloom and Tucson Meat & Provision, closed for the day.

The families of 42 young men from Southern Arizona probably did little celebrating that day. Their "boys" never returned.

The same could be said for another 116,666 Americans killed in what was then called the Great War. No one, after all, could imagine a successor.

"The world slept better last night for the first time in four years," were the words in a Star editorial published the day after the armistice was signed.

"Unlike anything of its kind in history, the ending of the great war was celebrated throughout the world. In all probability, no such spontaneous outburst of thankfulness, joy, enthusiasm and patriotism will ever be shown again in this or any other country."

Wild celebrations marking the end of World War II were a mere 27 years away.

WAR AND DISASTERS
3

Tucson High Class of '42

The dress was formal, the occasion the senior prom, and the night the last of carefree innocence the Class of '42 would ever know.

Saturday, Dec. 6, 1941. More than 100 couples swirl and sway across the floor of the Tucson High School cafeteria — transformed for one night and one night only into a "Snowland" wonderland.

Tucson High's Class of '42 celebrates its prom in the cafeteria on Dec. 6, 1941.

Never again would a group of Tucson teenagers be caught so clearly in the cross hairs of world events.

"In the middle of our senior year we were faced with decisions that would affect our future forever," said Katherine Reese Holsinger, member of the first THS class to graduate under the pall of World War II.

As high school classes go, it would turn out to be a fairly distinguished lot. Among its ranks: a future Tucson mayor and Pima County supervisor, as well as doctors, lawyers, artists and at least one almost-Brooklyn Dodger.

But the glue that would bind these men and women together for years to come was more than mere nostalgia. It was the stuff of war and loss and sacrifice — and of coming of age much too soon. And much too young.

"I remember hearing about Pearl Harbor from the family radio," said Holsinger. "I started to cry."

Others took the news with considerably more nonchalance.

"I don't remember hearing about it on the radio," said June Holmes Vance, who had attended the prom the night before. "I was probably sleeping."

Bud Grainger was goofing around in the back yard when his dad came out and delivered the news. "I thought, 'I guess that will shoot my baseball career,' " said Grainger, who had signed a contract to play ball for the Brooklyn Dodgers farm team, the Olean Oilers.

For many, the significance of it all would only begin to seep in the following morning, at school.

"I was in the band," said Ivan Hawkins. "First trumpet. That Monday morning, Professor Sewell (Arthur) — he was the head of the bands and orchestra — asked us all to stand up. Then the band hit 'The Star-Spangled Banner.' I'll always remember that."

And then at midmorning, the sonorous tones of President Franklin D. Roosevelt began to echo through the school's public address system. "It was the president declaring war," said Tom Moore.

First to heed the call from the Class of '42 were a handful of students who belonged to the National Guard.

"When the National Guard was activated, we had a school assembly," said Holsinger. "Those kids that were going went up on the stage in uniform. They had a ceremony and called their names off one by one as they left. And then they were gone."

More quickly followed. "You'd be sitting next to someone in class and before the end of the school year, he was gone," said Moore, who wound up flying combat missions over Japan during the last months of the war.

All through the late winter and early spring of '42, the Japanese swaggered through one conquest after another: Manila, Singapore, Bataan, Corregidor.

But for the Class of '42, this was also the last spring they'd ever spend in high school.

Which meant there was basketball to be played, dances to attend, plays to rehearse, and burgers and frosted root beers to be quaffed at the old Red and Blue Drive In.

"We were still doing all the things we'd always done," said Moore. "Why not?"

No one could deny, however, that this year's graduation was different. "I remember a lot of the guys were already gone," said June Holmes Vance. "They left their seats empty. I remember looking down the rows of seats and seeing those empty chairs."

"Graduation was very quiet," said Holsinger. "On that last day of school, we just knew we were leaving our whole future behind us."

Or at least the last remnants of childhood.

Right after graduation, Lew Donahue marched into the American Legion hall to take his Army physical.

But a missing left thumb quickly stuck him with a 4-F label. "I was shocked," said Donahue, already a crack shot and member of the National Rifle Association. "I wasn't very happy at all."

Meanwhile, Bud Grainger, who had graduated midyear in January of '42, decided to stick to his dreams of glory with the Dodgers.

"They offered me $75 a month," said Grainger, who only lasted a couple of months with the Dodgers' Class D team in Olean, N.Y.

By May of '42 he was back in Tucson. By February of '43 he was in a Marine uniform.

The coeds of the Class of '42 also did their part for the war effort. As soon as she turned 20 — the minimum age with a parent's permission — Martha Dadisman Menager signed up with the SPARS, the female branch of the U.S. Coast Guard.

It would be 1946 before she would return to Tucson. "My joke was that my mother signed for me to go in the SPARS so she could rent out my room," said Menager.

Holsinger sewed stomach bandages for the troops at the old Steinfeld mansion, which was turned over to the Red Cross during the war.

Alice Tully Raizk picked cotton. "I was working at Safeway as a cashier," said Raizk. "They were closed on Sundays. They asked if any of us would like to go out to pick cotton in Marana. We went out there in trucks. I had never seen a cotton field in my life."

Dina Panos Kwiatek, whose parents ran the Grand Cafe at the corner of Broadway and Sixth Avenue, wound up feeding soldiers, thousands of them.

"Our restaurant was three blocks from the railroad station," said Kwiatek. "The government contracted with us to feed the troop trains. Whenever the troops came in, we were given one hour's notice. They came in hungry."

Romance also loomed for the Class of '42, which quickly found out that while war may be hell, it's also quite an aphrodisiac.

In August, Katherine Reese Holsinger went on a blind date with a soldier. By October she was married. "It was my first and last blind date," said Holsinger, who promptly dropped out of classes at the University of Arizona.

Classmates Loretta Graydon and John "Sandy" McLeod began corresponding after Sandy joined the Army. "Every chance, I'd come back," he said. In May of '46, they were married.

Not all the letters that circulated among the Class of '42 were so pleasant. More than a half-century later, many still remembered how they learned of the deaths of classmates.

Bud Grainger lost two close friends, Frank Kempf and Cornelius "Corky" Moore. "There were four of us," said Grainger. "Frank, Corky, Arnold Chapo Riesgo and myself. We grew up together. If you saw one of us, you saw us all."

Corky was killed on Iwo Jima, Frank in Germany. "It was devastating," said Grainger.

June Holmes Vance, who had slept through the

frantic radio bulletins about Pearl Harbor, lost her sweetheart to a sniper's bullet.

"He was killed in action in 1944 on an island in the Pacific," said Vance. Notification was her last letter to the young man, returned unopened. "On the outside, they had marked with big printing: 'KIA.' That's how I found out."

After the war, June and Richard "Rusty" Vance, another Tucson High student who'd gone off to war, rekindled their friendship. They were married in 1948.

Tom Moore became a vice president with the Sundt Corp. Bud Grainger married the girl he met at Olean, N.Y., back during his Dodger tryouts. "I didn't strike out with her," he said.

Grainger, who retired as a bank vice president, played semipro ball and umpired games all around Southern Arizona.

Many from the Class of '42 went back to school on the GI Bill.

Ivan Hawkins, the boy who played "The Star-Spangled Banner" on the morning after Pearl Harbor, went from the U.S. Army Air Forces to the University of Arizona, courtesy of Uncle Sam.

"The war did change our lives," said Hawkins, who would become an attorney. "I don't think I would have gone to college without the GI Bill."

On the other hand, Katherine Holsinger said the war probably kept her from getting her college diploma. "If there had been no war, I would not have met and married a soldier. I would have probably completed college."

The Class of '42 would become filled with graying grandparents. Thirteen of its number, however, will remain forever locked into the memory of youth. They were the ones killed in action, in a war that began just hours past their last senior dance.

WAR AND DISASTERS
4

Food Giant plane crash

It fell from the sky seven days before Christmas.

If you were in Tucson, you still remember that night.

Monday, Dec. 18, 1967, about a quarter to 6.

Tucson Fire Capt. Ellis Franklin was on his way home from work.

Butcher Sam Des Jardin had just stepped into the meat locker.

Maria Lau was changing diapers on her newborn son.

And then her husband, Roger, heard it.

Wreckage of the Phantom that crashed into the rear of the Food Giant.

"It was a whining noise," said Roger Lau, former staff sergeant at Davis-Monthan Air Force Base. "Then I heard a loud explosion."

A U.S. Air Force Phantom jet loaded with more than 16,000 pounds of aviation fuel had slammed into the rear of the Food Giant grocery store at 1830 S. Alvernon Way.

Both crewmen safely ejected.

The high-set windows on the east side of Lau's house turned orange and yellow, reflecting the flames.

Outside it was raining.

The jet, which crashed after takeoff at D-M, sent fireballs into the market and into Lau's neighborhood, obliterating two homes.

"We got out of the house," said Lau, who lived at 1822 S. Winstel Blvd.

"I told my wife to get away with the baby and our young daughter. They headed west down the street and I went across the street to see if I could help."

But there was nothing that could be done for the young woman trapped inside the inferno at 1815 S. Winstel.

"The father was out there screaming, 'My baby. My baby.' "

Sherry Tilton, 19, was dead, along with Food Giant customers Victoria Palmer and Crystal Siemund, and meat wrapper Robin Bush.

Just seconds before, Bush, 34, had been chatting with the butcher.

"I needed to cut some liver," said Des Jardin. "So I went into the cooler."

The door automatically closed behind him. Then came the explosion.

"I felt a little jolt. When I went to open the door, fire came in."

He slammed the door shut and escaped through another exit that led to the front counter.

"I jumped over the counter and ran to the girl (Bush), but there was no way I could get in there. It was totally engulfed in flames."

He tried another way. "I couldn't get in there, either."

Seeing it was hopeless, Des Jardin ran for his car and drove home, shaken.

Seconds before, Fire Capt. Franklin had been heading east on 22nd Street.

"I spotted the fire and couldn't believe my eyes," said Franklin. "I called the Fire Department and proceeded immediately to the store." There he would stay for the next 20 hours, directing more than 100 firefighters.

"Our job was to get as many people out as we could and fight the fire at the same time," said Franklin.

Within minutes, news of the tragedy was flashing across television screens from New York to L.A.

Thousands of worried callers in and out of the city snarled phone lines.

More than a thousand blood donors swamped the local Red Cross center.

The next morning, only gutted shells remained of the market and two homes.

Yet at his home, "There were only a couple of minor cracks in the wall," said Lau.

He sold the house in 1974.

Sam Des Jardin went to work at another Food Giant.

Three years later, Ellis Franklin would fight the flames at the Pioneer Hotel.

For years, only a concrete slab marked the spot of the supermarket conflagration.

Today, the site is all parking lot and strip mall.

Said Des Jardin: "I look back on it now and think how lucky a lot of us were."

WAR AND DISASTERS
5

Jitterbugging at the Hacienda

They also served who danced.

"I hate to say what a good time we had, considering there was a war on," said Jeanne Glasgow.

War may have been hell elsewhere. But here in the desert, we collected tinfoil, sold bonds, gave blood and — if you were young and female — danced the night away with the soldiers at the old Hacienda, aka the GI Country Club.

Located about where Broadway Village is today, the Hacienda began in 1914 as a golf country club, fell on hard times during the Depression and was sitting vacant by the early '40s.

Jim and Jeanne Glasgow on a date in 1943 after meeting at the Hacienda.

That's when the local American Women's Voluntary Services stepped in, agreeing to pay the rent in the fall of '42.

It was up and running for the duration of the war, and AWVS volunteers did everything from scrap collecting to cotton picking.

But the activities that seem to linger longest in the memories of those who lived those years were those servicemen dances.

Actually, the dances began earlier in 1942, at a private home dubbed Leeward.

"They had refreshments, and music came from records," said Glasgow. "I remember a beautiful back yard, all grassy, and lawn swings with awnings."

Six months after they began, the dances switched to the Hacienda. By December of '42, homesick soldiers were thronging the place, which offered live dance band music on the weekends, female company — always chaperoned — and the inevitable refreshments.

"The soldiers called them ground gopher sandwiches. They were terrible," said Betty Hayden, another dance floor regular. Childhood chums, she and Glasgow both met their future husbands at the Hacienda.

"She danced by, and that was it," said Jim Glasgow, a sergeant at Davis-Monthan Field who played clarinet — but not that night — in the D-M dance band. He and Jeanne were married in March of '44.

Betty also married a musician she met at the Hacienda: Pfc. Ralph Hayden, stationed at Marana Army Air Field.

"She used to jitterbug in front of me," said Ralph, who admits being mesmerized by "those swaying hips." The two met on July 4, 1943, and married exactly one year later.

Both romances might never have happened, save for some parental relenting.

"During my first year of college, my dad would

not let me go out with servicemen," said Jeanne.

"But during my second year, a cousin of mine was stationed at D-M. My father suddenly realized that these servicemen were nice."

Meanwhile, Betty had a mother to win over. "I finally got to go to the dances, because one of the chaperons was friends with my mother," said Glasgow. "You never had to worry about sitting on the sidelines."

Open seven days a week, the Hacienda also offered pingpong, cards, tennis courts, shuffleboard and a swimming pool.

Not surprisingly, girls would date the fellows they met on the dance floor.

"We'd go to the Fox Theatre, or on Sunday afternoons we'd go to Sabino Canyon if someone had a car," said Jeanne. "Those fellows were so nice."

Music was alternately supplied by the dance bands from D-M and Marana, which the Star referred to as a "jive band."

Jim Glasgow shipped out to Tinian Island in January of '45, while Ralph left for Okinawa a few months after his marriage to Betty.

By then, everyone's dancing days, it seems, were numbered. In May of '45, the Hacienda closed, bought by the Shriners.

Open less than three years, it welcomed more than 125,000 servicemen, reported the Star.

Ground gopher sandwiches and all.

WAR AND
DISASTERS
6

Chatter

It gave us cornball comedy and small-town gossip, lists of the dead and the top tunes on "Your Hit Parade."

Chatter was its name; a breezy, over-the-back-fence-style newsletter published every second and fourth Sunday during the waning months of World War II.

Its initial publisher was the Spanish-American Mothers' and Wives' Association, also known as La Asociacion de Madres y Esposas Mexicanas.

Made up mainly of mothers and wives of military men, the club sold hundreds of thousands of dollars in war bonds here, mainly through Tucson's Mexican-American community.

Most of its newsletter readers were also Hispanic — servicemen slogging it out in the trenches of Europe or on the sands of some spitball of an island in the South Pacific.

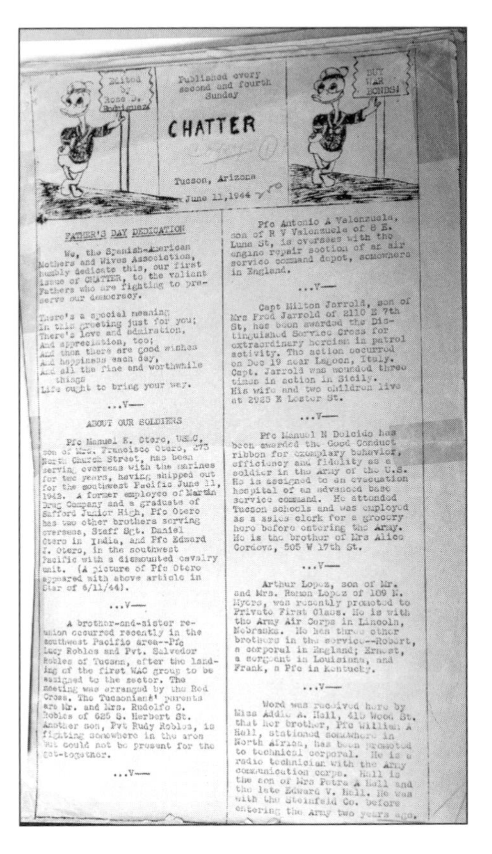

Edited by Rose D. Rodriguez

Published every second and fourth Sunday

CHATTER

Tucson, Arizona

June 11,1944

BUY WAR BONDS!

FATHER'S DAY DEDICATION

We, the Spanish-American Mothers and Wives Association, humbly dedicate this, our first issue of CHATTER, to the valiant Fathers who are fighting to preserve our democracy.

There's a special meaning
In this greeting just for you;
There's love and admiration,
And appreciation, too;
And then there are good wishes
And happiness each day,
And all the fine and worthwhile things
Life ought to bring your way.

...V—

ABOUT OUR SOLDIERS

Pfc Manuel E. Otero, USMC, son of Mrs. Francisco Otero, 273 North Church Street, has been serving overseas with the marines for two years, having shipped out for the southwest Pacific June 11, 1942. A former employee of Martin Drug Company and a graduate of Safford Junior High, Pfc Otero has two other brothers serving overseas, Staff Sgt. Daniel Otero in India, and Pfc Edward J. Otero, in the southwest Pacific with a dismounted cavalry unit. (A picture of Pfc Otero appeared with above article in Star of 6/11/44).

...V—

A brother-and-sister reunion occurred recently in the southwest Pacific area--Pfc Lucy Robles and Pvt. Salvador Robles of Tucson, after the landing of the first WAC group to be assigned to the sector. The meeting was arranged by the Red Cross. The Tucsonians' parents are Mr. and Mrs. Rudolfo C. Robles of 625 S. Herbert St. Another son, Pvt Rudy Robles, is fighting somewhere in the area but could not be present for the get-together.

...V—

Pfc Antonio A Valenzuela, son of R V Valenzuela of 8 E. Luna St, is overseas with the engine repair section of an air service command depot, somewhere in England.

...V—

Capt Milton Jarrold, son of Mrs Fred Jarrold of 2110 E 7th St, has been awarded the Distinguished Service Cross for extraordinary heroism in patrol activity. The action occurred on Dec 19 near Lagoon, Italy. Capt. Jarrold was wounded three times in action in Sicily. His wife and two children live at 2925 E Lester St.

...V—

Pfc Manuel N Dolcido has been awarded the Good Conduct ribbon for exemplary behavior, efficiency and fidelity as a soldier in the Army of the U.S. He is assigned to an evacuation hospital of an advanced base service command. He attended Tucson schools and was employed as a sales clerk for a grocery here before entering the Army. He is the brother of Mrs Alice Cordova, 505 W 17th St.

...V—

Arthur Lopez, son of Mr. and Mrs. Ramon Lopez of 109 N. Myers, was recently promoted to Private First Class. He is with the Army Air Corps in Lincoln, Nebraska. He has three other brothers in the service--Robert, a corporal in England; Ernest, a sergeant in Louisiana, and Frank, a Pfc in Kentucky.

...V—

Word was received here by Miss Addie A. Hall, 415 Wood St. that her brother, Pfc William A Hall, stationed somewhere in North Africa, has been promoted to technical corporal. He is a radio technician with the Army communication corps. Hall is the son of Mrs Petra A Hall and the late Edward V. Hall. He was with the Steinfeld Co. before entering the Army two years ago.

Its editor was Rose Rodriguez Caballero, one of the few single members (she was Rose Rodriguez then) of La Asociacion. "The club wanted me to be its secretary. But I told them, 'You can get anyone to do that,' " said Caballero, who was working as a secretary for City Treasurer Joseph D. McAllister.

Caballero had other club duties in mind. "I saw Oliver Drachman's Letters From Home, and I thought, if he could do it, I could do it," she said, referring to the homey newsletters that Drachman also sent out to local boys during the last years of the war.

Borrowing heavily from the morning and evening newspapers, Caballero typed up her news items at home, made up a stencil at work, then ran off 500 copies at a time.

Naturally, heavy play was given to local military newsmakers: new inductees, recipients of ribbons and medals, arrivals home on furlough, and the inevitable lists filled with the names of young men missing, taken prisoner, wounded or killed in action.

"I had envelopes for each category," said Caballero. "At first, I wouldn't put in who was killed in action, but the boys would write back saying, 'Tell us about our friends.' "

Happily, the four-page newsletter also contained frothier news. Chatter's first edition, published June 11, 1944, shared the masthead with a patriotic duck named Donald, propping up a sign exhorting readers to "Buy War Bonds."

"Willis Campbell did the illustrations for the first issue," said Caballero. "He was a young man with the city engineering department. I told him I was going to publish the newspaper and he came up with Donald Duck."

No one from the copyright infringement arm of Walt Disney Studios came calling, by the way.

Inside pages of that same edition gave the hours that local swimming pools were open, lauded the Tucson High School band for its "wartime musical activities," told of a fire that gutted the old Pekin Café, noted that Eddie Jacobs had recently sold the Riverside Auditorium to Herman Ray, sighed over the nuptials that united Miss Martha Leila Gallego and Sgt. Rudy W. Lopez, and listed the top nine tunes of "Your Hit Parade" for June 10 of '44.

"My 11-year-old niece, Alma, did that," said Caballero. "I asked her if she could stay home on Saturday nights. So she listened to 'Your Hit Parade' on the radio and wrote all the songs down."

In the beginning, either the club or Caballero herself paid for the raw materials — that is, until the day Caballero's boss asked her who was footing the bill. "I told him I was," she said. "He said, 'No way. The city will. We'll give you the paper.' And they did."

Helping hands from others in the community soon followed. Club Latino, a men's social club, offered to pay for all expenses. As a result, the paper was soon rolling off the presses of El Tucsonense, a Spanish-language newspaper.

Incidentally, although it was a club for women, La Asociacion and its wartime newsletter owed much to the men in the community, particularly El Tucsonense editor Ricardo Fierro, and Tucson businessman and community leader Rosalio Ronquillo, who was La Asociacion's founder and director.

With El Tucsonense presses producing the paper, the mimeographed pages Caballero had been running off down at City Hall gave way to slicker stock. Photographs of servicemen, wedding parties, even a mug shot of the editor, all started popping up in Chatter.

Despite its heavily Hispanic readership, only two copies of the newsletter were published in Spanish, though many contained a smattering of bilingual jokes.

"There was a language barrier," said Caballero. "Most of the ladies in the club didn't read or write English. They told me, 'Rosita, we don't understand a thing you're telling our sons. Please do it in Spanish.' "

"I thought to myself, 'Well, they're going to find out for themselves that these boys can't read Spanish.' You see, the schools were not bilingual. You were punished if you spoke Spanish."

Sure enough, said Caballero, after Spanish-language editions started arriving overseas, "The boys wrote and asked us to switch it back to English."

Once Chatter came off the press, Caballero toted the papers to La Asociacion meetings. "The ladies would buy copies and send them to the boys," said Caballero, who also sent out the newsletter to several servicemen on her list.

Chatter also wound up for sale in many of the stores that once lined Congress and Meyer streets.

Got a nickel? In '44 or '45 that would buy you Chatter at La Concha Drugstore, Reuben's Arizona Home Supply, Melwood Grocery Store and a dozen other once-thriving businesses, now long gone.

How many Chatters actually made it to the front no one knows, though Caballero heard from many servicemen during and right after the war, especially those in the 158th Infantry Regiment, known as the Bushmasters.

Joe Mendez, who quit high school in 1940 and lied about his age to get into the Bushmasters, got his edition of Chatter while serving in the South Pacific, near New Guinea.

"I though it was great," said Mendez, who saw action in four different skirmishes. "It gave all the information about what was happening in Tucson."

By May '45, Mendez was back home. One of the first things he did was look up his old Safford Junior High School teacher, Sara Marshall, who had sent him the little newsletter.

"I told her how much I appreciated getting that information," said Mendez, who went back to school, earned a degree in pharmacy from the University of Arizona, and opened up his own business, Medical Arts Pharmacy.

Among the photographs of servicemen that appeared in Chatter was one of Pfc. Carlos Caballero, who was captured in the Battle of the Bulge and spent the first few months of 1945 in a German prisoner of war camp.

After the camp was liberated, the ex-POW returned to Tucson. He and Rose, who had known each other for years, were married in September of '45.

By then, Rose had resigned as editor of Chatter, which in turn folded before the year was done.

La Asociacion, however, would continue to support other community causes for another three decades.

In 1976, dwindling membership finally forced its last four members to dissolve the organization that had once served as springboard for one of the town's best information lines. Next to the backyard fence, that is.

WAR AND DISASTERS
7

Supreme Cleaners Explosion

They all remembered the moment.

Stanley Salonic was boarding an airplane in Washington, D.C.

Arizona Daily Star Assistant Sports Editor Tom Foust was on his way to work.

Tony Tovar was sitting in math class at John Spring Junior High School.

"All of a sudden, the electricity went off and on. We felt something," said Tovar.

Minutes later, he was in the cafeteria. "I heard two ladies talking about an explosion at Supreme Cleaners. I dropped my tray, ran to my locker, got my things and took off."

Wreckage from the Supreme Cleaners explosion.

Tovar's mother, Carmen, worked at Supreme Cleaners. So did his aunt, Videlia Kingery.

"I ran back home to my grandma's home. Our eyes met, and we both knew something bad had happened."

Carmen Tovar, Videlia Kingery and four others died that day, March 29, 1963, in what police and firefighters would call one of the worst disasters ever to hit this city. A seventh victim died later.

A gas leak, sparked by the flip of a switch, created two explosions, followed by fire, at the cleaners' main plant at North Stone Avenue and Grant Road.

The north wall of the plant was blown into Grant Road, crushing three parked cars.

Two of the dead were blown into the street by the explosions, while chunks of concrete slammed onto cars, streets and into neighboring businesses.

It was a little after 11 a.m. when Foust, who was driving west on Grant Road, saw a 100-foot brown cloud rise in front of him, followed by a dull thud.

Ever the newsman, he pulled his car over, hauled out a camera he kept in the trunk, and started taking photos.

"My hand was shaking so bad I didn't know what I was doing," said Foust. He stayed until the Star's regular photographers arrived, then drove on to the Star's office, then downtown.

His photo ran on Page One the next day.

Thirty-two were injured that day, including Harris Salonic, who owned the cleaners, along with his brother, Stanley.

It was Harris who had flipped the switch in the basement vault of the building, igniting the leaking gas.

At that moment, Stanley Salonic, along with his wife, Teddi, was boarding a plane heading for Tucson.

Not until they landed did they learn what had happened. "Harris was supposed to pick us up," said Salonic.

The next day he was allowed to see his brother, swaddled in gauze, inside the burn unit at St. Mary's Hospital.

"He was madder than hell, hungry and thirsty," said Salonic. Two days later, Harris Salonic died.

"The disaster dumped right on top of him," said Salonic. "They were digging for hours to get him out."

The cleaners sued Tucson Gas and Electric Co., as it was then called. So did just about everyone else connected with the disaster.

In 1967, Superior Court Judge Robert O. Roylston ruled that the explosion resulted from a gas leakage from TG&E lines near the plant.

Long before then, Supreme Cleaners had rebuilt right on the site. Many who had worked at the plant returned.

"We had a very, very loyal group with us," said Salonic, then divorced and living in Las Vegas.

In the early '70s, Supreme Cleaners was sold. Over the years, it's housed everything from an opera company to a paint company, its current role.

"It took me years before I could go back there," said Tovar, who would go on to own Congress Street Hair.

Foust, who retired from the Star, also thought back to that day.

"I've often thought, 'Why did I stand around taking pictures, rather than helping people?' But then I thought, we needed someone to record this."

And to remember.

WAR AND
DISASTERS
8

Death of a President

Stunned UA students gather in front of a TV at Louie's.

Anyone of a certain age carries the memory — a memory that will last a lifetime. Where they were and what they were doing on the day President John F. Kennedy was shot.

It was just before noon, Friday, Nov. 22, 1963 when the terrible news started trickling into Tucson over the radio and television airwaves.

Downtown, at the corner of Stone Avenue and Pennington Street, a small crowd gathered in front of the American Airlines office, where a loudspeaker from KTUC mobile radio yammered out news of the shooting.

The continual bulletins coming in over the wire machines were taped to the windows, while people stood four-deep on the sidewalks to read them.

Above the Bank of Tucson, an electronic tape flashed out the message: "Pres. given last rites." A few minutes later the tape went blank, then started up again: "Pres. Kennedy is dead. Pres. Kennedy is dead."

At City Hall, Mayor Lew Davis was getting ready to go to the University of Arizona campus to greet a group of visitors in town for a convention.

"Bernard Garmire, who was the chief of police then, got the news up to me," remembered Davis. But the first bulletins had not yet turned devastating.

"The news on the radio said they thought he was going to be all right, so I went on over to the university. There, they said it looked like he was going to be all right, too, so we decided to go ahead with our luncheon."

Davis left word that he wanted to be handed a note, should any change occur. "At one o'clock they handed me a note, saying he had died. I asked everyone to please rise, then we said a prayer."

Rushing back to City Hall, Davis asked City Manager Mark Keane and his deputy, Roger O'Mara, about lowering the flag to half-staff. "Roger said only the governor could order the flag raised or lowered. So we got permission and sometime during the afternoon, we lowered the flag."

They lowered the flag that afternoon in front of Old Main as well. An Arizona Wildcat photographer, recording the scene for an extra edition of the campus paper, worked in tears.

As the news spread through the campus, classrooms were dismissed. Knots of students stared at a bulletin board in the Student Union as Associated Press dispatches were posted by the Wildcat staff.

Other students turned their faces toward the loudspeakers carrying the news. In between bulletins, Muzak continued to fill the air.

Downstairs, hamburgers lost their sizzle and Cokes went flat as Louie's Lower Level canceled its lunchtime service. A stunned crowd of 200 milled in front of the television set, eager for news about the fallen president.

The annual Military Ball was canceled for that evening. By midafternoon, chapels around campus were filled with students. The Newman Center held a requiem Mass for an overflow congregation — its largest ever.

Later that afternoon, the entire border between Mexico and Arizona was closed, trapping more than 3,000 people on the "wrong side." Even after borders reopened, travel to Mexico was banned for days.

All high school football games, as well as the Arizona-New Mexico skirmish scheduled for Saturday night in Arizona Stadium, were either canceled or postponed. The track at Greyhound Park was quiet that night and downtown merchants delayed turning on Christmas lights. Civil Defense authorities also called off Saturday's normal siren testing.

Most local radio stations adopted dirgelike music throughout the weekend and television stations dropped all commercial and entertainment in favor of an all-news format.

Tucson's nightclub scene was understandably dismal that Saturday night. The Skyroom used only dance music, while Saddle & Sirloin went on with its musical show — which entertained only a sprinkling of patrons.

Jack Lemmon in "Under the Yum Yum Tree" played before empty seats at the Fox-Tucson Theatre. Most of us preferred to stay home, keeping silent vigil in front of our television screens, watching sometimes-unbelievable images flicker past; the motorcade, the stunned young widow, Jack Ruby and his smoking gun, the rolling caisson, the salute of son to father as the casket went by.

On Monday, Tucson, along with the rest of the country, joined in mourning as the nation buried its president. All government offices and public and parochial schools were closed, as well as most businesses. Bars and many stores, including eight supermarket chains, also shut their doors for the day. City park programs were canceled and the municipal golf courses shut down.

Streets and highways were nearly deserted. What people there were out on the streets were mainly mourners, on their way to attend one of the scores of church services held that day.

More than 6,000 men gathered in formation for services at Davis-Monthan Air Force Base. Rifles also cracked out a salute beneath a half-staff flag during memorial services held at the U.S. Navy and Marine Corps Training Center in Tucson.

The late president was no stranger to the Old Pueblo. In 1958 and again in 1960, Kennedy paid brief visits. Both times he left town with a souvenir of our Western ways — a sombrero in 1958, a Stetson in 1960.

But long before he got into politics, Kennedy was into blue jeans and cowboy boots. In the summer of '36, he and his brother Joe worked at Jack Speiden's J-6 ranch near Benson — to toughen them up for Harvard athletics.

On the day of the assassination, Lew Davis said, "I never met him, but he was my president." That just about sums up how we all felt about Jack Kennedy.

WAR AND
DISASTERS
9

Wartime Housing

They slept in cars, in parks, in milk trucks. They were homeless. They were also soldiers.

Ask old-timers what turned Tucson from a sleepy cowtown into a bustling Southwestern city and they'll all say the same thing: World War II.

The boom began as soon as we found out in August 1940 that an air base was coming to town.

Trouble was, a new government edict declared that military family housing had to be at least two miles from any Army post or base.

By mid-January of '41, a site was selected. The Porter Womack Construction Co. would have 125 days to erect 135 housing units on the northeast corner of East Winsett Street and South Plumer Avenue.

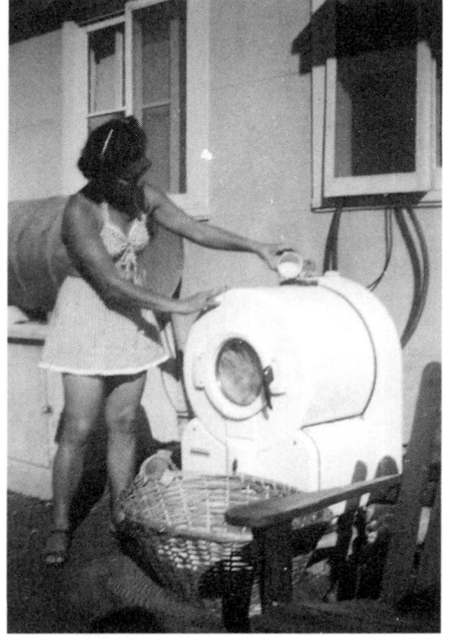

Josephine Lacagnina does laundry at the Consolidated Dwellings in 1946.

They did it in less than half that time. The name of the development: Rincon Vista, built for noncommissioned officers and some civilians working at Davis-Monthan.

The two- and three-bedroom units featured gas ranges, electric refrigerators and metal cupboards. Outside were paved streets and sidewalks.

Two months ahead of its July dedication, the $400,000 project had its first family, the Tanners, from Barksdale Field in Shreveport, La. "Too dry and dusty" were their first words about Tucson.

Housing was still at a premium when Ed and Peggy Kamienski and their two kids moved into a two-bedroom duplex in Rincon Vista in 1951.

"There was no carport, but we did have a driveway," remembered Peggy. "Each house had a lawn out front, and I think one mulberry tree."

Less than two years after ground was broken on Rincon Vista, 100 more dwellings, plus 70 rental trailers, were squatting nearby.

Built for defense workers and lower-ranked servicemen, the Davis-Monthan Dwellings and trailer park, as it came to be known, was soon packed to the rooflines — even after the war.

Cora Halpenny remembered the small trailer that she, husband Leonard and their two children shared until a dwelling opened up in late 1945. "The trailers were so small we had to keep our suitcases in the car."

Meanwhile, by August 1943, the first of 324 temporary dwellings south of town were being rented out to defense workers, many of them employed at the Consolidated Vultee plant.

As a result, the project, on the southeast corner of South Sixth Avenue and Irvington Road, quickly became known as the Consolidated Dwellings.

Monthly rents for the barrackslike units, furnished or unfurnished, ranged from $30 for a studio apartment to $39 for a three-bedroom.

Amenities included kerosene cooking range, oil-burning heater and icebox. Frills such as evaporative coolers were available for an extra $5 a month.

Next door, directly to the east of the rodeo grounds, sat 78 trailers, also filled to the max — during and after the war.

"We lived in a trailer for about six months until we could get a dwelling," Julius Cesare said about his post-war years as a young husband and father.

Coincidentally, Cesare, who lied to get in the Navy at age 15, grew up in the dwellings. "It was a great place to be a kid," he said.

The dwellings were laid out like the spokes of a wheel. In the center was a square where kids played kick the can while their fathers told war stories.

Marin Acosta, a Consolidated kid from 1943 to 1951, remembered dances, arts and crafts and pingpong games all taking place in the dwellings' recreation hall.

Most of the units came four to a building, said Michael Lacagnina, who grew up there during the mid-'40s.

"Paper houses, that's what we called them," said Lacagnina, who would later become a presiding judge in the Arizona Court of Appeals, Division 2.

Besides a judge, the old Consolidated Dwellings produced at least one future Pima County supervisor, as well as a home builder by the name of Estes.

"I lived in Consolidated Dwellings from 1944 to 1947," said Bill Estes Sr., who was working at Consolidated Vultee. "That one-bedroom apartment was our salvation."

The best thing about the dwellings, far as future County Supervisor Jim Murphy was concerned, was the rodeo grounds across the street.

"It was really our focal point for the community," said Murphy, who lived at the dwellings from '46 to '52.

Most of Consolidated's renters were grateful for the roofs over their heads. All made do.

"It was small, but we made it cheerful," said Anita Sigafus, who lived there as a young wife from 1945 to 1949. Her sister also lived in the dwellings.

"We painted the rooms, kicked out the roaches, made curtains for the windows, curtains for the cupboards — there were no doors. My sister and I were so clean we got a reward. When they finally put in toilet lids, we got the first ones."

Most of the cooking was done on kerosene stoves. "There were big barrels of kerosene outside each house," said Chris Craig, another resident. "A tube ran from each barrel inside to the stove. Our father forbade us to go near those things."

"Those tubes were dangerous," said Frank Udovich, one of a half-dozen maintenance men at the dwellings during the late '40s. "Copper was required, but there wasn't any during the war. They used plastic."

Another four or five men took care of the grass and trees around the complex, said Udovich. But Ray Gallego remembered no such greenery back when the complex was new.

"It was old dusty lots, no trees," said Gallego. "I moved to the Santa Rita Dwellings. They were much nicer."

Yep, if you wanted greenery, Santa Rita was the place to be. Located on East 20th Street at the northern edge of Santa Rita Park, the low-income project teemed with defense workers during the war, veterans afterward.

"We had a two-bedroom apartment, and the only door was through the kitchen," said Ruby Dawson, who lived at the Santa Rita project, along with her husband, Fred, and two children, from 1951 to 1954.

If the rodeo grounds were the draw for Consolidated residents, here it was the park.

"There were things going on all the time," said Dawson. "The firemen had their barbecues on the Fourth of July, and we'd all go. There were softball games we'd watch for free. We'd even go to the political rallies — to get in on the refreshments."

Kerosene and ice cooked and cooled the food. No laundry room, either. "We did have one big clothesline," said Dora Alvidrez, who lived at Santa Rita from 1949 to 1954. "One woman used to get up at 4 in the morning so she could beat everyone else to the clothesline."

War's end brought little relief to the housing shortage in Tucson, especially after Davis-Monthan was reactivated as a permanent base in 1946.

In November of that year, the downtown armory was thrown open to house soldiers and their families.

Lumber became so scarce there were reports that it was traded on the black market.

So critical was the demand for military housing in this town by 1949 that Mayor E.T. "Happy" Houston feared it would "foster the spread of communisim."

Soon after, the old policy of keeping homes off base was scrapped. Military housing started going up at Davis-Monthan.

Not until after the Korean War, however, did the old "temporary" dwellings go down.

"We got a notice in 1954 that we had to move out of Santa Rita," said Alvidrez.

Similar notices went out that year for residents living in the Consolidated and Davis-Monthan dwellings. Not until 1965, however, would Rincon Vista close down.

The area would later become Roy P. Drachman Stadium, which was only fitting, since Drachman owned some of the land upon which Rincon Vista was built.

Santa Rita Park expanded across its old namesake dwellings.

As for the Consolidated Dwellings site, many of the old buildings were auctioned off and hauled away. The land beneath them would become Joe Garagiola's Rodeo Park, later changed to Rudy Garcia Park.

Reminders of the old dwellings are never far away, however. "You can see them all over Tucson," said Marin Acosta.

Western Ways

Barbara Stanwyck and Robert Taylor at the swank Rancho Nezhone.

Way out West, we had pretend cowboys and the real deal. We also had an airstrip near Picacho Peak, a Mormon community called Binghampton, and a beloved mountain` lion named George.

WESTERN
WAYS
1

Botanical Gardens

Sophia and Grace with their nanny in 1937.

Back when Alvernon was called Maple and you could ride a horse to forever, they raised greenery and girls in the middle of nowhere. Today, we call "nowhere" the Tucson Botanical Gardens, a calming oasis in the midst of urban cacophony.

But once upon a time it was called home — home to Rutger and Bernice Porter and their three little girls.

"We were very much out in the country," said Cornelia "Nina" Ford, the youngest of those three little girls.

How far out in the country?

Well, said older sister Grace Hill, "For thrills, we used to lie down on Maple Boulevard and think, 'Gosh, maybe somebody will drive by.' "

Their father was a nurseryman. Their mother also knew her way around a garden.

Now deceased, Rutger and Bernice Porter live on through the legacy of their former home and gardens, now part of a five-acre compound of plants, trails and educational exhibits at 2150 N. Alvernon Way.

"I don't think our parents could have imagined all of that," said Ford. "It's gone beyond anything they hoped for."

As with so many of Tucson's transplants, Rutger Porter came west for his lungs.

Suffering from chronic pneumonia, he left New York City for Tucson in 1927 and soon found landscaping work at the winter home of Anna and Alfred Erickson.

It was the same Erickson fortune that helped start up the old Desert Sanatorium, forerunner to Tucson Medical Center.

Before long, Porter was helping landscape the sanitarium grounds as well.

In 1931, he married the former Bernice Walkley, who had moved here the year before. The two of them then moved to a parcel of property on Maple Boulevard, just south of Grant Road.

A small adobe house, tin barn and well were already there, as well as electrical lines and a 12-party phone line.

Three daughters quickly followed: Grace in 1932, Sophia (now deceased) in 1933 and Cornelia in 1936.

As the family grew, so did its quarters.

The little adobe house was enlarged, and a bedroom wing was added to the east. Eventually, the original house and bedroom wing were connected, with the enclosed space becoming a spacious living room and separate sun porch.

The family business was also expanding.

In the beginning, Porter, who had studied agriculture at Rutgers University, operated his nursery from home, growing many of his plants on fields he owned just west of Maple.

In 1936, he moved the business, known as Desert

Gardens Nursery, to Speedway near Country Club Road.

Two years later, a metal watering tank for cattle, 35 feet in diameter, was installed in the Porters' yard. Water from the tank was used to irrigate the surrounding grounds.

The storage tank also served as one of the town's first private swimming pools.

"It was a nice thing to call up friends and ask them to come over for a swim," said Ford.

Bereft of a filter, the water, of course, soon turned green.

"We'd drain it and have a party to scrub it," said Ford.

Hill remembered it a little differently. "It was a pain in the neck," she said.

Nature also created frequent havoc out of water.

"We used to have tremendous floods," said Ford. "Maple had drainage ditches on either side of the road. We had a narrow wooden bridge that crossed the ditch to our house. But sometimes it would flood over the banks."

But after the floods, said Hill, "We would dig for sand rubies that would wash up in the sand."

A combination reflecting pool and fish pond in the front yard attracted all sorts of wildlife over the years, ranging from coyotes and quail to the family's Scottish terriers.

In May 1977, Bernice Porter wrote of past visitors such as cottontails, gophers, roadrunners, scorpions, centipedes and at least one skunk.

"And we had a corral where the sensory garden is now," said Hill. Inside the corral were two horses, Red and Cavalier.

"It was wonderful," said Ford. "We would cross Grant — of course there was a little traffic — and then ride straight up to the foothills."

Both sisters remembered their mother as someone who loved company. "We had lots of winter visitors and relatives escaping the cold climate," said Hill.

"We used to call it 'Porterville,' " said Ford. "My mother was always encouraging friends and older relatives to live there."

A "family-values kind of life" was the way Ford recalled her childhood. "I remember us singing every song we knew at night out on the sleeping porch — where the offices are now."

During the war years, Rutger Porter went to work at the Consolidated Vultee aircraft plant south of town, though he kept the nursery going as well. "Those were long, hard hours," said Ford.

Decade after decade, the Porters enlarged and maintained their home gardens, tending and cultivating everything from orchids to low-water-use natives.

In 1958, Rutger Porter closed down his nursery business and retired. "I want to do some experimental work with shrubs that I have been putting off for years," he announced at the time.

"I can remember my parents talking about what they would like to do with the gardens after they were gone," said Ford. "I think something like what happened was very much in my father's mind."

Rutger Porter died in 1964, at the age of 59. "It was melanoma," said Hill. "He had that fair skin."

After her husband's death, Bernice Porter continued to live at home, opening it up to various garden clubs.

In 1968, she donated the house and surrounding 2½ acres of property to the city, with the stipulation that she could live on the grounds for the rest of her life.

That same year, the Tucson Botanical Gardens was founded as a nonprofit corporation. In 1974, it signed an agreement with the city to manage the property, moving its headquarters to the grounds.

In 1975, the Friends of the Tucson Botanical Society bought up an adjoining 2½ acres. Ten years later, the property was deeded to the Tucson Botanical Gardens.

Tony Edland, then director of grounds, remembered how it was back in the late '70s. "We were open to the public, but nobody knew about us," he said. "Mainly, it was members of visiting garden clubs."

He also remembered Bernice Porter's continuing interest in all things green and growing.

"She was a Vassar girl, but she would get right in there and dig in the dirt."

In 1983, Bernice Porter died at the age of 81.

Today, the Tucson Botanical Gardens contains 16 garden areas and exhibits, many of them new or remodeled.

It also hosts a variety of educational programs and special events throughout the year, drawing in thousands of visitors.

"I think my parents would be absolutely amazed," said Hill.

The same for Ford, who had the enviable position of being able to return to the home of her childhood.

Said Ford: "I was there one day, having lunch in

a little area. And there were all these children there from a day-care center, playing under the trees and having a wonderful time, the way I had and my children had.

"It was very, very moving to me. In a way, it's more preserved than if it had stayed in the family."

(Grace Hill died in 1999.)

WESTERN WAYS 2

Rancho Nezhone

The main pool at Rancho Nezhone circa the '40s.

Its name was Navajo — Rancho Nezhone. Beautiful ranch.

And so it was — from its velvety lawns to its gold-plated guest list. Liberace slept here. So did Kate Smith, Gen. John Pershing, and William Boyd, aka Hopalong Cassidy.

But when Hopalong came here, my dears, he left his spurs at home.

"This was not a dude ranch," said Beverly Manning, who grew up on the place back in the late '30s and early '40s.

Indeed not. Not with fine crystal and china in the dining room, a grand piano in the living room, and satin chaise lounges in the guest cottages.

"We dressed for dinner and never ate the same meal twice in 30 days," said Manning.

A half-mile west of Oracle Road, just south of a narrow dirt road called Orange Grove — this is where the ranch sprawled.

And all of it created by Leonie Boutall, a woman who could have been tapped straight from central casting.

"Think of Auntie Mame, and that was my aunt," Manning said about her mother's sister.

"She was a typical Southern woman. Five-foot-one and full of the dickens. She was a champion skeet shooter, a golfer, a bowler and deep-sea fisherman. In her 60s, she backpacked into Colorado with another lady, hunting for elk."

One of four sisters from Memphis, Tenn., Boutall was a career woman who never married. "She made considerable money in stocks and bonds before the crash," said Manning.

While living in Houston, Boutall developed bronchial troubles. "The doctor told her to come to a drier climate."

Both Boutall and Manning's mother had visited Tucson before. And so the two women moved to Tucson sometime during the early '30s.

"Mother was divorced at the time and lived with Aunt Leonie," said Manning. "My aunt's original plan was to build a large home for all her relatives."

Roaming through the desert northwest of Tucson, Boutall met up with Maurice Reid, who was developing the lush orchards of Rancho Palos Verdes just up the road. Impressed, she decided to do the same.

Turning more than 100 acres of raw desert land into an oasis took the usual sweat, toil and cash. Coincidence brought it all together around 1935.

For across the street from the future Rancho Nezhone, Juan Gonzales and sons Henry, Richard and Charlie were just finishing up a project on a banker's house.

"Leonie Boutall stopped and asked us if we'd like to clear her land across the street," said Henry Gonzales. "We said yes. My father was a stonemason, but he could do everything."

The land, he said, was "all hills and arroyos. We

cleared out the palo verde and mesquite and burned it in big piles. The cactus we saved."

Deer, javelina and coyotes were everywhere, said Gonzales. So were the snakes. "We killed hundreds of rattlers."

At the same time they were clearing the land, Juan Gonzales and sons worked on the stone wall out front — a 300-foot-long wall that still stands today. "It took a year to build," said Henry Gonzales.

"After we cleared the land, Miss Boutall said, 'Now we're going to make an orchard,' " said Gonzales. "It was pick and shovel work; no machines. We dug 5-by-8 holes by hand, about 1,000 of them."

Meanwhile, well-driller Carl Pistor set about finding water on the property. "He got an Indian guy, a Yaqui, and he put his ear to the ground and that's where they dug the well," said Gonzales.

Then came the trees — hundreds of citrus and date palms. "We brought the palms in on flatbed trucks from Phoenix," said Gene Reid, son of Maurice. "They were stacked like logs." A crane helped lower them into the ground.

It was a fight to keep the tender citrus from freezing during those first couple of years. "We would go down to Baum & Adamson and get old tires," said Gonzales. "Then we would go to the farms and get cornstalks and wrap them around the tree trunks. About 11 o'clock at night, we'd start burning the tires."

Toward the rear of the ranch, said Gonzales, "we planted six acres with everything you could think of. And we built a 100-by-100 slat greenhouse. We had vegetables winter and summer. We also had flowers and new buddings for trees."

The back property, said Gonzales, also contained a barn, corrals, 16 horses, eight dairy cows and "thousands of chickens." Turkeys, too.

While the Gonzales family worked on the stonework and landscaping, others worked on the buildings — initially one main ranch house, plus two guest houses.

"It was like a Spanish hacienda," said Gonzales. "There was a fountain in the center, murals on the front of the house, rock curbing everywhere." Inside were beamed ceilings, tiled floors covered by Oriental rugs, oak trim and wrought-iron fixtures.

Trouble was, here was a hacienda with no takers.

"My aunt built the two guest houses for her sisters in Tennessee," said Manning. "But she made one error: She forgot to ask them. They said: 'No, thank you. We're settled here.' "

And so Leonie Boutall got into the guest-ranching business. Joining her were Manning's mother, Marguerite, who by then had married Ventress Wade, a Westerner who'd once served as guide to author Zane Grey. Together, the couple helped manage the ranch — though, said Manning, "it was really Mother who ran the place."

Their young daughter, Yvonne, along with Manning, experienced a fabled childhood here on the ranch.

"It was a lovely place to grow up," said Manning, who would pose for pictures with guests such as Kate Smith, then hop on a burro's back for a quick romp around the ranch. "During the war I rode my horse from ranch to ranch, selling war bonds."

Young Beverly and Yvonne weren't the only ones growing up on the ranch.

"We had been living on Anita Street and coming and going to work every day in the truck," said Gonzales. "Miss Boutall said it was too far to go every day, so she had a contractor build two bungalows for us and we stayed there."

Here, Juan and Maria Gonzales would raise their family for a time — five boys, five girls. The youngest girl and boy were born right on the ranch.

Not long after the family moved onto the property, one of the Gonzales girls started taking care of Leonie Boutall's nieces. "I was like a nanny to them," said Naya Ortiz.

The ranch held as much charm for her as it did her young charges. "There were peacocks and tame deer we could go feed," said Ortiz. Monkeys and parrots also roosted in the trees.

All the children at the ranch attended Catalina Foothills School. "We used to buy our goats from the woman who drove the school bus," said Manning.

In the summers, the ranch was closed to visitors. "I used to travel with Mrs. Wade and her two daughters," said Ortiz. "We would go to Houston and Galveston, Texas, and to Memphis, Tenn. We stayed in beautiful hotels, and I had my own living quarters."

Ortiz's brother, Richard, also found work on the ranch as a chef. "If a chef quit, my aunt went in and did the cooking," said Manning. "She taught Richard Gonzales how to cook."

"He worked as a chef there for years," said Henry Gonzales, adding that Boutall also sent brother Richard to school for more training.

Swimming, sunbathing, horseback-riding and a putting green all beckoned visitors in the winter months. "Offhand, I'd say the ranch could accommodate 30 visitors," said Manning.

And despite its refined airs, Rancho Nezhone did manage to impart a somewhat Western atmosphere.

"In the early years, they had mariachis from Nogales come out every Friday night," said Gonzales. "And we'd have this hay wagon, drawn by horses that would follow the trails out in the desert. We had a barbecue, with all kinds of drinks and barrels of beer."

It took World War II to jolt the ranch into harsh reality — and make it ripe for change. Both Henry Gonzales and Naya Ortiz joined up — he with the Army, she with the Women's Army Corps.

Meanwhile, Juan Gonzales found work in the Southern Pacific roundhouse. He and Maria moved back to town. After the war, son Henry would join his father in the roundhouse for a time. "But the noise was too much," he said. "I went back to the ranch."

With him came a wife, the former Emilia Ramos, a widow nine years his senior. Here on the ranch, Henry Gonzales would live for the next 40 years, taking care of things.

"At first my brother Charlie and I were doing all the landscaping," said Gonzales. "Then Charlie left and it was just me."

In 1948, Leonie Boutall sold it all. "The novelty had worn off," said Manning, who by then was an 18-year-old coed at the University of Arizona. "My aunt wanted to do more traveling. She'd had several offers. Finally, she told my mother, 'I've decided to sell.' "

And sell she did, to an Eastern concern called Thermal Belt Resorts Inc. Selling price: $250,000. "The buildings, everything went," said Manning.

Leonie Boutall moved back to town. Marguerite Wade — by then divorced from Ventress Wade — stayed on for about four months, working for the new owners.

"But it just didn't work out," said Manning. "So Mother bought a house in town, while my aunt continued to rent. She wanted to be able to walk out the door anytime."

Meanwhile, back at the ranch, the new managers were trying to run the place as a kosher guest resort. The main ranch house was converted to apartments, and a new dining room was erected.

In 1950, the ranch was leased to Abraham Weinstein, an "Eastern spa operator" who tried to turn the place into a year-round resort and supper club.

Some 150 Tucsonans motored out for yet another grand reopening, this time with music provided by a group known as the Hollywood Rhythm Girls Orchestra.

Three years later, another change in ownership brought even grander plans for remodeling. This time, reported the Arizona Daily Star, the ranch would sport a new name: the Sahara.

Through it all, one constant remained: Henry Gonzales and the work to be done.

"I used to milk the cows at 5 in the morning and 5 in the afternoon," he said. "I'd feed all the animals, gather the eggs." Every 90 days he'd drain the pool and water the orchards.

One of the bungalows originally erected for the Gonzales family burned down. Henry Gonzales remained in the other one. "We used to go up there all the time and visit him and the ranch," said Naya Ortiz, who also kept in touch with the ranch's original owner.

"I used to visit Mrs. Wade and Miss Boutall all the time during the '50s. Miss Boutall would say, 'Remember, Naya? Remember how beautiful it all was?' "

She also kept in touch with Beverly Manning, who moved to California in 1964. One year, Manning wrote a letter to Ortiz brimming with memories: "I can close my eyes today and remember what it smelled like in your mom's kitchen when she made tortillas and tamales."

Time, however, kept up its relentless gnawing. By 1970, the place where generals and movie stars had slept was calling itself the Sahara Palms Motel.

Six years later, it fell to the wrecking ball. Henry Gonzales, still on the property, still on the payroll, moved into a trailer.

"They pulled up all the big trees with a scoop and dumped them all in this one big trench," said Gonzales. "I had to water the trench."

By then, the monkeys had all been dispatched to the old Pago Pago Cocktail Lounge down on Miracle Mile, said Gonzales. Same for the parrots.

Up went the walls of the property's new occupant — a massive apartment complex now known as Mission Palms. And still Gonzales stayed on, doing the landscaping and watering the trees — many of them personally planted by family members more than a half-century before.

In 1986, Gonzales, by then a widower, moved back to town. By then, Leonie Boutall and her sister, Marguerite Wade, had died. "They both died in Tucson in the same year, 1983," said Manning.

"My aunt outlived a lot of her friends, and she also gave away an awful, awful lot of money. She enjoyed it all."

A few years back, Manning returned to Tucson for a visit — and a nostalgic trip to the ranch of her girlhood.

"There was nothing left," she said, "except for the entrance, the palm trees, and the wall made by Juan Gonzales and his sons."

WESTERN
WAYS
3

Oracle Junction Service Station

Wide spot at the junction was all it was back in 1923.

And not a gas station in sight.

Jack-the-Well-Driller saw the possibilities. "In those days, 25 or 30 miles between watering places was a long way," he would later write in his journal.

Which is how the man whose real name was J.D. McDaniel started up a gas station where none had ever been before, at that curve in the road we all call Oracle Junction.

Logical name, of course. But it wasn't the first.

"Originally it was called Walnut Service Station," said Charley McDaniel, youngest son of the man who first pumped gas where the roads from Tucson, Florence and Oracle all meet.

Millard and Charley McDaniel in front of Dad's gas station in 1930.

"The story was, there was a big walnut tree in back that was hit by an airplane during World War I."

In 1926, the station was renamed Oracle Junction and expanded out back. In went a dance floor and restaurant, known far and wide for its ham.

"People would come out from Tucson for one of those ham sandwiches," said McDaniel.

Born at St. Mary's Hospital in 1925, Charley McDaniel grew up at the junction, living a boyhood few can imagine today.

He remembered roundups and sheep shearings, lion hunts and manhunts, barbecues and dances — dances so rowdy the cowboys brought their own jail.

But then, that's just the sort of childhood one would expect for the children of J.D. and Katie McDaniel, whose own lives could have stepped straight from the pages of pulp Western.

Born in Texas in 1879, J.D. made his way west to Arizona. Along the way he picked up a skill — well drilling — and a bride, the former Katie Hardcastle, 16.

Together, they roamed the West, he drilling for water or copper, she following her man and bearing the babies.

"Most of them were born in tents. I think I was the only one born in a hospital," said McDaniel, the youngest of eight.

After the first World War, his parents tried homesteading along Aravaipa Creek.

"If we could get flowing water there we had a promise of financial backing to grow fruit," wrote J.D. McDaniel. But the drill was still dry down 850 feet.

Then came the prospect of running a gas station — at the crook of the road most drove between Tucson and Phoenix.

"At that time, the closest gas station was the Last Chance at Oracle and River, or the Midway station between Florence and Tucson," said McDaniel.

As for the land, "I think Dad leased it, 40 acres, from the rancher who owned it."

In the beginning, the family lived in Oracle, till J.D. could build them a house next to the two-pump gas station he had built out of sheet iron.

"Some Mexican men were going by the station

when their car broke down," said McDaniel. "Dad said he'd fix their car if they'd make him some adobe blocks. They made the blocks. He fixed the car."

The house was a tin-roofed, three-bedroom adobe, with a big kitchen and an outhouse out back. "Later on, we had plumbing," said McDaniel. Electricity came from a generator.

Sinclair was the gas they pumped, said McDaniel, at "6 or 7 cents a gallon."

The help all came from within. "Dad knew how to fix things, and all the older boys helped out."

Good thing. "The station kept us busy day and night," wrote J.D.

"One time we had flat tires all up and down the road," said McDaniel. "Some convicts had escaped from Florence and stole a truck filled with roofing nails. They poured the nails from the kegs onto the road as they went. We fixed flat tires for I don't know how long."

Naturally, the road was dirt, said McDaniel. "But they kept it bladed. My brother used to run the blader from Oracle Junction to Florence. And Goodyear used to test its tires on that road."

Still, some wound up plodding the roads the old-fashioned way.

"This fellow came in with a Model-T that had thrown a rod," said McDaniel. "My brother traded him the car for a horse. The man rode the horse back to Tucson and my brother fixed the car."

By the time he was 13, McDaniel was driving.

"I got a special license that allowed me to drive to school in Oracle," said McDaniel, who arrived in style in a '27 Model-T truck. "All the other kids walked or rode burros."

In his spare time, he and his brothers hunted rabbits — and sometimes larger game.

"On weekends, I would go out with Dr. (William S.) Lackner, the dentist. We would go lion hunting with his bloodhounds. They would chase the lions up the trees. He did this for training his dogs. Then we'd let the lions go."

He also remembered hunts for higher stakes.

"Some convicts escaped from Florence, stole a car, came by the junction, then went up a little hill where El Conquistador Resort is now. They ran up over the mountains.

"My brother got his 30-30 and joined the posse, which had come back to pick up horses and bloodhounds. They finally found the convicts, on Miracle Mile."

Cowboys rather than convicts, however, usually provided the bulk of the excitement.

"All the ranchers would get together and have big roundups. They'd drive to Red Rock, which was the shipping point," said McDaniel.

"They'd always stop at the junction. The chuck wagon would come in in the early afternoon and they'd fix steaks, cream gravy and hot biscuits. We had big corrals then for the cattle."

Sheepmen also used those same pens.

"We'd have 2,000 head of sheep grazing there. They used to shear the sheep, then throw the wool into big vats 8 feet tall."

Rodeos came to the junction every Fourth of July.

"We barbecued seven whole beefs, had 50 gallons of beans, and sold 1,800 cases of beer, 2,200 cases of pop," said McDaniel. "We had to shovel the beer cans and bottles out of the dance hall before we could hold the dance."

Dances were held on a regular basis just about every Saturday night, with local musicians holding forth on bass fiddle and piano, accordion and violin.

And though music may have had charms to soothe the savage breast, it sometimes failed to work on your average cowboy, said McDaniel.

"One year Oracle Freight Lines brought in a truck with doors on it in back. Whenever anyone got rowdy, they'd lock them up in the truck till they sobered up."

In 1938 it all ended for the McDaniel family — as far as the junction was concerned.

"The Depression was still on; people weren't going up the road as much," said McDaniel. "I think my dad just walked away from it all. I guess he figured he had made his money out of it."

The family moved into Tucson, J.D. went back to well drilling, and young McDaniel enrolled at Sam Hughes Elementary.

Goodbye Model-T. "It really bothered me having to walk or take the bus to school," he admitted.

J.D. McDaniel died toward the end of World War II. But his well-drilling legacy lived on, with the family continuing to drill wells.

Meanwhile, others took over running the enterprises at the junction.

None of the original buildings, however, remains today, said McDaniel.

Later, two restaurants and a mobile home park would nestle in the crook of Oracle Junction.

But a service station is nowhere to be found.

"It's nothing like it used to be," said McDaniel.

WESTERN
WAYS
4

Westward Look

Remote? You bet. Fact is, they got lost the first time they tried to find the place.

"It was 10 miles outside of town," recalled Beverly Nason. "We stopped for gas and a couple there knew where it was. We followed them out."

Way, way out to what's still known as the Westward Look Resort, at 245 E. Ina Road.

Cool by the pool at Westward Look.

From 1948 to the early '60s, Beverly and her late husband, Bob, ran the resort — while raising four little girls in the process.

"We thought it was normal growing up there," said daughter Lani Nason Gianquinto, who rode horses rather than bicycles.

When portions of Walt Disney's "The Living Desert" were filmed on the property back in the early '50s, Gianquinto got a front-row seat.

"They kept trays of tarantulas down in the bunkhouse. They let us watch them filming them," Gianquinto said.

"Every morning at breakfast, we'd ask the guests what they wanted to do that day," said Nason.

Some days it was horseback riding, other days perhaps a trip to Mexico.

"We'd all go down to Nogales and have turtle soup at the Cavern," Nason said.

Once a week, said Gianquinto, her father would barbecue steaks and strum cowboy tunes on the guitar.

"We also had square dancing and Daddy did the calling. He was a wonderful host."

The lack of a liquor license inhibited cocktail hour not a whit.

"Guests brought their own," said Nason. "We had a locker system down by the pool. A bartender did the setups."

Actually, the good times started to roll here not long after statehood burst on the scene back in 1912.

That was the year William and Mary Watson bought 172 acres in the Catalina Foothills and hired Tucson architect Merritt Starkweather to build an adobe-style home.

Decades later, that same home still stood, enveloped by a much-expanded resort.

The initial expansion started with the Watsons, who put in 15 cottages and began operating a guest ranch in the early '20s.

The next owners were the Tanners, who in turn sold it to Bob Nason's father, Robert H., in the early '40s. In 1948, Bob and Beverly and their two oldest girls, Sancy and Lani, motored into Tucson, heading for their new digs.

"I remember it was so hot," said Nason, who was used to the cooler climes of San Francisco.

Still, she readily adapted to her new home. "I thought it was beautiful."

For a time, the family lived in the main house. "After we had the last two girls, we moved into one of the cottages," said Nason.

Ina Road was still dirt and First Avenue hadn't yet punched through to the north, said Nason, who did all her shopping downtown.

Rates from an old brochure range from $16 to $30 a night, meals included. Horseback riding was $2 an hour.

Up until 1956, when air conditioning was installed, the whole place shut down every summer.

That's when Bob and Beverly and the girls would jump in their convertible and head out on vacation themselves.

It was the same car Gianquinto literally fell into while perched in a tree. "I fell through the roof and landed on the horn," she said.

That same tree still shades what to her and her family was much more than a resort. To them, it was home.

WESTERN
WAYS
5

Tanque Verde Valley

There was no gas, no electricity, and the nearest neighbor was two miles away.

Heaven all right to Bryan Lyerly, who once homesteaded 500 acres in the Tanque Verde Valley.

Luxury homes now sprawl across that land at the north end of Soldier Trail, east of the Catalina Highway.

The Tanque Verde Valley before electricity.

"Oh, honey, I hate to tell you what I sold it for," said Lyerly. Maybe $20,000, he ventured.

But then, consider what he paid for it: zero.

"It was all federal land. I went to Phoenix to file. You had to do certain improvements. I built a road, had a well dug and house built. You had to live in it five years."

And live in it he did, along with wife Dorothy and their three little girls, born stair-step fashion between 1930 and 1933.

"The coyotes kept me awake at night. I couldn't sleep," said Lyerly, by way of explanation.

Born in Jonesboro, Ill., Lyerly rolled westward in 1925 to join a brother and two sisters already here. He got a job driving for Tucson Steam Laundry, a room at a boardinghouse, and a Ford coupe from Monte Mansfield.

In 1928, he met Dorothy Waugh, an out-of-towner visiting her parents. The following year, the newlyweds moved to the desert.

Home was frame, three rooms, plus a screened-in porch for sleeping.

Gas lanterns provided light. Lyerly provided the 300-pound blocks of ice, hauled home after work on roads he described as "cow paths."

Sometimes, he'd let the world intrude.

"I would drive my car to the side of the house, clamp the battery under the floorboards, and run a wire inside so we'd get a little radio at night."

He hunted deer and quail in the neighboring hills, fished for bass in the lake at Agua Caliente and palled around with men named Snyder and Cloud.

Lyerly's brother also took up homesteading near him. So did his parents, who'd moved here from Illinois.

Not everyone was happy with all this "development."

"Two rich people owned some property out there and they'd wire up the gate," said Lyerly.

But progress was coming.

In 1935, Lyerly let federal authorities set up camp on his land to house the prisoners building the road to Mount Lemmon.

"They had a lot of bootleggers there," said Lyerly. "One was a friend of mine."

After the camp moved to Vail Corral, the barracks remained.

"We made them into living quarters for the guards and a cook and his wife," said Lyerly. "I rented them out for $30 a month."

In the book, "Agua Caliente Chronicles," the Lyerly daughters recalled roller-skating in one of the deserted barracks and using another as a playhouse.

They also remembered trekking to a culvert installed during the building of the Catalina Highway and enjoying the cool breezes that swept from the mountains into the pipe.

After the Japanese bombed Pearl Harbor, Lyerly enlisted in the Seabees. When he returned, his wife asked for a divorce.

"I had no home. This real estate guy made me an offer for 150 acres and the homestead," said Lyerly. "I thought, 'Well, I'll take that money and buy me a house.' "

Some of his land had already been sold. The rest soon followed.

Years later and living in a retirement community, Lyerly took a field trip out to the old homestead. "They've got big houses where my front yard used to be."

Sad to say, however, there is no road anywhere out there bearing his name.

WESTERN WAYS 6

The Larsons at the Desert Museum

They got there a month before George.

In January of '53, Peggy and Merv Larson arrived at the little trailside museum west of town.

Maybe you've heard of it — the Arizona-Sonora Desert Museum?

Home was a one-bedroom house right on the grounds. A few steps away lived Bill Carr, co-founder — along with Arthur Pack — of the museum.

"Part of the deal was that Bill Carr would eat with us," said Peggy. "But I don't know if he knew about the quality of my cooking."

Peggy Larson mothers two baby bobcats in 1953.

Born in Nebraska, Peggy met Merv while in high school in California. After college and marriage, she taught school for a year while he studied for a master's degree in herpetology.

It was the snakes, of course, that lured Merv to the museum. There, he did everything from cleaning the cages to feeding the animals.

"Bill Carr felt we should all get involved," Peggy said. So naturally, when Carr asked her if she'd like to go along to the airport to pick up the museum's newest inhabitant, a mountain lion, she said sure.

It was love at first sight. "He was in a small cage, and we put him in the back of the station wagon," said Peggy.

Back at the museum, Carr and the Larsons stood inside the lion's enclosure as he extricated himself from the traveling cage.

"He came out of that cage and just expanded," said Peggy. "Bill said, 'I think we need to quietly leave.' "

But George L. Mountainlion was a love.

"He loved to have people scratch his nose," Peggy said. In the evenings after the crowds had gone, they would stand on the museum porch, calling out, "George, George," she said.

"He loved company and would begin to go, 'Yap, yap, yap,' in a cat's voice and then soon switch to purring."

George was certainly a draw, considering the museum had but one row of caged animals, plus a few bugs and reptiles.

No snack bar, no telephone, and Gates Pass was dirt road. "People would still drive out here to see it," said Peggy.

After six months of this, the Larsons returned to California, where Merv went back to school and worked as an entomologist.

In 1956 they returned to Tucson. Merv went back to the museum, building exhibits.

Already, the museum was evolving from "a snake on gravel with a dead stick" exhibit to more natural presentations.

Merv got involved with working on the tunnel exhibit, along with exhibits for otter, beaver and bighorn sheep, followed by the small cat habitat and the earth science cave.

Along the way, he went from curator of exhibits to director of the museum.

Though the couple now lived in town, young wildlife seemed to follow them home.

There was Franny the badger, who used to swim in the family bathtub before graduating to the backyard pool.

"I used to sit in the rocking chair at night and give her the last bottle of the day," said Peggy.

Merv also brought home a baby bighorn, who spent the first night in the Larsons' bed.

In 1976, Merv left the museum and founded and later sold The Larson Co., which specialized in building natural-looking habitats.

WESTERN
WAYS
7

King Anvil Ranch

Celia Elias King's ranching family goes back to the 1890s.

Forget Old Tucson. This is the real deal.

Way out West, where calves still bawl and fence lines always need checking, lies the King Anvil Ranch.

Fifty-thousand acres in all — some private, most state-leased — the ranch sprawls near Three Points, west of the road to Sasabe all the way to the ridge line of the Baboquivaris.

Four generations of Kings have ranched here in the Altar Valley, living in a compound of rambling, plastered adobes dating back to the 1890s.

John Wayne should come riding up any minute now.

"Some of it WAS like you see in the movies," said Celia Elias King, part of the second generation to ranch these lands.

"I saw my first roundup here in 1932," said Celia, who came to the ranch that year as bride to Joe King. It was Joe's father, Manuel, who started the ranch.

"The cowboys took their bedrolls to the mountains to bring down the cattle. They took a chuck wagon and cook, too," said Celia, who as a woman was forbidden to go.

The drive was one of the last to kick up dust all the way from the ranch house to the stockyards in Tucson.

"After 1933, they switched to trucks," said Celia's nephew, John King, who would later run the ranch, along with his son, John.

"People, government regulations, environmentalists," said the elder John King, ticking off a terse list of his most vexing problems.

Hardly even mentioned is the cow-killing drought — something every King has fought.

In the old days, they'd burn the spines off the cholla and feed the cactus to the cattle, said Pat King, one of Celia's five daughters.

Celia and Joe met at a dance in Tucson. After the honeymoon, Joe brought his bride home to the ranch, where Manuel also lived.

Though the ranch house had recently been outfitted with running water and a bathroom, power lines were still almost two decades away.

Celia cooked on a wood stove, cooled perishables with blocks of ice the postman delivered and quelled centipedes and scorpions with a well-aimed splat of boiling water.

"You had to be tough or you weren't going to make it," said Celia, who during one of her pregnancies drove herself to Tucson while well into labor.

"I was driving 65 miles an hour on that gravel road. I'd get a cramp and step on the gas."

Still, there were a few tenderfoot moments.

"The first week or so I was here, I thought I'd take a bath. It was so hot," said Celia, who went swimming in one of two 20,000-gallon tanks down by the corrals.

That is, until Manuel King ordered her out.

"When Joe came home, I told him and he said, 'My God, you were swimming in our drinking water.' One tank was for cattle, the other for us."

Joe's brother, John, brought his bride, Wilhelmina, to the ranch in 1939, settling in the house next to Joe and Celia's.

Their only child, John, along with all those girl cousins, would attend a one-room schoolhouse on land Joe set aside.

Teachers stayed on the ranch and let the kids out of school for the roundups.

In 1961, Celia and Joe bought a ranch in Sasabe, which Celia continued to run after Joe's death in 1979.

In later years, John King rounded up his cattle via helicopter and pilot. A few years ago, the whirlybird flushed out Celia's cattle as well.

This time, Celia got to go on the roundup — straight up.

"It was great," she said. "There were these two bulls fighting. The pilot had to go down low and kick up some dust to make them stop."

Guess some things have changed after all, back at the ranch.

WESTERN
WAYS
8

Picacho Peak Pilot Light

The two-bedroom home that came with the airport job seemed like a mansion to the Kisch children.

It juts up like a purple thumb hitchhiking across the desert, serving for eons as a signpost to the weary traveler.

More than 70 years ago, Picacho Peak also offered up beacon lights for pilots needing to put down in a hurry.

Four miles south of the peak sprawled Red Rock Airport, an emergency landing field that received everything from tiny single props to an American Airlines plane forced down by fog.

Brother and sister Lou Kisch and Irma Duttle bore witness to it all, living in a small frame house on the northern edge of the dirt runway.

To their father, Joseph Kisch, fell the job of periodically climbing Picacho Peak to change out the beacon bulbs.

"Daddy used to drive us to the bottom of Picacho Peak. We'd take a lunch. We had our picnic while Daddy climbed the mountain to check the beacon light," said Duttle.

"He told me one time he went up all the way and forgot the key to get to the bulb," said the son, who climbed the peak a few years back and still found remnants of the beacon that once flashed out across the valley.

The elder Kisch, who from 1935 to 1939 worked for what is now the Federal Aviation Administration, also checked the airport's landing lights.

"Daddy took me for walks to replace the bulbs," said Duttle, who remembered an airfield entirely surrounded by barbed wire. "The cattle ran loose all over the desert," she said.

She and her brother would also check for gopher and rabbit holes on the field for their father to fill. With the gophers and rabbits came the rattlers.

"Daddy would kill at least one a week," said Lou Kisch, who came to the airfield as a newborn and left four years later when his father's recurring tuberculosis forced a move back to Tucson.

"Daddy got TB in Haiti when he was with the Marines," said Duttle. Eventually, the "white plague" would bring the family to Tucson in the summer of '33.

"He had no pension, no assistance. He was very proud," said Duttle. Her mother finally persuaded her father to ask for help. "All they offered us was a bag of turnips," she recalled.

No doubt the Red Rock job Joseph Kisch landed in September of '35 was seen as a godsend.

Ditto for the house that came with it: two bedrooms, running water and electricity.

"We thought it was a mansion," said Lou Kisch.

School was two miles to the south in Red Rock: one room, grades one to eight. A potbellied stove and about 15 kids from neighboring ranches filled up the room, said Duttle.

"At Christmastime and at other get-togethers, we'd push all the desks together and have dances to a windup Victrola."

Summertimes, the family slept outside on Army cots, while a parade of humanity rolled up and down the nearby Casa Grande Highway, precursor to Interstate 10.

"We'd see those people from the Dust Bowl and their cars packed with their belongings, heading toward California," said Duttle.

Once in a while, a plane would land at the L-shaped airfield, including a rather large passenger craft that the family posed in front of in 1939.

Later that year they moved back to Tucson, where the elder Kisch would eventually be cured of TB, living to age 85.

Meanwhile, the Red Rock field developed back in 1927 reverted to wind-swept desert by the mid-'50s, its "mansion" trucked to Tucson, where it still stands today, said Lou Kisch.

Two miles south of the old runway, 18-wheelers on I-10 roar by the spot where Duttle once went to school.

It's disappeared as well — replaced by a newer building a few blocks away.

"It's all gone," said Duttle.

All but the memories.

WESTERN WAYS 9

Link and Lutie

They kept chickens by the thousands, drank water from a natural spring and fenced out the cows that roamed where a golf course now sprawls.

In the mid-1990s, Link and Lutie Wilson, still lived on the land — surrounded by million-dollar homes whose occupants would no doubt be aghast at the thought of an actual chicken scratching nearby.

We know that land today as a portion of Coronado Foothills Estates, up so high in the Catalina Foothills it actually looks down on Skyline Country Club, my dears.

Lutie and Link Wilson pioneered high in the Santa Catalina Foothills.

Sixty years ago, however, it was little more than busted dreams — played-out mining claims honeycombed with old tunnels.

"We still water our citrus and pecan trees with water from the mines," said Lutie, whose front yard butted up to an old mine shaft, complete with pump.

It was Link's uncle, Miles Carpenter, who put them up, up, up where they would eventually live, she said.

A mining man, Carpenter worked the old Texas Arizona Copper Co. mine in the foothills back when this century was new.

"He had tunnels all over," said Lutie. "One of the shafts is straight in front of us."

Other mines, other claims also dotted the area: The Pontatoc, the Saratoga, the Pemberton and Don Jose.

From them came mainly copper, along with a little silver and a trace of gold, said Nyal Niemuth of the state's Department of Mines and Mineral Resources.

"It was relatively weak copper along the Catalina Foothills fault," said Niemuth about the foothills mines in general. "It was handpicked ore. What looked good, they put in a sack, loaded on mules and shipped. What didn't look good they dumped there."

By the 1940s, however, the mines had long played out, Carpenter was dead, and his widow was looking for a deal.

"She got his mining claims as clear property and in 1947 we bought it from her — 116 acres — for $20,000," said Lutie. On the property stood Carpenter's former assay office, as well as a cook shack.

At the time of the sale, Lutie was teaching in Marana, Link was working for the railroad. They rented out their house in town and became pioneers. "We moved into the cook's shack," said Lutie. The "shack" would form the middle of their house, which was greatly expanded.

Light came from a kerosene lantern, and later by generator. Water came piped in from Pontatoc Springs, less than a mile from their house.

"It was a good force of water," said Lutie. "I ran a washing machine with it."

At one time, Indians camped near the springs, but by the time the Wilsons moved into the area, it was covered with a pump house, said Lutie.

Pontatoc Road, which once led to the mine, was one lane and rocky — and the only road to their place.

"We practically rebuilt the road," said Lutie, describing how she and a daughter-in-law would stand on railroad cross ties that had been chained to a truck and dragged slowly across the road.

"We gave the cross ties leverage," she said.

Thankfully, they only did that a few times. "Then Link found out that Pontatoc was a dedicated road and he got the county to maintain it."

The closest grocery store was miles away. Same for the telephone. Deer, bobcats, coyotes, snakes and skunks were plentiful. Human neighbors were harder to come by.

"Once in a while we'd see people on horseback," said Lutie. "They'd come up to our door, lost, and say, 'Do you know where I am?' "

Artist Ted DeGrazia also came calling. "He drove up here one time and about scared me silly," said Lutie, who invited him in. "He wanted to buy our property." The answer was no.

During storms, water would course down from the mountains, filling the gullies.

"The arroyos were much deeper and more active then," said Lutie. "Water would come flying down."

Some of that mountain runoff was later trapped in a three-sided basin large enough to contain a speeding motorboat. "Link and our son Larry used a bulldozer and a scraper to build up the fourth side," said Lutie.

Eventually, the county breached the dam, said Lutie, because neighbors south of it were afraid it would break.

After Link retired in the '50s, the Wilsons got into eggs. Big time.

"We called it Pontatoc Ranch," said Lutie. "We decided to raise chickens for the eggs. We had as many as 4,000 hens." But the venture only lasted a few years.

For progress was coming — in the form of developers.

"They were going to cut up the land in lots. We were on the edge of it. Rather than oppose it, we decided to join in," said Lutie.

In 1961, the Wilsons sold all but five of their acres to a group of Eastern businessmen. The lots would become part of Coronado Foothills Estates.

"Before this happened, we were thinking of reopening the mine. But we decided we couldn't have a mine in the midst of all this prosperity," said Lutie.

Just down the road, more plans were unveiled for a swanky new country club and homes to be built east of Swan Road — where cattle once grazed. Its name: Skyline Country Club.

"The shoulders for Swan Road just below Skyline were made from the ore bed in our front yard," said Lutie.

Over the years, Link and others also engineered many of the other roads snaking through the foothills. "Link could hold onto a jackhammer longer than any of the men," said Lutie.

But road development also meant the end of the lovely springs that had pumped water to the Wilsons for so long.

"By that time, the pump house was gone, and engineers ran the road right over the springs," said Lutie, whose home by then had been connected to a regular water utility.

By the mid-'90s, the Wilsons' ranch house would be dwarfed by multimillion-dollar monuments jutting here and there on the cliffs.

Asked how she felt about that, Lutie replied: "They are castles. They're so pretty. It's all right as far as I'm concerned."

(Link Wilson died in 1997, Lutie died in 2000.)

WESTERN
WAYS
10

Tumbleweed Ranch

When old-timers harp on and on about how this shopping center or that car lot used to be nothing but desert, believe.

Believe that the intersection of Swan and Speedway once looked like the middle of nowhere a mere seven decades ago.

Believe that there were no stoplights, no traffic, no sprawl.

Believe that you could ride a horse east all the way to the rising moon, easing itself up over the Rincons.

Scrap Roberts, astride his beloved horse, War Chief.

A.W. "Scrap" Roberts believed.

"I had the idea to build some stables," said Roberts, whose previous encounters with a horse consisted mainly of ROTC cavalry drills at the University of Arizona.

No matter.

In 1936, he started buying up real estate along Speedway just west of Swan Road — then a dirt strip just aching for a landing.

A few years later, a friend with an airplane would do just that, with Roberts sitting next to him in the cockpit. "There were no cars then," he said, referring to today's hectic traffic.

A California boy, Roberts had come east to Tucson in 1934 to enroll at the University of Arizona and play a little football under J.F. "Pop" McKale. It was McKale, by the way, who first called him "Scrap."

The following year, he bought the old college hangout known as the Varsity Inn. His involvement didn't last long. "Too much time and not enough money," said Roberts.

Besides, there was all that desert out there. All those financial possibilities.

"My mother and dad had come out here by then, and we started buying up more and more land," said Roberts.

By the time they were done, they owned everything from Swan Road to Venice Avenue, Speedway to Fairmount Street. Forty acres altogether, snapped up, he said, for $2,000 an acre.

One of the lots they bought fronting Speedway already held a house.

"We paid $16,000 for the house and one acre," said Roberts, who made that the family home. Electricity was in. So was the water, supplied from a well.

"We put in two more wells, dug down 100 feet. Back then, the water was good."

Into the ground went Aleppo pines, pepper trees, oleanders and a hand-dug swimming pool.

"It was the only one for miles around," said Roberts. "It cost $700 to build."

By the early '40s, he was calling the whole thing Tumbleweed Ranch, named for the stickery bushes regularly rolling on by.

Coyotes and javelina ambled by the front porch. Out back, behind the property, squatted a turkey farm and a former speak-easy.

If it was neighbors they wanted, neighbors they soon got — residing in small rental cottages Roberts and his dad, Floyd, built on the property.

"There were seven little houses — two-bedroom,

one-bath, brick and plaster," said Roberts. "We rented them for $50 a month. Later it went to $75."

Among the tenants: Hollywood film crews, "an opera singer who came out here from New York" and plenty of health-seekers.

"They brought one woman out in a car with the seat turned down. She was lying down," said Roberts. "Pretty soon she had a couple of crutches. She left us walking."

On the southeast portion of the property, Roberts put in his stables and riding arena, offering instruction in both English and Western riding.

Tenderfoots and tourists showed up, along with students from St. Joseph's Academy and Arizona Sunshine School.

One Saturday night, Roberts asked a young woman to dance at the old Desert Shores supper club.

"For crying out loud, there he was wearing cowboy clothes, with stuff on his boots," said Virginia Roberts. Nevertheless, she accepted his invitation to dance. They married in 1942.

Out to the ranch she went. "I was a wrangler right from the beginning," said Virginia, who also helped out Scrap's mother, Anne, with the cooking.

"We had two cowboys, Shorty and Ed, who lived in the bunkhouse," said Virginia. "But we fed them in the kitchen."

Sixty head of horses lived on the ranch at one time, including Scrap's beloved War Chief. "We hauled in our hay all the way from Yuma," said Scrap.

Friday nights were reserved for steak rides. "The horses used a trail off of Swan Road that went clear to Wilmot Road," said Virginia.

On the way back, Scrap and the riders would stop at the old Venice Gardens (later known as the Palomino) for a beer.

"That's when he'd call me and say, 'Put on the steaks,' " said Virginia. Total cost for the ride and the grub: $2.50.

During wartime, said Virginia, "we had a time getting the steaks, but we saved our stamps."

While steaks may have been scarce during the war, not so tenants. "Houses were hard to come by," said Scrap. "All the cottages were filled."

By war's end, Scrap's parents had moved back to California, and Scrap and Virginia were busy raising two boys.

Another kind of growth was also occurring, as others discovered the eastside.

"We started noticing there was less access to the horse trails," said Virginia. Again seizing opportunity, Scrap leased out a corner of the property for a gas station.

Despite civilization's inroads, Tumbleweed Ranch still tried to keep it horsey.

"Every year at rodeo time, we'd take all the horses down to the rodeo parade for others to ride," said Virginia. "People would pay us $3. We saddled every horse, 60 of them, then took them down 22nd Street."

Speedway, it seems, had become too citified for horses' hooves.

Looming assessments for road improvements finally forced them to sell in the mid-1950s. "People were circulating petitions to have the roads paved," said Scrap. "It would have cost us a fortune."

So they sold it all to an out-of-town buyer — the property, the main house, the cottages, the stables. "We sold the horses and 100 saddles," said Scrap. "The hardest was selling War Chief."

"The new owner tore it all down," said Virginia. "That killed us when he tore down the houses and filled in the swimming pool."

For years, said Virginia, the land stood vacant. "The new owner got offers, but nobody could get financing."

Meanwhile, Scrap and Virginia built a new home not far from the old Tumbleweed Ranch.

Today, the ranch where Scrap saddled up and Virginia cooked steaks so far out in the desert is filled with commerce.

WESTERN
WAYS
11

Tohono Chul

The family home built in 1937 for John Wack.

Never underestimate the power of a mint julep.

John Wack remembered what they did to him. "We had a luncheon with Rev. and Mrs. George Ferguson." He was the founding rector of St. Philip's In The Hills church. "After the mint juleps, they took us out and showed us some land for sale. Between their powers of persuasion and the mint juleps, we bought the land, 80 acres."

The ice long ago melted in those frosty glasses. But the legacy of the land and the house Wack would build upon it almost 70 years ago lives on in that refuge from urban life that we all know as Tohono Chul Park.

Today, it's a 49-acre nature preserve, complete with winding desert trails, exhibitions, art and gift galleries and a tearoom. A corner of desert treasure tucked behind the busy intersection of Ina and Oracle roads.

Eighty-five years ago, only cattle roamed through the brush and the cacti there, on land homesteaded by T.T. Muzzy. Then along came Sam W. Seaney, who homesteaded 640 acres and subdivided it into large, multi-acre lots that would one day bear the rather civilized name Catalina Citrus Estates.

Seaney's daughter Cornelia Lovitt remembered a few rather uncivilized aspects about the property, however.

"My father built a little cabin right behind where Tohono Chul is now. He homesteaded there. My mother and I would come out on the weekends. Oracle was not paved and when the Rillito was running, you couldn't cross.

Her father drilled the property's first well on, of all things, a hill. "What's amazing is that he didn't have to go down very far for water."

Desert creatures, of course, abounded. "I had a little dog I loved who was yapping outside the door of the cabin," recalled Lovitt. "We opened the door to let him in and a coyote came running in, too, stopped in the middle of the room, turned around, and ran out."

Polo brought Wack, who played on the Santa Barbara, Calif., team, to town and to that auspicious lunch with the Fergusons in 1936.

Maurice Reid, who developed the oasis of palms and citrus on Orange Grove Road, is the one who sold them the land — $200 an acre, Gene Reid, Maurice's son, remembered how it was done back then:

"We had a little 10-horse Caterpillar tractor. We'd cut a little trail so we could get vehicles in there to show prospective buyers. That's why the roads are so crooked out there; we worked around the major plants.

The Reids landscaped the property with an orchard's worth of grapefruit trees trucked in from Phoenix, along with more than a dozen date palms.

Using the plans of a Santa Barbara architect, the Wacks hired Paul Holton to build their house. Adobe blocks for the 18-inch-thick walls were made on the site and massive ponderosa pine ceiling beams were hauled down Mount Lemmon's rustic back road.

French doors to catch the breeze and that rarity known as a private swimming pool were the home's only cooling devices.

But progress was on the march. By the time the home was completed in 1937, electric lines and pavement were both snaking up on Oracle Road.

Ironically, the home's first owner spent little, if any time there. "We ended up building the house for my father, Henry Wellington Wack, who was the founder and first editor of Field and Steam magazine," said John Wack.

Other likewise esteemed occupants would follow.

By the end of World War II, the elegant home so far out in the desert had passed through the ownership of two more out-of-town families, one from Boston, the other from Pittsburgh.

How much time either spent in the house, no one seems to know. But just about everyone in America knew the popular radio shows created by the home's next occupant, scriptwriter Clifford Goldsmith.

The man who introduced the character Henry Aldrich and his trademark, "Coming, Mother," into the American consciousness, rented the home on 1946.

His son, Barclay Goldsmith, who lived in the house as a child, remembered his father banging out scripts for "The Aldrich Family" in an office that would later house Tohono Chul's gift shop.

"My father had spent so much time away from home. I think this was an attempt to be more of a family. It was a treat for him," said Goldsmith about the man who, indeed, would make his home in Tucson until the day he died in 1971.

He remembered lots of back-and-forth calls between New York and Tucson, and a steady stream of visitors — some of them world-famous. "Claude Rains stayed there. I know."

Ten years after its adobe walls went up, the home was still very much out in the middle of nowhere. "Ina was dirt, two-lane and like a washboard," said Goldsmith.

Tom Peterson, a classmate of the younger Goldsmith's, remembered what visiting his friend entailed. "It was so far away that my dad would take me downtown and I would get on a Greyhound bus for Phoenix — that's when they went through Florence. And for a quarter, I would ride the bus to Oracle and Ina."

After two years, the Goldsmiths built a home of their own farther west on Ina Road. The home they had rented went on the market — and sold in 1948 to Col. Robert Bagnell and his wife, Eugenia Sullivan Bagnell, formerly of St. Louis.

With them came their butler, Levan Bell, who years later remembered picking grapefruit off the trees and taking the family's Airedale into town to have porcupine quills removed.

Of all the families associated with the house, the Bagnells lived there the longest. She died in 1962, he two years later.

Jane Sullivan, the widow of Mrs. Bagnell's son, John, remembered the home — both the way it was when she first saw it as a newlywed back in the late '40s, and the way it looked 15 years later.

"It was a beautiful home, the house never changed," she said, recalling the rose garden, the night-blooming cereus and the elegant dinners served by Levan Bell.

Not long before Robert Bagnell died, John and Jane Sullivan moved into a new home on the property, designed by Tucson architect Louis Hall. Known as the West House, it would later serve as Tohono Chul's gift gallery and tearoom.

Upon his death, Robert Bagnell's home and property went to John Sullivan. Before long, the Sullivans and their children were living in the old adobe-walled home.

But the Sullivans were interested in buying a ranch south of Tucson. Once again, the property changed hands. By then, much of the 80 original acres had been chipped away.

In 1966, the new owners, Richard and Jean Wilson, began buying some of it back — 36 acres in all.

Although they lived in West House for a time, the Wilsons never lived in the main house. After the bookshop they built on the far eastern strip of the property was completed in 1979, the Wilsons decided to put in a nature trail to the west.

The rest, as they say, is philanthropy.

In 1985, the massive house — built, it would seem, on a whim — was lovingly renovated.

Rooms where butlers served canapés at elegant soirees and radio scriptwriters turned out next week's coast-to-coast guffaws were turned into administrative offices, exhibit space and a gift shop.

Some who once called the place home would see that that reincarnation. Some did not. All are glad it survives.

Said Jane Sullivan: "I just loved that house. I could have lived there forever."

WESTERN
WAYS
12

Binghampton

Wagonload after wagonload of Mormons raised kids and crops in Binghampton.

Credit Pancho Villa with this one.

When the wily revolutionary started stomping through northern Mexico, folks started packing. Among them: wagonload after wagonload of Mormons who would raise kids and crops in a town so far from Tucson it had its own name.

The place also had ponds big enough for rowboats, orchards groaning with fruit, and a dust-in-your-toes way of life that can make strong men weep with nostalgia.

Binghampton, they called it. We know it today as the area bounded roughly by Country Club and Swan roads to the west and east, Fort Lowell Road to the south, the Rillito River to the north.

Nephi Bingham was the town's namesake — which is one of the "perks" for getting there first.

Just before the turn of the century he moved to a farm where Dodge Boulevard now dead-ends into River Road. Add on another 50 or 60 years and it would be Gov. Raul Castro's place.

It was also Nephi Bingham who rode south into Mexico to urge his fellow Mormons — most of them relatives — northward.

"In December of 1909 here they came, in covered wagons," said Millard Bingham, Nephi's nephew and one-time family chronicler of a history about as rich as they come.

Before the Mormons from Mexico got here, the Binghams were it, said Millard. "From 1893 to 1909 we were the only Mormon family in Tucson."

The saga begins with Millard's grandfather, Erastus Bingham Jr., who sired 16 children with his second wife. The youngest child was Jacob, Millard's father.

When Jacob was 12, the family sold its dairy farm in Mancos, Colo., and started south. "Grandpa was getting old and he had two grown sons, Nephi and Daniel, who were already living in Arizona," said Millard.

Horseflesh brought them south. They either rode it or sold it. "They traded horses at all the Army posts on the way down," said Millard.

The travelers crossed the Colorado at Lees Ferry, then climbed into the mountain passes. "I've heard Dad talk about having to take his herd of horses and tromp them through the snow, packing it down so the rest could get through," said Millard.

Once in Tucson, the family settled east of town in an old house near Fourth Avenue and Ninth Street. Then they set up a dairy at the end of Congress Street, where the old Rialto/Paramount theater would later rise. "Nothing was up that far east," said Millard.

Jacob sold ice cream from the dairy, ran with the local boys — who taught him fluent Spanish — and went all the way through the third grade in an adobe schoolhouse set up on Uncle Nephi's land north of the Rillito.

By his late teens, Jacob Bingham was cowboying at a ranch in Vail and courting Frances Lavana Harris, whose family had moved into the area from Silver City, N.M. "My father met my mother when she was a 14-year-old girl," said Millard.

Eight children would be born to them. Millard was No. 6. By that time, the family was living on leased farmland near Fort Lowell and Swan roads.

Uncle Nephi also branched out. "He owned a dairy farm at Fort Lowell and Columbus," said Millard.

Nephi also donated some land behind his River Road farm for the inevitable burials. The first was in 1899: John Harris, age 91. Jacob Bingham did the digging.

All through 1910, 1911, 1912, the Mormons kept trickling up from Mexico. Among the families was one named Nelson. After several years in St. David, they moved to Binghampton. Fourteen children were born to Alvin and Elsinore Nelson. No. 11 was a daughter, born in 1918 near what is now the north end of Country Club Road.

They called her Pearl. Nineteen years later she would marry Millard Bingham, who was five years her senior. The two grew up together, in Binghampton.

"She was just a little girl, but so pretty," said Millard. "I used to say, 'Save her for me.' "

Like Millard, Pearl, too, had vivid memories of a childhood spent along the rich bottomlands of the Rillito.

"I was only 3, but I remember taking the salt shaker out to the tomato patch, salting a tomato and eating it right off the vine," said Pearl. "We had peaches and apricots, and corn and potatoes."

With the richness of the land came the threat of flood. "I remember once when the river jumped the bank," said Pearl. "I can still see the water bubbling all around in our yard. We moved our lumber house to higher ground."

Still, the farmers of Binghampton stayed close to the river, which, after all, was responsible for plumping up all those peaches and tomatoes.

With redwood flumes, they channeled water from the river at what is now the Craycroft bridge, westward toward their crops.

"From my first memory as a boy to about when I was 16 or 17, I remember a big stream of water coming all day long," said Millard. Two enormous water ponds sat side by side near the north end of Alvernon Way and the river, to catch the surplus.

By 1913, Binghampton's population had quadrupled. The community decided it was high time to build its own concrete-lined swimming pool. "They ran clean water to it, but after a few years it began to silt up," said Millard. "It became a swimming hole for us naked boys."

Life in the community revolved around work, church and school — with the latter two activities held for many years in the same building.

In 1905, a real estate investor by the name of Alexander Davidson donated the land, and the Mormons hammered together a frame school building near what is now the intersection of Alvernon and Fort Lowell.

In 1912, a larger frame building took its place. By 1916, an adobe building also stood on the property. Here is where the Mormons of Binghampton worshipped — and where the children of Davidson School would attend assemblies in what became the school auditorium.

In the early '20s, discord flared in the community over the Mormons using the same property for church and school.

A compromise was worked out. In 1928, Davidson School was annexed into what is now Tucson Unified School District. By then, the Mormons of Binghampton were building another church, known as the First Ward, at 3700 E. Fort Lowell Road.

"We started it in 1927, but we didn't dedicate it until 1936, when it was paid for," said Millard.

Nineteen twenty-seven was also the year vast tracts of Foothills land north of the Rillito were opened up for homesteading. Most of it was gobbled up by developer John Murphey — including Binghampton's 40-acre cemetery.

"Murphey told us to move the bodies," said Millard, who was about 14 at the time. "My mother was in there — she died of the Spanish influenza in 1919. We were all upset."

A meeting was held at the church, and a man by the name of Orrin Williams was elected to go to Phoenix to try to persuade the Bureau of Land Management to let the Mormons buy their cemetery for homesteading fees — $1.25 an acre.

"He had the gift of gab," Millard said about Williams. Apparently so. For he came back with rights to the land where generations of Binghampton residents now lie — including Pearl's and Millard's parents.

Self-sufficiency colored every aspect of life in Binghampton. "My mother churned her own butter, kneaded and baked her own bread, and pieced and made all the quilts on our beds," said Pearl.

"I can still see her at that old Singer sewing machine, feet working the pedals and her singing at the top of her voice."

Every scrap of clothing was hand-sewn. "In the schoolyard, we had a pole with handles that you could grab and swing out," said Pearl. "All the little girls wore dresses then, and when they swung way out, you could see the panties their mothers had made. They all said Gold Medal Flour on them."

Water was drawn from a backyard well — or maybe pumped by hand out by the back door. Light came through kerosene lamp. Children made extra money by hiring out in the onion fields — when they weren't trying to sneak into the strawberry patch, said Millard.

Most of the children were born at home — attended by Binghampton's own midwife, Louisa Done.

In the summertime, said Pearl, everyone slept out under the stars. And sure as the heat, every year at least one rabid dog — sickened by the skunks or coyotes — would snap and snarl through the community, sending men scurrying after their shotguns.

Friday nights, there was usually a potluck and dance, held to raise money to pay off the new church. "Erastus Wheeler would play the fiddle and Maude Clawson — she was married to the principal of Davidson — would play the piano," said Pearl.

"We made our own fun," she continued. "We had plays, musicals. We'd go down to the riverbed and have corn roasts, wiener roasts."

But the land alone could not support most of the families of Binghampton. Both Millard and his father Jacob wound up working for the railroad. "By the '30s, some of the old Mormon families were moving out of town," said Millard. "Moving closer to work."

During World War II, Binghampton gave up two of its own. "George and Ellis Hardy," said Millard. "They were brothers." Both rest at peace in the Binghampton cemetery, which Millard and Pearl would later oversee.

Today, the lush fields and orchards of Binghampton have given way to a mishmash of homes and businesses. Pearl and Millard moved away and the home where they raised five children would become a lapidary business.

Though a few of the old-time families still live in what was once a thriving farm community, none of them, said Millard, are Binghams.

WESTERN WAYS 13

Depression life in Tucson Mountains

Hard to say if any other boy-grown-to-man had a better childhood — hardscrabble times notwithstanding.

"I grew up with the javelina and the antelope," said Joseph F. Carithers, whose dad — also named Joseph — served as superintendent of Tucson Mountain Park in the midst of the Great Depression.

Home was a two-room rock house on Kinney Road, not far from the present Arizona-Sonora Desert Museum.

No water, no electricity, no cooling, no matter.

"We used to lie with our heads under the icebox, to keep cool," remembered Rebecca Ferguson, Joe's younger sister.

Tuberculosis in the elder Joseph Carithers' lungs brought the family from Mississippi to Tucson in 1932. Couple of years later, the head of the family was well enough to take the Tucson Mountains post.

Everyone, including the children's mother, Doris, moved to the little rock house so far from town.

Water was hauled from a Civilian Conservation Corps camp down the road. Light came by lantern, heat from a fireplace. Winter and summer, the kids slept on the front porch.

Two CCC camps sprang up in the area — one to the south, the other in the Picture Rocks area.

When they weren't building trails and ramadas throughout the park, many of the men from the Picture Rocks camp, said Carithers, could be found on the family's front porch.

"I can remember them eating my mom's fried chicken and watermelon and listening to a Joe Louis fight on our battery radio," Carithers reported in a written account of his childhood.

In return for the hospitality, said Carithers, the men would haul in desert firewood for the family's cookstove and fireplace.

Not all of the men, however, were forced into bachelorhood. For the families of some, said Carithers, followed them to the desert, renting out whatever homestead housing was available.

That may explain why in 1933 — the year the CCC began — a spare, whitewashed frame building by the name of Homestead School, District No. 52, sprang up northwest of the Tucson Mountains.

About half of its student body of 30 or so were the children of CCC workers; the rest were ranchers' or farmers' kids.

Scuffed shoes and worn jeans were the uniform of all in this classroom, whether Anglo or Mexican-American, said Carithers, who first attended the school as a third-grader, back in '35.

The Depression, he wrote, "was a great equalizer. There was no snobbery or despair. We were rich in ways that I didn't fully appreciate until I was grown."

The school's landscaping was native mesquite and palo verde, its play area an open field, and its school bus a farmer's pickup truck, outfitted with canvas backing and two rows of benches for the human cargo.

The owner of the truck also served as bus driver — when he wasn't hauling livestock to market in that same truck, that is. "He was thoughtful enough to hose out the bed occasionally," said Carithers.

Reduced to splinters decades ago, the old schoolhouse would still hold powerful memories for its one-time scholar.

Most vivid of all, perhaps, were his memories of Homestead's schoolmarm, a Mrs. Simpson, who was, said Carithers, "a person to be reckoned with."

Here was a teacher, wrote Carithers, who firmly believed that "the inability to communicate, cipher and reason would result in a wasted and unhappy life."

No such thing for the pupils at Homestead, who were kept busy not only with the three R's, but with plays and pageants that revolved around the holidays, ranging from Armistice Day to Christmas.

"It was all done as a group, all equal, all of us shy and gangly and self-conscious," wrote Carithers. But when it was over, "all felt a great flow of accomplishment."

Learning, coupled with ingenuity, frequently leaped beyond the boundaries of this Depression-era classroom.

One Christmas, said Carithers, the class decided to decorate the school's interior with desert mistletoe, painstakingly gathered on a cold afternoon.

But during the night, a cow gorged down the entire cache, which had been temporarily stored next to the school.

"We all referred to it as the year that the cow ate Christmas."

Harsher lessons awaited. Pressed to come up with funds for a new set of encyclopedias, Mrs. Simpson enlisted the class to round up rattlesnakes for a Tucson man who was paying cash for the venom.

"After lunch every day in the early fall and late spring, we made the rounds of the countryside," wrote Carithers, adding that a good week's harvest might yield six to eight rattlers.

Snakes were placed in a gunnysack in Mrs. Simpson's car, which she drove to Tucson on Fridays, after school.

And then one Friday, the inevitable happened. While getting ready to enter her car, which was always parked in the shade, Mrs. Simpson heard the unmistakable sounds of a rattle — several of them, matter of fact — coming from under the seats and the dashboard.

Enterprising as ever, the class rolled the car into the sunshine and opened all the doors. By Monday, Carithers reported, the car was clean — save for a gunnysack with a small hole in it. The incident, however, marked the end of Homestead's rattlesnake roundups.

After a couple of years at Homestead, young Carithers transferred to the Preventorium, by then up and running at the old CCC camp where Gilbert Ray Campground is today.

The Preventorium was a county-run institution set up for children at risk of contracting tuberculosis. Carithers, however, was there strictly for the tutoring, in subjects he knew he'd soon be tackling at Roskruge Junior High.

All through junior high and high school, he commuted between town and the little rock house in the Tucson Mountains.

He served in the Army during World War II, then returned to Tucson and enrolled at the University of Arizona.

Meanwhile, the elder Joseph Carithers had quit his post as Tucson Mountain Park superintendent and, along with Doris, began running an Old Tucson concession known as Ward's Saloon.

Stepping into the post was C.B. Brown, the former Pima County agricultural agent who was a major force in establishing the park back in 1930.

But Brown was clearly there on a temporary basis, said Carithers, who applied for and got his father's old job in 1949.

Carithers, his wife, Hildegarde, and their two children would live in the same rock house where he had spent so many happy childhood years.

"We enlarged the house and I raised a family there," said Carithers, who during his tenure oversaw the building of the Gilbert Ray Campground on the grounds of the old Preventorium.

In 1958, Carithers left Tucson to become assistant Western representative for the National Parks Association. A lifetime of various jobs in parks administration would follow.

Later living in Texas, Carithers would recall a visit to the old Homestead school site sometime during the '60s. "I tried to locate it, but all I could find were the front steps, made out of poured cement."

Institutions

The adult choir at Mount Calvary sang on the radio in the 1940s.

They healed the sick, educated the young, and saved our souls. Hospitals, schools and churches: All played a role in this, our town.

INSTITUTIONS
1

Laguna School

Children during a break from readin', 'ritin' and 'rithmetic at Laguna School.

The mesquite grew into brambles and the trains screamed like banshees the year Laguna School came into being.

Out of adobe and dreams for a better life, a little schoolhouse took shape, close by the railroad tracks. One room, one teacher, eight kids, in the year 1889.

Ten years later, in 1899, the Rillito School District, as it was then known, split. Half became the Laguna School District No. 17, the other half became the Flowing Wells District.

Time marched on. By 1915, Laguna had a four-acre site and a brand-new red-brick schoolhouse, still essentially one-room.

This was the school Gene Shannon attended as a sixth-grader in 1930. By then the school had two teachers and two classrooms, separated by a partition that was removed when the kids all put on their bedspreads and wings to play shepherds and angels in the annual Christmas play.

Most of the 30 or so students, first through sixth grade, were the children of either farmers or railroad men living in section houses near the tracks. Shannon's father, Lester, who served on the Laguna school board, ran a dairy farm on the south banks of the Rillito River.

Down the two-lane dirt road that ran in front of the schoolhouse, young Shannon would ride his Indian pony to school, bareback: "Other kids rode their horses to school, too," said Shannon, who would later move to Prescott. "There was a big bank in front of the school with grass and water. We'd let our horses out there."

Two potbellied stoves kept the schoolhouse toasty in winter." A section gang from the railroad used to gather the wood," said Shannon. "Across the street it was a jungle of mesquite."

To the north of the building stood two outhouses — one for the girls, one for the boys — and the original adobe schoolhouse.

Readin', 'ritin', and 'rithmetic were top priorities for Laguna's faculty back then. Act up and you might find yourself stuck in the coat closet for a half-hour or so. Or get a note pinned to your shirt, for your father.

But even the teachers found it hard to keep order above the din of the trains coming through. "The trains then were steam engine," said Shannon. "When they'd blow the whistle for the crossing at Ruthrauff, everything came to screeching halt."

Barbed-wire fencing ran along the schoolyard, said Shannon, keeping the students from straying too close to the tracks. "The kids from the section houses walked home along the tracks, but they were pretty wise about the trains."

When the weather turned warm, they'd open all the doors and windows and let the breezes flow through. "It was a big, high-ceilinged room," said

Shannon. "With the breezes it wasn't too bad. Nobody thought about coolers back then."

After school, there were cows to milk and hay to load, and then if you got through and it was still daylight, rabbits or quail to hunt along the Rillito, or, in warm weather, irrigation ditches to cool off in.

The schoolyard where the children took turns tossing a basketball into a lone hoop was dirt and gravel. Shading both playground and schoolhouse were several cottonwood trees.

When Shannon went to Roskruge Junior High School the following year, he had to leave his horse at home. "I would catch the bus due west of our house," he recalled. "It ran out Silverbell Road almost to Rattlesnake Pass. Then it went on Sunset Road and the Casa Grande Highway, which was two-lane and very narrow back then."

In 1948, the Laguna district bought more land around the school, bringing the total area to 12 acres. Two frame barracks from Fort Huachuca became classrooms.

During the next few years, the school would grow from 43 students to almost 400. Still "out in the country," Laguna also served as a community center. Saturday nights often found square dancers twirling through their do-si-do's at the school.

Two classrooms and a cafetorium were added in 1963. The following year, Laguna School District No. 17 was annexed to the Flowing Wells School District.

Today, the trains still rumble just to the west of the schoolyard. But the shriek of the steam whistle that once brought readin' and 'ritin' and 'rithmetic to a standstill is only a memory.

INSTITUTIONS
2

Mount Calvary

The roads were ruts and caliche, the horse was the preferred mode of transportation and statehood was still a dozen years away in 1900.

That was the year a series of revivals led by an out-of-town preacher sparked the beginnings of Mount Calvary Missionary Baptist Church.

Parishioners at Mount Calvary.

What is now Arizona's oldest black Baptist church began with a bedrock of 10 men and women. Services were held at first in a building at North Ninth Avenue and West Fifth Street.

As the congregation grew in numbers, it began sprouting the usual arms of a thriving church — missionary society, Sunday school, choir, Bible study group.

By 1921, Mount Calvary had again outgrown its rented quarters. This time it would build its own house of God and bricks, on the southwest corner of North 10th Avenue and West Fourth Street.

Air conditioning came from ceiling fans, heat from a free-standing stove visible from the pulpit.

Preaching from behind that pulpit in the late '20s was the Rev. P.B. Cornelius. And there among the congregation was his niece, Eugenia Wells, future lifetime member.

"My mother played the piano in church, and they carried me in there when I was a baby," said Wells, who was born in 1928.

Eight years later, she would be baptized in the standing waters of the church — directly beneath the choir stand.

"They had to move the choir and pick up the folding chairs," Wells recalled. "There was a wooden floor, like a trapdoor, that you opened. Steps led down to the water." The congregation, said Wells, would then gather 'round to watch the baptisms.

"There was a time when we also used one of the swimming pools for baptisms — the one that allowed us to swim there," said Wells.

Segregation reared its head at that most innocuous of all activities: the Sunday school picnic. "We were not permitted in the parks," said Wells. "So we would go out to the Indian reservation."

Church, says Wells, "was where we socialized and worshipped. There was no other place to go."

To help fill the summertime lull, vacation Bible school became part of Mount Calvary's myriad youth programs.

Meanwhile, Sunday school classes met in the church basement, or else gathered in the sanctuary.

Greeting the children for more than 40 years was Sunday school teacher Monie Bell. "We always had a little Bible story, and everybody had a verse to say," remembered Bell, who joined the congregation in the fall of '36.

Favorite song among the children: "Jesus Loves Me."

Boys age 12 or so could serve as junior deacons, said Bell. "They would participate every fourth Sunday, lead the devotional and help with the offering." Girls sang and ushered.

Reading Scriptures in front of the entire congregation was not as scary as it sounded, said Willie Fears, who joined Mount Calvary as a child in the late '30s. "Everybody knew everybody, so we were not nervous. We were all like family."

Of all the joyful noises offered up to the Lord at Mount Calvary, the choir most closely identified with the church was its Gospel Chorus, later known as the Cathedral Choir.

The exuberance of this choir regularly soared past the confines of the church.

"We would go to different hospitals and sing," said Elsie Hood, who joined the church in 1937 and worked in its day-care center. "We also went out Christmas caroling — to hospitals, nursing homes and the shut-ins."

When World War II erupted, Mount Calvary swelled with the ranks of black soldiers, many of them stationed at Fort Huachuca.

Once peace was declared, the church — just like about everything else in this town — experienced phenomenal growth. "On Easter and special Sundays, we'd have to put folding chairs down the aisles," said Fears, whose church could hold no more than 300 souls.

Crowded or not, one spot remained "reserved" in the pew where church stalwart Missouri Nobles sat.

"Mother had a special place where she sat in the church, on the right-hand side," said daughter Laura Banks, herself a member for more than 50 years. "Everybody knew that was Sister Missouri Nobles' place. No one else sat there."

At least not for long, "A woman did sit there once," said Banks. "Mother said, 'Excuse me, Madam, but that's my seat.' The woman moved."

A former Sunday school teacher, accompanist for the Junior Choir and director of the church's Baptist Young People's Union, Banks joined Mount Calvary at the relatively late age of 12.

"At special services, I remember having to sit on the mourners' bench, which is where you sat if you were not a Christian," said Banks.

"Mainly, the mourners' bench was used at revivals, for people who had not joined the church," Fears remembered. "My uncle used to say it would be pretty embarrassing if you sat on that bench the whole week without finding the Lord between Monday and Friday."

When Mount Calvary went looking for a new location in the late '40s, it still faced some restrictions, said Fears. "We had to find property in the 'colored' areas. There were only certain areas where we could build."

Fried chicken fed to the multitudes by the women of Mount Calvary contributed mightily to the church building fund.

"We cooked up a lot of chicken dinners in the basement of the old church to get into the new church," said Hood. "We delivered a lot of dinners, too. A lot of white people we worked for, and friends, would order."

Less than a dollar is what Wells remembered the dinners costing. "The women contributed the food, too. The foundation of Mount Calvary is the black mothers and their cooking."

The reward came on July 31, 1955, when Mount Calvary broke ground at its new location, 201 E. Lester St. Seven months later, on Feb. 29, 1956, the first services were held in the new church.

A Sunday school wing, large choir room, secretary's office, pastor's study and nurse's office were just some of the amenities of the new Mount Calvary, built to hold 600 worshippers.

Integration, the civil rights struggle, Martin Luther King's assassination — all would be addressed from the pulpit of Mount Calvary Missionary Baptist Church. "As times have changed, the church has changed," said Fears. "But the church is still the rock."

INSTITUTIONS
3

Fort Lowell School

Lots of older folks remember the teachers in their schools. Few, however, are ever able to pore over the scrapbooks with them.

In the fall of '26, Lutie Wilson started teaching at the old Fort Lowell School, near the crook of what was then a narrow, dirt road by the same name.

Lutie Wilson taught here when it was the site of the old Fort Lowell School.

It was your typical country school. Wood-burning stove, outdoor plumbing, dinner pails at noon.

Also starting school that fall was Dorothy Kellogg, who was then Dorothy Messner. "I was there for the sixth and seventh grades, but I didn't have Lutie for a teacher," said Kellogg.

Little matter. In a school with only 60 or so pupils, everyone knew Lutie Wilson.

Seventy years later, Kellogg and Wilson were still able to prod each other's memories — laughing over the good times, gingerly tiptoeing over the delicate.

Like the time Kellogg was caught smoking in the outhouse — and how Wilson personally drove her home to face the music.

"We didn't say a word all the way home," said Wilson, who became principal during her second year at the school.

"Whenever I had trouble with a student, I took them home to their parents and let them explain what had happened," said Wilson. "For the most part, that was worse than a whipping."

Kellogg wholeheartedly agreed.

"I don't remember any really great punishment, but the fear of not knowing what my father would do was worse than anything."

Wilson and her husband, Link, moved to Tucson as newlyweds in 1922 to attend the University of Arizona. In 1924, she began her career substitute-teaching at Laguna School, near Jaynes Station.

By the summer of '26, she was a wife and mother of two young boys. Necessity soon had her scouting around for another teaching job.

"We were living on practically nothing," said Wilson.

Hearing of a job vacancy at Fort Lowell School, Wilson put the family Buick coupe into gear and motored east on Fort Lowell Road.

Destination: The home of Frank Jordan, who was a member of the Fort Lowell district's governing board.

"I really didn't know how to drive then. I didn't have a license," said Wilson.

She drove on one-lane dirt all the way. No traffic lights, no stops, no street signs.

Despite all that, Wilson found the Jordan home, did a little visiting and left with the promise that the job was hers.

Salary: $90 a month every 20 working days.

Annie Daniels, Pima County school superintendent, saw it differently.

"I had to go to her for her approval," said Wilson. "She said, 'This won't do. I have 250 applicants.' I said, 'Won't you make it 251?' "

Somehow, Wilson talked herself into the job —

along with some extra chauffeuring.

"I had to pick three children up at an old dairy farm on Country Club Road, then two more children a couple of blocks farther on. We managed all right."

The "bus service" also put an extra $50 a month in her pocket.

As for child care, a neighbor took care of Wilson's two sons in exchange for a gallon of milk a day, courtesy of the Jordans, who kept cows. "Mrs. Jordan brought it to me at the school," said Wilson.

Altogether, three teachers taught at the school, which went from grades one to seven.

One class held forth at a little adobe-walled school built in 1908. Two more classes, including the one Wilson taught, were held at the old Fort Lowell Union Church, just west of the school.

"It was one big room with folding doors between the classrooms," said Wilson. Come Sundays, desks were moved to accommodate the preaching, then scooted back into place.

To the east of the adobe school was a teacherage, where teachers lived on and off over the years.

No running water, no electricity, no cooling of any kind at the school.

If there was a perk, it went to the principal, who had the privilege of ringing the bell every morning to signal the beginning of class.

Pupils came from as far as Sabino Canyon — and as near as the little farms that sprang up in the area after the soldiers from Fort Lowell moved out in 1891.

"It had a country atmosphere," said Kellogg. "People wore whatever they had. Some wore work clothes made from flour and feed sacks. But everyone wore shoes."

During the noon hour, the children would often explore the chile and corn fields to the north of the school.

"There were wild burros in the mountains," said Wilson. "On cold days, they'd come down and get in the bushes behind the school."

One of those burros managed to kick a student square in the chin.

"There was blood all over him," said Wilson, who tore off part of her blouse to make a bandage for the boy's head, then drove him into town to the doctor's office.

"He was so good. On the way home, I got him an ice cream cone."

In the summer of '28, Wilson had a third child, a girl. "She was born in July. I taught up until May," she said.

That fall, Wilson was back at school, teaching, thanks to yet another neighbor's help.

"Her kids were in school all day, so she came to my house, watched my children and cooked for me, for a dollar a day."

By then, two of the school's teachers had moved on, leaving Wilson with seniority — and the title of principal.

She also taught music — "public school music, they called it" — and helped the students put in a garden.

Hot lunches finally came to the school by accident, after somebody's mother showed up at the school one day and announced that a nearby field of turnips was being cleared.

"You bring the turnips and I'll clean them and we'll give these children turnip soup," Wilson told her.

And so they did.

"We cooked them on the stove at the teacherage," said Wilson, who talked Abe Myerson, of Myerson's White House, into donating tin cups and spoons for the children's soup.

"After that, we started cooking regularly at the teacherage," said Wilson.

"Parents would bring in the food and Evalyn Bentley, the Pima County home economist, gave them help. That was the beginning of our hot-lunch program."

In 1929, Fort Lowell School moved to its present location at 5151 E. Pima St. Many of its pupils carried portions of the old school — from books to desks to erasers — across the desert on foot to the new school.

Gone was the outhouse where Kellogg had so recently gotten into trouble. This new school had electricity, running water and indoor toilets.

The new school would remain with the Fort Lowell District until 1948, when it was annexed by what is now Tucson Unified School District.

As the 1920s folded into the 1930s, Wilson moved on to other teaching jobs in other districts. Among them: a one-room school in Catalina, three years in Amphitheater Public Schools, and a stint of substitute-teaching in Continental.

"I substitute-taught at Continental during the cotton-picking season from September to the end of

February," said Wilson. "The school was full of children from migrant families."

In the latter years of World War II, Wilson started teaching at Marana Unified School District. She would stay 19 years, retiring in 1963.

Meanwhile, Kellogg continued on with her schooling, first at Davidson School, then at Tucson High School.

In 1938 she married and began raising a family. Children, school, church and community became her life. Her husband, Don, died in 1977.

Wilson gave up the chalk and blackboard for good in 1963. Two years later, she and Kellogg rekindled their relationship after discovering both belonged to the same women's club.

"I feel very privileged to have her as a friend," said Kellogg.

INSTITUTIONS
4

VA hospital

The VA hospital, when it was new.

For eight decades now, veterans have come here to be healed.

Here, the walls are always pink, the walkways arched, the grounds a soothing mix of palms and cypress, roses and citrus.

In an age of throwaway boxes that pass for buildings, the Tucson Veterans Affairs Medical Center — as it's called these days — still serves as one of Tucson's most visible grace notes.

What we all think of as the veterans hospital sprawled along South Sixth Avenue north of Ajo Way actually had its origins in 1919, several miles to the north.

Known as Pastime Park, that 11-acre site once supported an amusement park and beer garden near Oracle and Roger roads.

In 1919 the Tucson Red Cross Chapter leased it as a likely spot to house the hundreds of tubercular World War I veterans flooding the city's Tucson's hospital wards.

On March 15, 1920, U.S. Veterans Hospital No. 51 opened with 50 wooden four-man cottages, mess hall and clinic.

Within a year, the place was filled to capacity, with more than a thousand other veterans clamoring to get in.

"The government must take at once some definite steps in regard to the shameful conditions of the kind existing at Tucson," thundered the national commander of the Disabled American Veterans.

Tucsonans, along with Congress, agreed.

In the fall of '27, Congress appropriated $1.4 million to build a permanent hospital on 117 acres of southside desert donated by Tucson department store owner Albert Steinfeld.

Thank Tucson architect Roy Place, who also gave us the old Pima County Courthouse, for the hospital's Mission Revival style, complete with courtyard, cupola and red-tile roof.

"Acme of perfection," trumpeted the Arizona Daily Star on the day the hospital was completed, Aug. 18, 1928.

Less than two months later, Oct. 13, thousands of Tucsonans showed up for guided tours of the 260-bed hospital.

Soothing the milling crowds was an almost continuous outpouring of background music, provided by the bands from Tucson High School and the University of Arizona.

Formal ceremonies that evening were marked with appearances by the usual assortment of dignitaries, whose speeches were periodically interspersed with violin music.

A few days later the patients moved in, shuttled from Pastime Park in ambulances loaned from every mortuary in town.

All went smoothly, save for one patient whose appendix ruptured during the move.

Doctors quickly shifted from moving furniture

to clearing out the operating room for the hospital's first surgical procedure.

The operation was a complete success.

An occasional appendectomy aside, the hospital's main function was to serve tuberculosis patients — with sunshine, bed rest and collapsing of lungs serving as the primary avenues of treatment.

Hardly had the congratulatory din settled from the grand opening when Congress appropriated another $280,000 for a 98-bed addition.

It opened in 1932, marking what would become an almost continuous round of additions and improvements over the coming decades.

At one time, the hospital site also held nurses quarters, as well as quarters set aside for aides, dietitians and medical officers.

Like every hospital in town, Tucson's vets hospital was filled to overflowing during World War II.

Edward Deiboldt remembered the first time he laid eyes on Tucson's VA hospital in the spring of '45.

Medically discharged from the Army Air Forces with rheumatoid arthritis, Deiboldt arrived here in a wheelchair.

Waiting for him at the Southern Pacific depot was an ambulance sent out from the VA hospital.

"We got about two blocks past downtown Tucson and the driver said, 'There's the hospital.' It was a pink building out in the middle of the desert," he said.

Since its specialty was tuberculosis, the Tucson hospital only kept Deiboldt for a month before finding room for him at the VA hospital in Prescott.

But he remembered the six-man wards, the communal showers and bathrooms, and the open-roofed sleeping porches at the old Tucson VA.

"The docs made the rounds every morning and said, 'Howdy, Ed.' I knew all the nurses," he said. "It was a very friendly gathering. We had potlucks and coffee breaks."

After receiving treatment for his arthritis in Prescott, Deiboldt went on to earn a master's degree in industrial education and taught school in Tucson for 30 years.

Streptomycin was first used at the hospital in the summer of '47. Other "wonder drugs" soon followed, returning hundreds of TB patients to normal lives. Still, as late as 1958, 181 of the hospital's 208 general medical beds were reserved for tuberculosis cases.

INSTITUTIONS
5

St. Mary's School of Nursing

Students at St. Mary's Hospital School of Nursing circa 1915.

I left my tonsils there in 1954, my appendix in 1962.

What made both ordeals bearable were the nurses who stood at my bedside, sliding Jell-O into my mouth, cool cloths onto my forehead.

These were the nurses of St. Mary's Hospital, gliding down the halls in their white caps and uniforms or — for the nuns — long flowing habits.

Many of them got their professional start at the hospital's school of nursing — the first in the state.

It began in 1914 with four students. It ended 900 graduates later in 1966, replaced by a four-year college program.

In between were two world wars, a Depression, and changes, both medical and societal, that took nurses from caring for tomahawk wounds — when the hospital first opened — to changing mustard plasters to administering the latest in miracle drugs.

When the school opened, St. Mary's Hospital was already in its 34th year, started in 1880 by the Sisters of St. Joseph of Carondelet. But it was not until year's end, 1914, that a facility would be built to accommodate the student nurses — something Mother Mary Fidelia McMahon, a superintendent of the hospital, had insisted upon.

The course of study took 2½ years — later lengthened to three — and included everything from anatomy to urinalysis. Even through the 1920s, however, applicants did not need to produce a high school diploma.

Much of the training came from hands-on experience in the wards. "We worked 12 hours a day. Fours hours of class, eight hours in the hospital," said Cecilia Grondin, a 1956 graduate.

That was nothing. According to written historical accounts, until the mid-1930s, registered nurses on private duty routinely worked a 20-hour shift.

Before being allowed to go near the patients, all student nurses got in some practice during class.

"Nursing arts," Grondin called it. Everything from turning out a mean hospital corner on the bedsheets to practicing injections on oranges. "We also did some bandaging and put intravenous needles into each other," she recalled.

Everyone lived in the dorm, even the Tucson residents, said Grondin, who nursed at the hospital for years. Curfew was 10 p.m., though you got one late night a week — all the way to midnight.

Uniforms were light blue, starched, with a white bib. White stockings, too, and caps that began with a beanie and ended with a nurse's cap. Three black stripes ran around the front, symbol of the registered nurse.

When the first group of nurses graduated from St. Mary's in 1918, legislation to register them did not exist in the state. Sister Mary Evangelista Weyand, director of the nursing school, prodded the Legislature into establishing a state board of nurse examiners. For her efforts, she received Arizona Registered Nurse certificate No. 1.

The class of '23 was the first to take its state boards. In 1939, another milestone was reached. The school graduated its first two male nurses. Many others would follow.

During the '30s, with nurse's aides and practical nurses still in the future, student nurses formed a large portion of the hospital staff — working their way through school in lieu of tuition.

Before sulfa and penicillin came into use, nurses and nurses-in-training had to be adept in changing hot packs, soaking linens in disinfectant and changing mustard plasters. Student nurses also helped out in the hospital's sanitarium, built in 1900 for tuberculosis patients.

When World War II began, the Cadet Nursing Corps was started, with the government paying fees and other expenses of trainees in nursing schools. Each trainee agreed to continue in nursing — civilian or military — for the duration of the war. St. Mary's enrolled 54 students into the program during its first six months. Refresher courses for inactive graduate nurses were also begun.

After the war, the hospital could no longer afford the practice of earned tuition for its student nurses. Scholarships and loans were established instead. In 1956, student nurses were allowed to live at home. Still, many could not meet the fees.

Declining enrollment and the establishment of a degree program for professional nurses at the University of Arizona cast the future of the hospital's three-year school in doubt.

Requirements and surveys became more rigid and exacting. In 1962, St. Mary's School of Nursing — the first to receive state credentials — was able to gain only temporary accreditation.

Though the school met all requirements for full accreditation two years later, the handwriting was on the wall. On May 24, 1966, the school capped its last class of 17 graduates.

INSTITUTIONS
6

Escuela

We bowl and bank and buy our groceries where once it stood — the stately brick campus known to three generations of students as Escuela. The school.

The rest of us knew it as Tucson Indian Training School, a complex of red-brick buildings and elm-shaded grounds long since replaced by a sprawling shopping center at Ajo Way and 16th Avenue.

When the students weren't in school, they were generally doing chores.

Operated by the Board of National Missions of the United Presbyterian Church, the boarding school's history goes way past its 1908 groundbreaking — all the way to 1887.

That was the year the Presbyterians opened their first Tucson school for Indian children, in a rented adobe building at the corner of Congress Street and Sixth Avenue.

One year later, the school leased from the city approximately 15 acres of raw land just north of where Roskruge Middle School stands today.

A new two-story building soon began to take shape, and in the fall of 1888 the Rev. Howard A. Billman became the school's director.

A firm believer in "civilizing the Indian by teaching him the beauty of the blistered hands," Billman oversaw a curriculum heavy on the farming and manual arts. In 1894, he resigned to become president of the University of Arizona.

The school he left behind continued to prosper, however, as did the town of Tucson, which was soon crowding the school's boundaries.

Through a complicated arrangement, the school bought the property from the city, and then sold it to a housing developer at a handsome profit. The proceeds were used to buy up property and build a new complex south of the city.

In 1907, students began clearing 160 acres of ranch land on the site of what would be the town's Indian boarding school, just east of the Santa Cruz River.

When the children arrived for their first day of school in the fall of 1908, they found a small village complete right down to its own post office, aptly called Escuela. It would operate for the next 35 years.

The village held two cottages — one for the superintendent, the other for the ever-important farmer — identical boys' and girls' dormitories, infirmary, classrooms, kitchens and dining rooms.

Every brick that went into the building was made and baked in a kiln right on the property.

Until a chapel was built on campus in 1922, students and teacher worshipped at Trinity Presbyterian Church, whose own links to Tucson go back to 1876.

As the years rolled by, Escuela began to focus on academics as well as the practical. With more and more government-run day schools taking hold on the reservations, the school began dropping its primary classes while adding high school grades.

In 1939, the school held commencement for its first crop of graduates. No longer did aspiring high schoolers have to trek to Tucson High.

Because the school was not accredited, however, students who wished to go to college or take classes such as algebra and geometry continued to be bused to Tucson High for a fifth year of studies.

Driving that school bus from 1938 to 1940 was Roy Tombaugh, who also served as dorm supervisor for the senior boys' cottage.

He remembered a still-bucolic campus on a road called Indian School, later renamed Ajo Way.

"We had a well, dairy farm, our own milk and chickens, a print shop. Everything was done there," said Tombaugh.

The school even grew a crop of cotton, which everyone helped harvest.

"I remember bringing a busload of kids back from Tucson High, and everyone, including the teachers, was out in the fields picking cotton," said Tombaugh. "We all went to help. That's the first time in my life I ever picked cotton."

John Hamilton, who would later write a thesis on the history of the school — on which much of this column is based — also remembered those days.

"We grew our own corn, and every fall we had a big corn roaster," said Hamilton, who coached football, basketball, and baseball at the school in the late '30s and early '40s.

In 1940, the coach came up with winning season in all three sports. The basketball team, which only suited up junior high players, took the city championship.

Besides organized sports, the campus also boasted its own swimming pool, built in 1926 through the largess of a Mrs. Gamble, as in Proctor and Gamble.

Almost all the staff lived on campus, said Hamilton. "We slept on sun porches summer and winter," he said. Though canvas was rolled down over the screens in the winter months, "Nobody liked getting out of bed on those cold mornings."

In 1940, 18 tribes, ranging from Apache to Zuni, were represented on campus. The emphasis, however, was still on assimilation.

Class plays and glee clubs songs reflected little if any Indian culture. During Thanksgiving, some of the students posed for the high school annual dressed as Pilgrims.

Practical educations still held a mighty sway. Girls learned to sew, knit, weave and crochet. Mending was so demanding that it followed a rigid schedule: sheets, bedspreads and pillowcases on Mondays, towels and nightgowns on Tuesdays, and so forth.

Students also learned to butcher steers, cook meals, bake the bread and do the laundry.

Laundry was still part of the curriculum 10 years later when Marjorie Puella, a Shoshone originally from Nevada, graduated from Escuela.

"We washed all the clothes by hand and hung it on the line. And the boys got to have their clothes washed by the girls," said Puella.

By then, the school, which numbered about 130 pupils, had only junior high and high school-age students. But the day still followed a regimen that began with a dawn wake-up, followed by breakfast, chapel, chores, school, lunch, more classes or chores, sports, dinner and two hours of homework.

"You went to school a total of four full days a week," said Puella. "The rest was chores."

Not that every minute was spent industriously. There were picnics down at the riverbed, or hikes up Cat Mountain, outings into town, and weekend movies at school.

"Every Saturday night they played 'Lloyd's of London,' with Tyrone Power," said Puella.

Dancing, however, was strictly forbidden. "We had square dancing one time and someone kicked up a fit," said Puella.

In lieu of a prom, the school held an annual junior-senior banquet. "The girls picked out their own material and made their own formal dresses," said Puella. "The boys wore coats and ties."

In the spring of '50, Puella put on a cap and gown and marched to "Pomp and Circumstance" with the rest of her class. She would later become a registered nurse at the Department of Veterans Affairs Medical Center.

"For me personally, if I hadn't come to Tucson, I don't think I would have graduated from high school," said Puella, who had "bounced around" both public and government-run schools before enrolling at Escuela. "The teachers at Tucson Indian school really cared about the students."

In 1957, Paul Parker hired on at the school as tutor and program director. Three years later, he would help close Escuela's doors forever.

"Not much farming was going on by the time I got there, but I remember all those beautiful eucalyptus and elm trees," said Parker.

Just north of the school was the brand-new Pueblo High School campus. "Only two of our students went there in the fall of '57," said Parker. "The next year, they all went."

The writing was more than on the wall. All over the West, high schools were being built inside or else right up on the fringes of the Indian reservations. In the spring of '58, the National Board of Missions ordered Escuela closed.

"We spent two years doing inventory and closing it down," said Parker. During those years, high school students still boarded at the school, while junior high pupils continued to take their classes there.

In June of 1960, the school closed for good. "The kids went back to their hometowns and assimilated into public schools," said Parker.

Today, nothing remains of the pastoral "village" that once boasted its own post office, farm fields and dairy cattle.

"I do have an old branding iron from the school," said Parker. "I found it in a trash heap."

INSTITUTIONS
7

Pima County Hospital

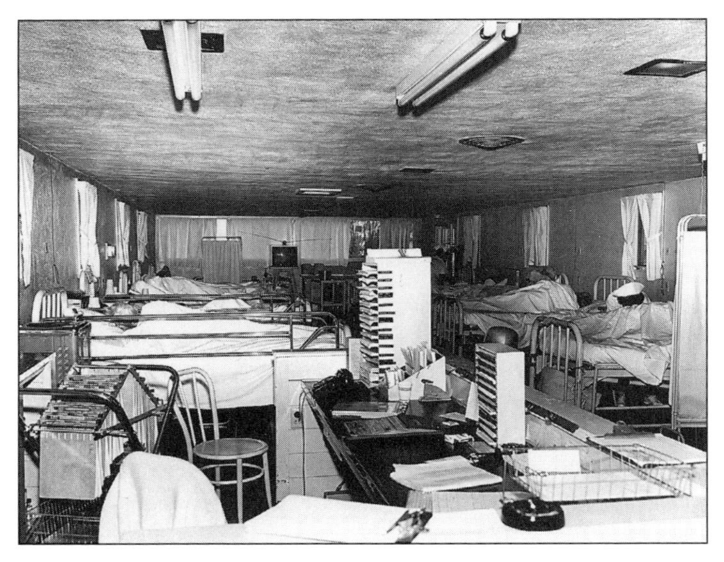

The Pima County Hospital, 1967.

She had been warned. The place was old to the point of ramshackle.

To the newly transplanted Easterner, however, it looked like something straight out of the movies.

"I loved it," said Mary Ellen Tatro, a medical technologist who went to work in 1971 inside that maze of adobe buildings on South Sixth Avenue known at one time as Pima County General Hospital.

"I had never seen anything like it back East," said Tatro. "You could see the adobe and straw through the plaster, and there was a hitching post out front. It was like working out of a history book."

That it was. The hospital got its start, as did so many in this sunny clime, from a cough. In 1916, a private tuberculosis sanitarium was built on the property — then little more than a patch of desert on Tucson's southern skirt.

Two years later, the front part of the building was bought by Pima County. Meanwhile, the rear of the building became a small maternity hospital.

It took the Great Depression — and 75 men working under the Works Progress Administration — to turn it all into a true community hospital, capable of caring for Tucson's indigent, as they were then called.

First came the nurses' quarters, followed by a men's ward, heating plant, surgery and administrative offices. The walls were stabilized adobe, the floors concrete. Total cost: $100,000.

The 147-bed hospital was dedicated in 1937. And from then on, it seemed, the place was in a constant state of flux, as here a ward, there a room, was either added onto or carved from the original buildings.

"Rabbit warren" was the way patient Constance Kress referred in print to the jumble of one-story adobe buildings "spliced on, added to, set down and jammed in with desperate expediency."

"We called it the old dump, but it was a wonderful place. People were so well-treated there," said Gladys Wittwer, a volunteer at the old county hospital who later ran the gift shop at its replacement: Kino Community Hospital.

Steam heat kept the place warm in winter. Nothing, for years, kept it cool in summers.

"They had a cooler in the hallway, but not in the rooms," said Norma Fraser, who worked as a nurse's aide, off and on, from '47 to '75. "The patients, God love 'em, never complained. They'd lie there and perspire like a duck splashing water."

In 1947, the hospital was spruced up with paint, and asphalt tile was laid down over the bare concrete floors. In 1958, a new wing featuring an expanded outpatient clinic was added.

Clarence W. "Red" Brown, who like his father before him served as director of maintenance at the hospital, remembered trying to saw through those adobe walls whenever a remodeling project loomed.

"That adobe was not crumbling," he said. "Quite the contrary. Those walls were 16 inches thick."

Some things just couldn't be modernized. Such as piping in oxygen and other gases that patients might need. "We had cylinders we had to carry around," said Tony Ruiz, then manager of special services at Kino.

Special clinics abounded for a time at the hospital. Among them: a crippled children's clinic, as well as one devoted to conquering arthritis.

Victims of knifings, shootings and barroom brawls often wound up in the hospital's emergency room. So did those who came to grief on the Nogales and Benson highways.

"It was often chaos," said Mary Helen Allison, a registered nurse who worked the 3-11 p.m. shift. "We just had one room with four stretchers, and a holding room with one bed across the hall."

Working the shift with her was one orderly and one intern. Out in the hallways, a mass of humanity — squalling babies, distraught women, surly men — milled about. "It was not unusual to see 50 to 75 people on that shift," said Allison.

She especially remembered the children. Children who had been poisoned, children with burns, children obviously neglected. And, once in a while, children being born.

"We didn't have a maternity ward, but we did have emergency deliveries," said Allison.

"It was a madhouse," said Dr. Warren Eddy, who, like many practicing physicians in town, volunteered regular hours at the hospital.

He remembered one memorable New Year's Eve, when a carload of accident victims showed up in the emergency room. "I was up all night," he said.

As for Allison, she was working the shift that cold night in December of 1959 when a Greyhound bus and a cattle truck collided on the Benson Highway, killing nine people, injuring 32.

Pima County Hospital took in its share of the victims. "We just flew that night. It's hard to describe," said Allison.

The hospital is also where the county's psychiatric patients were temporarily housed. "It was the hospital's only locked ward," said Allison. Most, she adds, only stayed a few weeks, and then were either released or committed to the state hospital.

Talk to those who knew the place well and one theme starts to emerge: a feeling of closeness, of home.

"Everybody was good, friendly and eager to help each other," said former nurse's aide Norma Fraser. "And the grounds were beautiful, with a big old cottonwood tree in back."

The Eastern transplant who loved the hospital's Western ways also loved its Sunday buffets. "They made huge rolls. And they had white tablecloths and candles on the tables," said Mary Ellen Tatro.

If the staff loved the old wreck of a place, so did the patients. One, a trapeze artist named Tiny, who'd been admitted with spinal injuries, later became a volunteer.

Here, too, is where doctors such as Harold Rowe, who worked at the hospital all through the '50s, saw things they never saw anywhere else:

"I was trying to diagnose one woman who'd come up from the interior of southern Mexico. Most of her nose had been eaten up. There were no records. One of the fellows working there was from Mexico. He said, 'Oh, Dr. Rowe. This woman has leprosy.' "

Time did its little marching number. In 1961, the Pima County Medical Society ceased its volunteer staffing of the county hospital. "Our future course will be to increase the full-time staff," Pima County Supervisor Pete Rubi told the press.

In 1970, the 13-year-old Kress School of Practical Nursing graduated its final class. The school, located in back of the hospital, was being closed to provide — what else — more patient room.

During the early '70s, the hospital's pediatric clinic moved to University Medical Center.

The writing was soon all over those stuccoed adobe walls.

In 1972, Pima County voters approved an $11 million bond issue to build a new southside hospital.

On March 5, 1977, patients and staff members made the move to the new Kino Community Hospital.

Not everyone was happy about the move. "The patients were lonely in their private rooms," said Ruiz, remembering the old eight-patient wards.

He, however, felt right at home. "When we moved to Kino, we found they had forgotten to pipe the gas into the emergency room."

For years, the old adobe buildings sat vacant while county powers dickered about what to do with the place. Finally, South Tucson bought it all. A fire burned several of the buildings in 1980. Years later, what was left was razed and carted off. In 2000, a shopping center was built on the site.

INSTITUTIONS
8

TMC

The home of Anna and Alfred Erickson, who financed the beginnings of what is now Tucson Medical Center.

Take dedicated doctors working on the somewhat jagged edge of medical technology. Throw in great wealth, guest appearances from the famous, a whiff of scandal.

Electronic soap? Not this time.

What we have here is the beginnings of the town's largest hospital — Tucson Medical Center — back when it was a cluster of sun-baked dwellings known as Desert Sanatorium.

It began with a cough. "The White Plague," they called it. Tuberculosis. By the late 1800s, hundreds were seeking its cure in the dry Arizona air.

Medical facilities, such as they were, were ill-equipped to handle the numbers.

In 1925, young doctor Bernard Langdon Wyatt came to Tucson from New England to set up a sanitarium and research the sun's effect on various ailments.

The seed money for Wyatt's dream — a $25,000 donation — came from New York adman Alfred Erickson, reputed during the early 1920s to be worth more than $48 million. Erickson's wife, Anna, also happened to be good friends with Wyatt's wife, Minnie.

Though Wyatt initially had two physician partners in the venture, they soon bowed out. The Ericksons wound up financing the entire package.

The Wyatts went looking for land in Tucson. In an old car belonging to Walter Lovejoy of the Arizona Trust Company, they headed out one day toward a section of land near old Fort Lowell.

With no boundary markings in sight, the threesome depended upon the car's odometer to signal when they'd traveled a half-mile across what is now the northwest corner of Grant and Craycroft roads.

One hundred and sixty acres. Out in the desert. Miles from town. Sold to the doctor for $25 an acre.

A well was dug and a water tower erected. Patterned along the lines of Hopi architecture, the original structures included four eight-room courts, as well as a two-story main dwelling that housed patient rooms, offices, laboratories, dining room, kitchen and a veranda-turned-solarium — billed as the world's largest.

Opened on Nov. 15, 1926, the sanitarium was the first in the country to attempt to cure tuberculosis by direct solar radiation.

Using a process called heliotherapy, doctors would write "prescriptions" for sun exposure. Patients, usually wearing sunsuits and smoked glasses, would expose various parts of their bodies to the sun for carefully allotted times.

Special lenses directed concentrated doses of sunlight to the body, while a radiometer, mounted telescope-fashion inside a dome, measured the intensity of the sun's ultraviolet rays.

The wealthy flocked to the place. Though some indeed were suffering from TB or arthritis, most came to rest and relax in the Arizona desert.

Despite the easy Southwestern décor, elegance was de rigueur. "They dressed for dinner," said Reba Grubb, TMC's history consultant. "They had two dining rooms, meals on silver trays to those who stayed in their rooms. One woman, said Grubb, "brought her mink coverlet and satin sheets."

All for $35 a day, including meals and therapy. Most patients, however, were tended by their own private nurses.

Among the famous guests were writers Ring Lardner and Booth Tarkington, actor Gary Cooper, and Gen. John J. Pershing, admitted while wintering at the nearby El Conquistador Hotel.

Though he lapsed into a coma and elaborate plans were made for his funeral, the general resolutely refused to die. He lived another 10 years, during which time he had two considerably more enjoyable stays at the sanitarium.

Throughout the late '20s, construction continued on new roads and buildings on the property, including a home for the Ericksons, who by now had assumed all of the sanitarium's financial obligations.

The year 1929 was not a good one for the sanitarium. In January, patients with pulmonary tuberculosis were no longer accepted after research showed that heliotherapy was of no benefit. Gradually the emphasis shifted from tuberculosis to the study of arthritis.

Then in April of that year, Dr. Wyatt resigned after divorcing his wife — who, remember, was Anna Erickson's good friend — to marry Laura Mae Wright, superintendent of sanitarium nurses.

During the Depression, the Ericksons lost some of their great wealth, though none held in trust to support the sanitarium.

Fewer patients basked under the desert sun during the '30s. Yet the country club atmosphere prevailed, complete with two swimming pools, croquet, even horseback riding at a nearby stable at Speedway and Swan Road.

On Nov. 3, 1936, Alfred Erickson died. Anna Erickson succeeded him on the sanitarium's board of directors.

By decade's end, business at the sanitarium, like elsewhere, was picking up. With the influx of service families at Davis-Monthan Field and a shortage of beds elsewhere, the sanitarium started accommodating maternity patients.

World War II, however, brought more local patients — and took away more staff — than the sanitarium could handle. Catering to the wealthy became an impossible luxury. On May 15, 1943, the Desert Sanatorium closed for good.

A growing Tucson, however, could ill afford to lose a hospital. After Anna Erickson indicated that she would consider giving the sanitarium to the community, a group of citizens immediately launched a fund drive to raise $250,000 for remodeling and operating costs.

By Christmas Eve 1943, most of the money had been raised. The Desert Sanatorium was formally deeded to Tucson Medical Center on March 2, 1944.

Anna Erickson kept the title to her home and a five-acre tract on the property. They, along with another 60 acres of land opposite the hospital to the south, were willed to TMC upon her death, Feb. 7, 1961.

INSTITUTIONS
9

Square and Compass

This wood and tin shed was supposed to be the backyard playhouse for Walker's daughters.

Maybe it was the potholes. Maybe it was the heat.

And maybe the rocky road to Phoenix really did lead to a Tucson institution credited during the past six decades with helping hundreds of thousands of youngsters with special health needs.

One thing's for sure: Hollywood couldn't have come up with a better script than the one that gave us the Square and Compass Crippled Children's Clinic.

Take one trailer dealer used to cutting red tape and getting the job done. Add a wife who understands, and two daughters willing to give up their brand-new playhouse. Now bring the children, ones struck down by polio.

The first came in 1946. As former trailer dealer Ted Walker explained it: "A child with polio might be in the hospital two or three weeks, but then there would be constant therapy afterwards. The theory then was to keep muscles alive; don't let them die."

Trouble was, about the only outpatient therapy treatment then available for Tucson's needier children lay 120 dusty miles away in Phoenix, at a 50-bed hospital for crippled children.

Walker, already fast becoming an inveterate organizer around these parts, was asked by state health officials to get involved with the transporting.

"We had a station wagon rigged up with a bed. Every time they had a bed or two available in Phoenix, my wife, Daisy, would take the children up there for outpatient therapy. But going up there on that hot, bumpy road for a half-hour of therapy was doing the children more harm than good."

By 1947, Walker was looking around for something closer to home. "I tried to find a vacant building. But back then everyone was scared to death of polio. Nobody would rent to us."

And then he looked — ta-dah — right in his own back yard. " I had just completed a recreation hall in our back yard for my two daughters and the rest of the neighborhood children," Walker recalled.

The next step was calling the health authorities for a look-see. Charitably speaking, what they found was a well-built shack, hammered from tin and plywood. But it did boast a shower and sink. Paint it white and it'll do, said the authorities.

The state provided the medical staff and equipment, Walker paid the utilities, and Daisy baked the cookies that daughters Joan and Lois shared with the young outpatients. "We'd get up to 105 children a week," said Walker.

Within a year, plans were well under way for a more permanent center — this time involving much of the community.

The property, at 2916 E. Broadway, would come from the Shrine holding company, which for 25 years would donate it to the clinic on a $1-a-year lease until the Masons bought the land outright.

Meanwhile, an architecture business donated its services and the local trade unions council contributed $55,000 to pay for the labor needed to build the clinic.

"Churches held socials, clubs held dances, fraternal groups held fund drives, roller skaters skated, musicians played, labor unions worked, a radio announcer plugged the drive for 18 hours one day … everybody got into the act," reported the Arizona Daily Star prior to the clinic's opening.

Even the wheels of government turned a little faster for this cause. "The city rushed through the zoning for us," said Walker. "We didn't have the bureaucratic red tape then. Everything was done on a handshake."

Sunday, Dec. 18, 1949. Gov. Dan E. Garvey, Mayor E.T. "Happy" Houston and a thousand onlookers helped dedicate the building. During the ceremonies, clinic president Frank Minarik remarked: "It is my hope that this clinic will be so effective in its treatment of children that in a few years it can be made a bowling alley for them to play in."

Priorities changed. In 1950, Walker was appointed to the state welfare board and began expanding the crippled children's program from its initial orthopedic focus. "We integrated health into the program, and took children from birth to 21."

Still, the clinic did not lose sight of its first patients. "Even after the Salk vaccine came out, doctors still felt that a person had to be free from polio for seven years to be cured," said Walker. "So we had a considerable backlog of cases."

Today, Square and Compass works hand in hand with Children's Clinics for Rehabilitative Services, leasing to the clinics a 52,000-square-foot building at 2600 N.Wyatt Drive, on the Tucson Medical Center campus.

About 4,500 children throughout Southern Arizona with birth defects or other chronic or disabling conditions receive medical care from the clinics, with funding from the state.

(Ted Walker died in 1993.)

Teen Times

"Red" Greth tucked inside his "slingshot" dragster at the D-M strip. Left to right, are Don Maynard, Mason Downey and Jim Ashenbrenner.

Buddy Holly came to town. So did Elvis.
Then there were the drag races, the garage
bands and a drive-in called Johnie's.
Swell time to be a teen in Tucson.

TEEN
TIMES
1

Elvis

It would be a scorcher — 108 degrees before the day was done.

Sunday, June 10, 1956. Ike was in the White House, hamburger was selling for 30 cents a pound, and here in Tucson, a new three-bedroom home could be had for $42 a month.

Tucsonans who weren't out house-hunting that day could pick and choose from among several diversions. Among them: a veal scaloppine dinner for $1.75 at the Tucson Inn, a triple horror show at the Apache Drive-In for a dollar a carload, or over at the rodeo grounds, a young performer billed as "the nation's only atomic-powered singer."

Deputies escort Elvis to his car after a press conference at the rodeo grounds in June 1956.

His name: Elvis Presley. His price: $1.50 in advance, $2 at the gate. And well worth every penny.

"We saved our lunch money," said Vicki Douglas-Otto, one of 2,000 mostly screaming fans who witnessed Presley's Tucson debut on a field usually reserved for bucking bulls or runaway jalopies.

Sweet 14 and a sophomore at Catalina High School, Douglas-Otto got in to see the future King through the time-honored way. "I spent the night with a girlfriend. We told our parents we were going to the movies."

Instead, the two hopped a westbound bus heading for downtown. "Then we took the Old Pueblo bus to the southside," said Douglas-Otto. "It was absolutely packed with teenagers."

After a quick Coke at the Lucky Wishbone, the two crossed South Sixth Avenue and funneled into the surging crowd, all eager to see for themselves this polite young man with the dangerous ways.

"Elvis represented everything that was rebellious," said Douglas-Otto. "Our parents called him bad and sexy, and of course that just made us like him all the more."

They made their way to their seats along the west-side bleachers of the rodeo arena. Not 20 feet away was the makeshift wooden stage.

"It seemed like forever for the show to start," said Douglas-Otto, who first had to endure — according to the next morning's review in the Arizona Daily Star — "a halfhearted comedian, a less-than-adequate girl vocalist, and a sometimes Irish tenor."

But at last, there he was, this thin, young Southerner with the slick black hair, bashfully mumbling into the microphone. "I don't know what I was expecting," Douglas-Otto admited. "He said something very polite, very humble."

And then the screaming began. "It was absolute pandemonium," said Douglas-Otto, whose vocal cords also contributed to the cause.

"Well, you just got caught up in the moment. He was moving quite a bit. That, of course, was what we wanted. Girls were fainting. It was quite hot. I was dizzy."

As for what lyrics were coming out of young Presley's mouth, Douglas-Otto was a little vague.

"I know he sang 'Heartbreak Hotel.' He didn't have to name any of the songs. As soon as we heard the first couple of chords we started screaming. The speakers were squawking. But he could have been lip-synching and it wouldn't have mattered."

Down near the stage, Arizona Daily Star photographer Jack Sheaffer was struggling to capture a writhing Presley on film.

"He wouldn't stand still," said Sheaffer. "All those bumps and grinds and twists. And he was doing the jitterbug with the microphone. He was wearing a cheap tuxedo. There was one white-hot light on him, and he perspired through the whole show.

"Oh, he was definitely hard to shoot. I only shot him when he was straight up, when I could see his face."

Earlier that afternoon, Sheaffer had an easier time of it during a press conference held in a small room under the rodeo arena bleachers.

"He was just a young, handsome kid with big eyes that could stare right through you. He was talking to me about my camera. He had come here on a plane, and the girls and his band came in a bus."

Girls?

"They were hired screamers," said Sheaffer. "A brunette and a blonde. I first noticed the blonde at the press conference."

And again at the beginning of the concert.

"At first when Elvis started singing, it was all as quiet as a church mouse," said Sheaffer. "Then up pops this blonde in the stands, yelling and screaming. People were watching her more than Elvis. Then all the little girls started screaming, too."

Positioned so close to the stage, Sheaffer, unlike the fans up in the stands, could actually hear Presley's singing. "Everybody said he would be a flash in the pan, but I thought he had a good voice."

Twenty feet away, Douglas-Otto was caught up in her own sort of reverie. "The concert itself was a very personal experience," she said. "Even with all the screaming and the frenzy, it was if he were singing to each of us alone."

After the concert, said Douglas-Otto, "we stood around talking for a while, hoping to catch a glimpse of him." Security, however, had whisked the teen idol away.

Douglas-Otto and friend rode the northbound bus to downtown, had a chili dog at Art's, then caught the eastbound bus for home. "We talked half the night and wrote about Elvis in our diaries."

Also scribbling into the night was Star reviewer Shirley Phillips, who would describe Presley as "a tall, good-looking boy with a heavy Southern accent," but one who could "hardly be classed as a singer — unless one is familiar with the trade term 'exotic singer,' which includes writhing, twitching, squirming and exercising the entire body along with the vocal cords."

Not that such scathing criticism would deter Douglas-Otto and her friends. "When 'Love Me Tender' came out, all the reviews panned it," she said. "But we all went to see it. And we all cried when Elvis died."

In 1960, Douglas-Otto graduated from high school. She went to college, did some "girl Friday work," married, had a couple of kids, even appeared as an extra in a few movies filming around town.

"I got older; my life changed," she said. "I continued to buy Elvis' records, but I didn't keep up the scrapbook I'd started."

The concert in '56 was the only time she saw Presley live and in person. Not so for Sheaffer, who tried to shoot Presley's Tucson concerts in 1972 and 1976.

"They didn't allow cameras," said Sheaffer, who nonetheless captured a considerably heavier Presley during his last Tucson appearance.

"He was fat and perspiring, and you could hear him gasp for air. But people still loved him. He must have thrown out 50 of those silk scarves into the audience."

When Presley died on Aug. 16, 1977, the moment for Douglas-Otto — as for millions of fans — caught a fast train to the past.

"I had been in the grocery store. I got in the car with my groceries, put my 4-year-old daughter in her car seat, started the car, and the radio came on with the news almost immediately. I cried. He was a part of my growing up — for all of us. It was like we'd lost a friend."

All over the city, the mourners came forward. Radio stations began playing nonstop Elvis. Fans lamented their loss over the airwaves. And, in a hint of what was to come, some started heading toward the record stores.

The next day's Tucson Citizen noted: "Employees of several Tucson record stores, whose sales of Presley albums sagged in recent years, reported that customers were buying them in droves yesterday afternoon and evening."

Not every fan, however, would become ensnared in the ensuing commercialism. "No, I never went to Graceland," said Douglas-Otto. "It's all become so much hype. It's kind of unreal.

"But going to that concert in 1956 — that was real."

TEEN
TIMES
2

Johnie's

You never had to ask.

After the show, the game, the dance — you knew where they'd all be. Jimmy and Joe and Mary Lou. The whole gang. At Johnie's.

"Oh won't you stay-ay just a little bit longer..."

If you turned teen in this town during the '50s or '60s you were there, too. Sitting in your Chevy or Ford, radio turned to KTKT, collar up, hair greased or sprayed into obedience, sipping your Coke, trying to make it last, hoping — ooh, baby, baby — hoping you looked as cool as you felt.

Hungry? Thirsty? Got a dollar? That'll get you two "Famous Fat Boy" hamburgers. With change back. Or five bags of French fries. Or 10 cokes.

Entertainment? Sure. All free. "Look there's Eddie and Joey in Eddie's '57 Chevy. Cruising. Shhh. Don't look. They're pulling in next to us.

"Hey, Ricky, who's the new carhop? Oh yeah, baby. Shake that thing."

"Uh-oh. There's Donna with that new guy in school. And here comes Jimmy in his car, with a bunch of guys. I didn't know they broke up. Look, Donna's ducking down in her seat. Do you think Jimmy saw her?"

"Don't be cruel to a heart that's true..."

High drama among the tailfins. That was Johnie's all right.

In the beginning there were two, then four, then none. The last one, where all the southsiders used to cruise, sat at East 22nd Street and South Alvernon Way. And then it was gone.

No sign of the Fat Boy, making goo-goo eyes at his double patty. No orange plastic seats. No Ventures playing on the jukebox. No carhops in candy-striped blouses and short red skirts, balancing a beehive hairdo and a tray full of Cokes.

Carl Wright bought the first two Johnie's at 2545 E. Speedway and at 945 N. Stone Ave. back in '57.

"Oh, little darlin', hup hup hup-doowad-duh..."

"The original owner was Frank Johnson," said Carl's son, Will Wright. "That's where they got the 'Johnie's' from."

Open 24 hours a day, both restaurants had indoor dining and curb service. "That was the California touch," said Wright. "Everyone had drive-ins."

In 1959, the California touch oozed into a brand-new Johnie's on 22nd Street, near Alvernon. Orange and blue interiors. Terrazzo floors. Lots of glass.

Three years later a fourth Johnie's popped up at East Speedway and North Craycroft Road. Even more glass and color inside. Outside, illuminated menus and speakers sidled up next to the cars. Customers learned to tell a machine to hold the onions. The carhops came out only after the deep-fat fryer had had its way.

"Duke, Duke, Duke, Duke of Earl..."

Ever any trouble in teen paradise? Sure, said Wright, who appeared to be a man who'd seen enough ducktails and heard enough be-bop to last him a lifetime.

" There were laws for drive-ins, to keep the neighbors happy," said Wright. "We had rules about lights, about noise, and squealing tires. You weren't supposed to get out of your car unless you were going to the bathroom." Curb service stopped at 2 a.m., 3 on the weekends. "We'd still be full at 2," said Wright.

Off-duty cops or lot attendants kept order on the curb. "If certain kids got too bad, we'd just ban them," said Wright. "Remember, the four Johnie's in this town were just about it back then. If you kept a kid away you were really cutting off his social life."

"Come on baby, light my fire..."

Times changed. A rougher element moved in. Johnie's on Stone closed in 1957; the one at Speedway and Tucson Boulevard followed not too long after. The two new Johnie's stayed, but curb service stopped. Kindly sip your malted inside.

It was never quite the same. Then the golden arches hit town. "They put one in a block away," said Wright. "That really killed us."

December 1973. Arab oil embargo. Lines at the pump. Skyrocketing gas prices. Johnie's sold out to Jord-Inns of America. "They operated for 18 months," said Wright.

"I remember when rock was young, me and Susie had so much fun..."

The economy got no better. Jord-Inns gave 'em back. Up, up, up went the old signs. But the Fat Boy was down for the count. Sold for scrap. "We adopted Jord-Inns menu," Wright explained.

The East Speedway eatery became a full buffet. Great business in the winter, lousy in summer, said Wright. He gutted it, turned it into a boat shop.

The last Johnie's stayed on. But Wright couldn't buy the land underneath.

Eventually the building was razed, the orange booths long gone at the last old hangout.

"Louie, Lou-ay, oh yeah, we gotta go now..."

TEEN TIMES 3

The Ramblers

"The Ramblers" (above), who play regularly at the Latin-American Club at 146 So. Main, will donate their music on Friday, Dec. 18, when the Latin-American holds its 28th annual Christmas benefit dance. "The Ramblers" will furnish dance music from 9 pm to 1 am and the admission fee is 75¢ per person. The total collected from admissions for this non-profit enterprise will be donated to the Comstock Childrens' Hospital for crippled children. Join the fun this Friday at the Latino where "The Ramblers" will entertain you with the music you like, for they play everything including Mexican and Latin-American styles, Corridos, Rock 'n Roll and just about anything you want to dance to . . . and, you have the satisfaction of knowing you are helping a worthy cause. Some of the recipients in the past 27 benefits have been students who received scholarships for college, House of Neighborly service, Tucson Boys Club, Cerebral Palsy and Arizona Children's Home, just to mention a few.

Club officers for 1965 are; Harry Cooper, pres.; Santos Andrade, V.P.; Alvaro Alvarez, Sec.; M. V. Morales, Treas. and the Board of Trustees are A. Sandoval, Emilio Carrillo and Frank Urias. The new business manager for the club is Edward Montiel.

The Ramblers: Bottom, from left, Frank Vargas, Dickie Marmion. Top: David Foust, Raul Castro, Frank Catalano, Gilbert Guerra.

They had the band. Now all they needed was a name. "We were trying to think of cars," said Frank Catalano. "We came up with the Ramblers."

Of course. After all, the Cadillacs and the Edsels were taken.

Then again, a band by any other name would have worked just as well for any of us who bopped, swayed or tried a little cha-cha-cha during the Ramblers' reign back in the '60s.

"We were the band," said Catalano. "Nobody was as popular as the Ramblers."

No argument there from lead guitarist Gilbert "Guero" Guerra: "We were so popular because we could play anything — rancheras, cumbias, rhythm and blues."

It began in 1960 when a group of guys — mostly Hispanic, mostly graduates of Tucson High — drifted together and started playing music.

"We would go to Bob's ballroom and listen to the other bands play," said Catalano, who played drums and sang.

Besides Bob's — a dance hall located about where Furr's cafeteria would later stand on St. Mary's Road — the Ramblers also played El Casino Ballroom, Sunset Rollerama and even the tony Skyroom one New Year's Eve, remembered Guerra.

Then there were those gigs from the backs of pickup trucks. "We'd do grand openings," said Catalano.

Out-of-town music was also in the mix — everywhere from Morenci to Douglas to Ajo.

"When we left Ajo, we needed gas to get home," said Guerra. "We stopped at this gas station on the way out of town at 1 in the morning. We had to wake the woman who was sleeping upstairs. She told us, 'I'm not coming down there for 50 cents worth of gas.' "

The Ramblers made it worth her while, filling up their cars for two bucks a pop.

Though the going rate for a four-hour gig in Tucson was $18 apiece, the Ramblers also played many a benefit.

"We were willing to play free for everyone," said Guerra. "Finally someone asked me, 'Do you always play for free?' I said, 'No, last week we played for money, but the check bounced.' "

On his wedding day, Catalano played drums with the band at his own reception after the drummer hired to sub for him showed up hours late. "I played the drums and everybody danced with the bride," he said.

At some gigs, of course, fights would break out, particularly at Bob's. "The owner would wave to us to keep on going," said Catalano. "We'd play polkas till the cops came."

Guerra remembered it a little differently. "We'd hold up our guitars to shield us from the beer bottles."

Either way, this was a band that hung around for an entire decade — an eternity in garage-band years.

Sure, band members came and went. Celia Marie Felix sang with the band its first three years. Guitarist Eddie Cocio, and pianist Jimmie Vindiola, who went on to lead the popular Los Caballeros, played a year or so.

Others who stuck around longer included Raul Castro on sax, David Foust on sax, Dickie Marmion on bass guitar and Frank Vargas on guitar.

In '65, Catalano left the Ramblers, joining Los Caballeros and later, other bands.

"The guys started going separate ways," said Guerra, who kept the Ramblers going until 1970. Then he, too, started playing with other bands.

While Catalano, retired from Raytheon Missile Systems, long ago put away his drums, Guerra, who retired from the city of Tucson, kept on playing up until 2001.

Even so, he and Catalano played together after that. Said Guerra: "I just can't quit the music."

TEEN
TIMES
4

Hot Rods

"I had a '39 Ford coupe. One night, I was running a '40 Ford, two-door. And I was beating him pretty bad. When I hit the cattle guard at the bottom, the hood came unhitched and wrapped itself around my windshield. I was going 100 mph. My lights went out. Everything went black." — Former drag racer Fred Blackmore, who walked away unscathed.

Racing at Tucson Raceway was downright respectable.

Born to be wild? Maybe. Maybe not. One thing's for sure, though. These boys loved speed.

Pedal to the metal. Nothing but blacktop and bugs ahead, bouncing off the headlights. Roll across that first cattle guard. Thrrump. Hit it. Faster, faster. You're neck and neck. Here comes the second cattle guard. Thrrump. Ease off. Steady, steady. Ha, ha. Headlights behind you. Hot damn! You won.

Even better, you lived.

"I get chills at times thinking how it could have been," said Gary "Red" Greth, another former drag racer and member of The Lords car club. "We had no helmets, no roll bars, but cars weren't as fast then."

Fast enough, however, to send Pima County Sheriff Waldon Burr and his deputies fanning out across the desert back in the mid-'50s, in hot pursuit of the young lawbreakers.

"We raced between the cattle guards on the cutoff to Mount Lemmon on Friday nights, real late," said Greth. "There was nothing out there then."

Nothing, that is, but the chance to prove who had the fastest flathead Ford or Chevy. And who got swaggering rights on Monday morning out in the high school parking lot. Wearing your colors on a sateen jacket. The Lords, the Outcasts, the High Rollers, the Lowriders.

Hot rod clubs. Back in the '50s there were more than a dozen in this town. Most formed early in the decade, about the same time that drag racing started taking off around the country.

Not all racing was done illegally on desert back roads. In the early '50s, the old Southern Arizona Timing Association held time trials and drag races on a regular basis on one of the old landing strips out at Marana Army Airfield.

One dollar for racers, free to the public. "You wore a white T-shirt and Levi's, maybe some goggles. And you run what you brung," said Blackmore, an Outcast who claims he "brung" to the Marana races the only car ever banned. "Roger McCluskey (future Indy 500 competitor) was on the tech committee. He banned it. It was atrocious."

Meanwhile, the midnight rubber continued to burn at Mount Lemmon and elsewhere. In 1955, 50 hot rodders were discovered by sheriff's deputies on what was then known as the Papago Reservation. Five were injured in a rollover, trying to flee.

Something's got to be done, said the cops, the

media, the general public. Meetings were held to discuss the feasibility of starting a legal drag strip. In attendance were government officials, law enforcement, business leaders, members of the Tucson Junior Chamber of Commerce and hundreds of hot rod enthusiasts.

Finally, after months of debate and considerable pulling of strings, an unused Davis-Monthan Air Force Base runway became Tucson's official drag strip in the spring of '56.

Sponsored by the Tucson Jaycees and sanctioned by the National Hot Rod Association, the monthly drag races were conducted by members of the Tucson Timing Association, made up of members of the various hot rod clubs.

"It was really a community effort," said Greth, a former Tucson Timing Association president. "It was all volunteer."

"Barry Goldwater got the permission for us to use it. I think we were the only ones in the country to race on a SAC (Strategic Air Command) base," said Jack Burnett, former manager of what would be known as the D-M Drag Strip.

"We had a trailer, with the timing clocks and the gear," said Burnett. "We rented a PA (public address) system. After we made a little money, we went out and bought a PA system and a better set of clocks."

Safety, at last, became a factor. An ambulance and driver were hired to stand by. All cars were inspected. Drivers in the faster cars had to wear helmets and flame-retardant suits.

Classifications ranged from top fuelers gulping down nitro methane to high school kids in regular street cars. "Some raced their parents' cars and their parents never knew it," said Greth.

Sunday, April 29, 1956. Opening day for the D-M Strip. More than 3,000 spectators plunked down their 50 cents, settled down on their car hoods and cheered on 169 racers in 23 categories competing down the quarter-mile.

Fastest time of the day went to Greth, who clocked in at 130 mph in a "slingshot" dragster that he and fellow Lords Don Maynard and Lyle Fisher owned.

To the victors went trophies and $25 Savings Bonds. A year later, there was at least one kiss, awarded in '57 by Susie Born, a.k.a. "Miss Tucson Drag Strip."

"That was my sister," said Greth's wife, Marge. "We needed someone to kiss the trophy winner. As far as I know, she was the only queen of the drag strip."

D-M is where Roger McCluskey raced before moving on, as well as a host of racers from Phoenix and California making the circuit. "We'd pay the big names to race, and use their names in the advertising before the race," said Burnett.

The Greth-Fisher-Maynard team was also making a name for itself, both on the circuit and in Tucson. In October 1957, Greth would steer the team's class A modified roadster down the D-M strip to a new world's record of 169.11 mph.

Times were good for hot rodders in Tucson through the rest of the '50s and into the early '60s. Car dealers unveiled the next year's models out at the strip. Races for various charities were also held from time to time.

Drag racing had become downright respectable. The D-M strip also squelched most of this town's illegal drags, since hot rodders caught racing on the street were immediately banned from the strip.

"The Tucson Timing Association probably saved us a lot of lives out at D-M, getting us off the streets," said Greth.

The record at the D-M strip: no fatalities, one bad burn, said Burnett, who managed the strip through most of its existence.

And then in April 1963, Davis-Monthan announced that the drag strip was needed for military purposes, immediately. Once again, hot rodders were left searching for a drag strip to call their own.

A year later, they got it at Tucson Dragway, which Lyle Fisher helped start and then managed.

In 1985, that too shut down, after the state called in its lease on the land, on Tucson's far southeast side.

By then, drag racing had evolved into a multimillion-dollar sport. "Today, it's all computerized engines," said Greth. "You don't build an engine now, you buy everything."

A piece of the old strip that he and Blackmore and countless other speed demons once roared across still exists, however, not far from the Golf Links-Swan Road intersection.

"I can see it when I'm driving down Golf Links," said Greth. "It still gives me a thrill."

TEEN
TIMES
5

Lewallen Brothers

A mid-1960s record cover, shot near Soldier Trail: from left, Bobby Lewallen, Tim Lewallen, Dennis Gamble, Cal Lewallen and Keith Lewallen.

They may have known their way around a pipe wrench. But it's their way with a guitar chord that Tucsonans of a certain age remember.

Heck, you may have danced to their tunes at the old Sunset Rollerama or Hi-Ho Club.

Their name was Lewallen. As in the Lewallen Brothers — one of the hottest bands rockin' in the Old Pueblo back in the '60s.

Three of their songs got considerable airplay on Tucson radio. They also won a TV gig on the Dick Clark show, "Happening '68," featuring such luminaries as James Brown and Glen Campbell.

"It was really amazing to be on a show like that," said Cal Lewallen, oldest of the clan.

If that name rings a bell in a different way, perhaps someone from Cal's Plumbing has unstopped your drains a time or two.

Unstopping drains and strummin' guitars — both are a family tradition going back to Cal's father, Cal Sr.

In 1936, Cal Sr. came to town with a wife and a promised gig with a band whose guitar player had taken sick.

"The guy stayed sick, Dad kept the job," said Cal Jr. And then one fateful day, the business agent from the local plumbers union talked Cal Sr. into an apprenticeship.

By 1948, he had his own company, Cal's Plumbing. Even so, the man kept his guitar pick in the music game. He also encouraged his sons to play, buying them guitars and a few lessons.

First to take their dad up on the offer were Keith and Tim. Before long, Cal Jr. was joining in on bass guitar.

Meanwhile, sister Gayle was singing with a band, the Marsades.

"Their guitar player got drafted, so Tim and I started playing with them," said Keith. So, before long, did Cal Jr.

Cal Jr., Keith and Tim started a band in 1963 called the Cokats, with Dennis Gamble joining them on drums.

Besides the usual teen hangouts, they also hit the bar scene. "I was playing in bars when I was 15," said Keith.

In 1963, they recorded their first record, "Tough He Was," written by Cal Jr.

They sent the song to record producer Bob Keane. A promoter with Keane told the band to change their name to the Lewallen Brothers. By that time, brother Bobby had joined them on keyboard and vocals.

Two more records followed: "It Must Be Love," and "Only a Dream," both recorded in 1967.

In 1968, the Lewallen Brothers won a battle of

the bands contest at Old Tucson. First prize: an audition on "Happening '68." They made it through two shows, losing on their third appearance.

So they hit the road — everywhere from Oregon to Wisconsin. Drummer Dennis Gamble dropped out, replaced by Mike Ramsey.

Less than a year later, they were back in Tucson, where they became the house band for the Cedars and backed up everyone from the Turtles to Gary Lewis and the Playboys.

"We also played with Chuck Berry," said Cal Jr. "He always wanted the local band to play with him."

Years before, Cal Jr. had taken up the pipe wrench — plumbing by day, strumming by night. Keith and Tim followed that route around 1970.

In 1981, Bobby died of cancer. The band quit for a decade.

But by the early '90s, they were back on stage at various spots around town. Somewhere along the way, Tim dropped out to become a full-time plumber.

Their latest gig: a high school reunion in the spring of '05.

Asked if he still gets recognized when he makes house calls, Keith said, "All the time. I go there as a plumber and we wind up talking about the Lewallen Brothers."

TEEN
TIMES
6

Junior Assembly

Some still speak of it with a shudder.

For two generations, pubescent boys and girls from Tucson's proper families spent their Saturday afternoons learning the waltz, the rhumba and their how-do-you-do's in a little exercise known as Junior Assembly.

"You dressed like you were going to Sunday school," said Jim Turner, who attended Junior Assembly from grades six through nine.

Jim Turner, left, takes the lessons he learned at Junior Assembly to this punch bowl gathering in 1964.

Held for years at the Tucson Woman's Club downtown, the dance and deportment lessons were by invitation only.

"You had to have the right connections," said Turner, who would later work at the University of Arizona.

The grand doyenne of all this was Isabel Drachman, who for 28 years ruled Junior Assembly with a stern look, an authoritative voice and a pair of killer stilettos.

"She would stalk across the dance floor in those high heels," said Lynn Harris, another Junior Assembly alum from the early '60s.

Naturally, there was an "enforcer."

"Mrs. Drachman hired the head usher from the Fox Theatre to holler at us and get us in line," said Turner. "He was tall and skinny and had a Duane Eddy hairstyle."

All the boys and girls, said Turner, "were coupled up to enter the wood-floored ballroom via a serpentine march."

At the north end of the room was a piano, held down, said Turner, by a "blank-faced old man pounding out 'On Wisconsin,' 'Buckle Down Winsocki' and other inspirational marching songs."

Ethel Fritschy, who for years ran a dance studio here, taught the children all the right moves, including the waltz, fox trot and cha-cha-cha.

Boys did the asking, said Turner, except during holiday parties, which featured "Ladies' Choice."

In between dance lessons, Drachman expounded on proper etiquette.

"At least three times every Saturday she would interrupt her lectures to remind the girls to keep their knees together," said Harris.

Meanwhile, boys would be boys.

Turner remembered how he and a few other culprits stuck toy caps under their heels, which exploded when they stepped on the dance floor's metal heater gratings.

A generation earlier, it was chickens, stolen from the UA farm and let loose in the ballroom.

"Class was called off for fear someone would slip on you-know-what," said Ruth Corbett Cross, whose Junior Assembly training harks back to its beginning years in the late '30s.

Cross, mother to Lynn Harris, remembered classes held in a variety of venues, taught by a predecessor to Drachman.

The winning formula was already in place: Sunday-best clothes, an old man pounding the piano, and sweaty palms.

"We learned the two-step, the rhumba and the tango," said Cross. "But no dipping."

Deportment lessons came in "five-minute blasts," said Cross, followed by punch and cookies, served by the boys.

Even so, Cross finagled her way free after four years. "I finally convinced my father I wouldn't be good on the athletic field if I did this every Saturday afternoon."

Yet she still insisted her daughter attend. "I felt it did me good," said Cross.

In 1973, Drachman died of cancer. Junior Assembly, with others at the helm, carried on until the mid-'80s.

Similar purveyors of propriety, such as Desert Juniors, also stepped in.

But for many a Tucsonan, it will always be Junior Assembly that taught them the intricacies of the receiving line, the rhumba — and how to sit like a lady.

TEEN
TIMES
7

Buddy Holly

Never say never.

Once upon a time, I wrote that, far as I knew, Buddy Holly never played this burg.

Wrong, wrong, wrong. That was the word from the readers who took the time to inform me differently. And boy, am I glad they did.

Otherwise, I might never have learned about what may very well have been the greatest rock 'n' roll show to ever play this town.

Buddy Holly rocked the Catalina High School gym.

Fats Domino, Chuck Berry, Frankie Lymon, Lavern Baker, Paul Anka, Clyde McPhatter, the Drifters, Johnnie and Joe, the Bobbettes. Oh, yes. And a group the Arizona Daily Star referred to only as "the teen age crickets," featuring Buddy Holly as lead singer.

All on one stage. Playing one night and one night only at the gym of Catalina High School.

Oct. 10, 1957. Be there or be square.

"It was the rock 'n' roll concert to end all rock 'n' roll concerts," remembered Bill Risner.

Later on, Risner, would practice law. No doubt in a three-piece suit. But back in '57, he was just your average high school rock 'n' roller — one who knew history before it even rounded the corner.

"I knew this was a once-in-a-lifetime thing," said Risner. "I even made my parents go. They went to a church that didn't allow dancing, but they liked the show."

So did 3,000 other "hepsters," according to the next day's review by the Arizona Daily Star.

Headliner of the 2½-hour "Show of Stars" was Fats Domino, who wowed 'em with a raspberry-colored suit and a string of hits that included "Blueberry Hill" and "I'm Walkin'."

Chuck Berry strutted through "School Days" and "Maybelline." Sixteen-year-old Paul Anka pleaded, "Oh, please stay with me 'Diana.' " Lavern Baker sang of "Jim Dandy," while the Bobbettes preferred to stick with "Mr. Lee."

Johnnie and Joe were there, too, singing "Over the Mountain; Across the Sea," which may be the best slow-dancing-in-the-cafeteria-after-the-football-game song of all time.

But it took a skinny man in a pair of horn rims to blow Risner away on that warm October night so many years ago. "He looked like a nerd. He was so improbable-looking," said Risner. "But Buddy Holly stole the show. I had heard some of his songs, but I really didn't know who he was. The suddenly, Boom! Everyone was saying, 'Who is that guy?' He won my allegiance."

Many years and many rock 'n' roll shows later, Risner would still say this one's the best. " I don't know what the acoustics were in that gym, but they rocked that night."

Retired educator Bill Kemmeries had his own concerns about the gym that night. As Catalina's basketball coach, his main worry was the floor. "We covered it with canvas," he said.

Why a rock show in a high school gym? "We had no community center," said Kemmeries. "The Catalina gym was built big. They had a rental agreement to hold acts there. The acoustics were great. Marian

Anderson even sang there."

But not on this night.

Tickets to the "Show of Stars" were sold at the door — or at Grabe Electric downtown. (How many of you old-timers remember that store?)

"I'm not sure of the price of the tickets, but they were a deal when you think of who was on that stage," said Kemmeries.

The high school lettermen did the ushering, good for one free ticket to the show. Refreshments were sold outside. No posters, no rock T-shirt souvenirs.

The stage was set up at the west end of the gym, said Kemmeries. Locker rooms became dressing rooms for the stars. "I remember finding the Bobbettes in the boys' locker room. Smoking."

Although most of the fans were teenagers, the Star's review noted approvingly that, "The show moved smoothly with nobody dancing."

Afterward, Kemmeries found his gym floor unscathed by its fleeting encounter with rock 'n' roll.

Not everyone, however, was pleased about rock 'n' roll history made that night in the basketball gym of Catalina High School. Especially Principal Rollin T. Gridley.

"During the cleanup," said Kemmeries, "the janitors uncovered a few empty whiskey bottles around the stands."

The principal was there when it happened. "He was mad," said Kemmeries. "He said, 'That's the last time we *ever* have that wild crazy music here.' "

Holidays

This crowd came to Stone and Congress on the Friday after Thanksgiving in 1955 to welcome Santa Claus.

We crowned a king and queen on Halloween, sang Christmas carols on horseback, and oohed and ahhed at the fireworks at Arizona Stadium. You bet we knew how to celebrate the holidays.

HOLIDAYS
1

Fireworks at Arizona Stadium

Arizona Stadium, courtesy of the Tucson Jaycees.

Eyes closed, fingers in the ears, mouth turned resolutely downward.

Now that was the way to greet a fireworks display. Or so I thought the first time one ever burst over my pigtailed head. It happened — where else — inside the University of Arizona football stadium.

In time, the fingers came out of the ears, mine eyes lifted skyward to the bombshells, and my mouth, like everyone else's in Arizona Stadium, became a slack-jawed vessel for one "ohh-ahh" after another.

For 49 Julys, Tucsonans craned their necks at those bombs bursting in air, just above the old scoreboard that read "Arizona" on one side, "Visitors" on the other.

The pyrotechnics, which came courtesy of the Tucson Jaycees, stopped in 1979 — two years after the fire chief proposed a ban on fireworks, and three years after a cannon explosion injured five spectators at a UA football game.

For a while the Jaycees carried on elsewhere, first at the Pima County Fairgrounds, later at Tucson Dragway. Then they officially bowed out.

The rockets' red glare, however, continued to show up over new terrain. At ballgames and resorts, and, finally, on top of a mountain named "A."

Arizona Stadium now sits dark and empty on the Fourth of July. Free, it would appear, of fire danger and liability suits. But not, necessarily, of memories:

Hot, that's the way the day usually broke. Clear too. Until midafternoon, when the thunderheads would start piling in from Nogales.

We'd hear the distant rumbles. "No, Mom, that wasn't thunder. Must have been a plane."

Please, please. Don't let it rain tonight. Not on the Fourth of July.

Usually, our pleas were answered. We'd have an early supper, then pile into the old station wagon — adults, kids, neighbors. Anybody who liked things that go boom in the night.

The sun would just be sliding behind the Tucson Mountains by the time we spread out our quilts over the wooden bleachers down at the south end of the stadium.

Might as well make ourselves comfortable. Matter of fact, one year my youngest brother was so at ease that he slept through the entire show.

That wasn't hard to do at the beginning of the program, when the only salvos being fired came from the mouths of the officeholders. "We'd invite 15 or so politicians to speak," recalled Greg Jamieson, past Jaycee president. Blessedly, only two or three of the bunch ever accepted.

Speeches were to be kept short and patriotic. There was no attention to what was being said anyway. Entire bleachers, in fact, seemed to undulate with the squirmings of the bored and restless.

Finally, the dark sky told us it was showtime. Red, blue and white — the great gobs of phosphorescence would start bursting above our heads. One, two, five at a time.

"Oooh-ahhh. Oooh-ahhh." And, sooner or later, "Uh-oh."

Lordy, how I hated the duds. The ones that flashed over our heads like busted headlights. No sparkle, no color. Just a loud "bang."

Come to find out, the loud ones weren't duds at all. "The duds didn't have any sound to them," said Jamieson. "But the ones with the big boom were deliberate."

Salutes, Jamieson called them. "We'd send off a salute at the stadium beginning at noon and continue one every hour until the show started."

Work at the show actually began in January — mainly on the ground displays.

Elaborate numbers, they'd flare out momentary pictures of everything from stagecoaches to moon landings to Republican elephants and Democratic donkeys — wagging appropriately sparkling appendages at exhortations such as: "Get Out And Vote."

In all, 32 displays were interspersed among the aerials. "Every year we'd pick a theme," said Jamieson. Disneyland one year, history of Arizona the next, and so on.

They'd plot their pictures onto graph paper, then transpose them onto 8-by-8-foot-square wooden lattices.

Then they'd go looking for oleander bushes. "We'd bend the green limbs to frame the pictures," said Jamieson. Small flares, similar to those used on the highway, supplied the candlepower. Gunpowder supplied the punch.

"The crowds loved those displays," said Jamieson. "And this was one thing only the paying crowd could see."

Alas, free aerial shows have pretty much spelled the demise of the fizzling pachyderms and other such ground displays.

HOLIDAYS
2

Downtown holiday spirit

Only Christmas Eve could top it.

The night after Thanksgiving. The night when the lights all over downtown Tucson twinkled on — and Santa Claus swooped from the skyline on a hook and ladder.

Cars and shoppers filled downtown the Friday night after Thanksgiving in 1955.

Lights strung across the streets, shiny red boxes, the faces of happy shoppers, a red velvet knee to sit on — this was the Christmas of my childhood.

And it all took place downtown — before the cold steel and glass boxes went up.

Back when you did your shopping not in faceless chain stores, but shops where the owners, often as not, waited on you personally. Stores like Jácome's, Steinfeld's, Cele Peterson's, Myerson's White House.

Tell me you remember what it was like to shop in these stores during the Christmas seasons of the '40s and '50s. Before the malls began their sprawl across the desert.

Alex Jácome Jr. remembered. "The Friday night after Thanksgiving, all the lights went on downtown. The stores were all outlined in lights and there were lines strung across the streets."

Santa Claus, usually a Tucson fireman, came down from a rooftop courtesy of the Tucson's Fire Department hook-and-ladder crew.

"The mayor would pull the switch and all the lights would come on at once," said Jácome. "Then the stores would open until 9 every night till Christmas."

But never on Sundays.

"J.C. Penney would turn over in his grave to see the stores open on Sundays now," said Herb Bloom, who with his brothers, Dave and Ted, went straight out of high school in the '30s to work in their father's men's apparel store, corner of Congress Street and Sixth Avenue.

Ted Bloom remembered the crowds at Christmas, especially during the war years. "The servicemen would wait for the buses in front of our store. They'd be 10 rows deep. One time there was such a crush they fell right through our store window."

Every store had its own trademark of the season. For the Blooms it was the 2,000 ties they'd hang from the ceilings every Christmas.

For Jácome's, it was shiny red boxes — already assembled — handed out to all the customers.

"Those boxes were so expensive," said Jácome. "At Christmas, the family, of course, had all their gifts wrapped up in Jácome's boxes. But we didn't use any tape on them. The day after Christmas, all the boxes went back to the store, to use again."

Just across the street from Jácome's final location was Steinfeld's corner window — the best Christmas display in town. What would you give to press your nose against that glass just once more, to watch those dancing elves?

"We spent $6,000 on that window every year, and that was the early '50s," said Lee Davis, nephew of Mrs. Harold Steinfeld.

Added Lee's brother, Jim Davis: "Our display man, Ralph Egurola, was very talented. Every year, he'd go to New York to see the new exhibitions from the great stores along Fifth Avenue. Many times, he'd buy their displays for us to use next year."

In fact, those dripping-with-elegance chandeliers we all remember at Steinfeld's were originally part of a window display. "Everybody liked them so much, we decided to hang them indoors," said Jim Davis. "At Christmas we'd decorate them with holly and mistletoe."

Steinfeld's sweeping red staircase going up to its mezzanine also figured in many a Tucson Christmas card. "Around October, people would start coming in with their kids, even their dogs, asking if they could pose on the staircase for their Christmas card," said Jim Davis.

Ever accommodating, Steinfeld's clerks would snap the shutters on those family cameras.

Though several Santas set up shop around town, the one whose knees every kid of the '50s wanted to climb on lived in the basement of Steinfeld's.

Known in real life as Clive Bardine, this Santa turned out to be irreplaceable. "When he died," remembered Jim Davis, "we could never make ourselves get another one."

They didn't have a Santa or a fashionable window display. But Myerson's White House, at the corner of Congress and Church, had something even better: an X-ray machine.

Hey, kids, how many of you broke away from your mother's hand so you could climb up that piece of machinery, stick your foot under the light and watch your bones light up?

The machine, of course, was intended to show customers just how well that new pair of Myerson's shoes fit. "They made us take it out in the '60s. Said it was dangerous," said Saul Deitel, who started with the store back in '42, back when the customers still tied their horses up to the parking meters out front.

Remember Myerson's brothers Abe, Hymie, Joseph? Remember those creaky wooden floors? Remember those narrow, crowded aisles, the smell of new leather and unwashed denim?

"One of our biggest sellers at Christmas was Western apparel," said Deitel. "And Levi's. I remember the Christmas after the war, they were lined up around the block — for silk stockings and Levi's."

Cele Peterson, who owned dress shops in this town for more than 75 years, remembered the days of doing business on "fashionable Pennington" during the holidays.

"It was such a fun thing. Everything was so Christmasy. The Salvation Army was out with the bell ringers. And their bands would play on the corners. I remember the women, their capes with red lining.

"There was none of that harried look you see now on the faces of the shoppers. There was such a spirit that you just couldn't be sad.

"Everything was full of joy."

HOLIDAYS
3

Halloween Mardi Gras

They were royalty for a day, er, make that a night.

"What I remember is me and Bettie sitting all night on a makeshift stage in front of the Valley National Bank on Congress while all these kids passed in front of us in their costumes."

Such were the royal duties of Jim Pfersdorf, king of the 1936 Mardi Gras, and his queen, Bettie Houston.

Don't think New Orleans here. Don't even think pre-Lent.

No, we're talking Halloween — and an annual downtown party that reigned for almost two decades.

Jim Pfersdorf and Bettie Houston Crawford as Mardi Gras king and queen.

Started by pool hall owner Dooley Bookman, Tucson's own Mardi Gras lured thousands of kids and grown-ups downtown for merriment, prizes and plenty of tooth-rotting treats.

Even radio came. Imagine: Thousands of Tucsonans with their ears glued to the radio dial, perhaps waiting to hear whether little Johnny or Susie had won a prize for the most hideous head.

Yep, that was one of the categories. So was tallest girl, smallest boy and least costly costume.

Hey, haven't you heard? There's a Depression going on.

Prizes ranged from fur scarves to $1 savings accounts to a 2-pound box of Martha Washington candies.

Neither Pfersdorf, nor Bettie, whose married name would be Crawford, remembered exactly how they even got on the ballot.

But there they were, along with the names of a few other kids.

"You went into Jácome's or Penney's and there were boxes there with ballots," said Pfersdorf. "When you bought something, they gave you a ballot to fill out. This went on for a couple of months."

Long enough for each of the winners to rack up more than 3,000 votes.

"They called my mother and told her I was king," said Pfersdorf.

His Andy Hardy response: "Gee, Mother. You aren't kidding me, are you?"

It didn't take long for kingly obligations to start weighing heavily on Pfersdorf's 9-year-old shoulders.

There were newspaper interviews, photo sessions, and oh, yeah, getting fitted for his crown and costume, which vaguely resembled some sort of band uniform.

"My mother didn't make it," said Pfersdorf. "I don't know who did. But I got to keep it."

Meanwhile, Crawford's mother was busily stitching together her white satin gown, complete with stand-up collar and matching crown.

"I carried that thing around until a few years ago," said Crawford, who would eventually move to Paradise Valley.

Halloween night, both were whisked to their stage, the better to survey the ghostly subjects passing by in parade.

"We sat on little thrones," said Crawford, then 9, who was described in a Tucson Citizen article as "dark-haired, dark-eyed, and round cheeked."

"I think I got a perm that morning," she added.

"I combed my hair," said Pfersdorf.

Though neither one remembered receiving any sort of prize for winning, the glow, said Crawford, lasted for several days past the event.

The next year, Pfersdorf revisited Mardi Gras. "I wore my king outfit as my costume and I was part of the milling crowd."

But he would enjoy other moments of fame. The first boy to sign up with the Tucson Boys Chorus, Pfersdorf also won a singing contest at the Fox-Tucson's old Mickey Mouse Club.

"The winner would get a quart of ice cream. I wanted that ice cream," said Pfersdorf, who belted out "You Must Have Been a Beautiful Baby."

As for Crawford, she continued trick-or-treating as an adult — with her grandchildren.

HOLIDAYS
4

The finest of celebrations

St. Augustine Cathedral is illuminated by the glow from the annual fireworks display on "A" Mountain.

Tucson was 101 years old, the U.S.A. a year younger, when saloonkeeper George Hand summed up the day that had just passed: July 4, 1876:

"The day broke with the firing of guns, including a 12-pounder cannon from the post. The band from the post played, and a Mexican band also. They all went to Levin's Park.

"It was the finest celebration I ever saw in this town. I kept sober all day."

Whether it was with one-legged races and band concerts, or firecrackers and rodeos, Tucsonans have usually managed to celebrate a bang-up Fourth around here.

The eats weren't bad either.

Witness this July 4, 1890, bill of fare from the Tucson Restaurant, 12 N. Meyer St.:

Chicken soup, roast chicken, roast beef, boiled ham, champagne sauce, fresh salmon, string beans, fresh tomatoes, new potatoes, cucumbers, tea, coffee, ice cream and jelly cake.

All for 25 cents.

More delicate palates could partake of the ice cream social at 7:30 that night on the lawn of the Methodist parsonage. Music and literary exercises to follow.

Oh, yeah. As a public service, the Star also cautioned readers "not to shoot off fire crackers in the streets when horses are passing by, as accidents may result."

By 1910, the city had clamped down hard with its no-fireworks edict.

"Heretofore, the Fourth has been celebrated in Tucson with an unusual amount of noise and din, but this year it is going to be safe and sane," the Star pontificated.

Ah well. You could still "explode with fun" down at Nogales.

Or stay in town and take in two days' worth of ballgames, band concerts, and sack races over at the Elysian Grove — where Carrillo Intermediate Magnet School sits today.

And if all that activity left you hot and out of sorts, why not send over to the Owl Drug Co. for a bottle of Digesto? ("Just like a trip to the mountains. Cooling as a fresh breeze. 25 cents.")

By 1930, Tucsonans were getting their fireworks fixes in Arizona Stadium, courtesy of the Tucson

Jaycees.

For one thin dime you also got Yaqui dancers, a "machine gun sham battle," and — alas — a three-bomb rocket misfire that injured five, none seriously.

Two years later, the Jaycees added a little pulchritude to the program: 14 — count 'em, 14 — "lovely blondes, brunettes and redheads" competing for the title of Miss Southern Arizona.

Bicycle racers, some coming from as far as Wilmot Road, also wheeled into the stadium's oval track for a thrilling finish that night.

During the '30s, Tucson's Chinese community put on a series of Independence Day celebrations over at Wetmore's Grounds — just east of where the Tucson Mall now stands.

Swimming, barbecues, fireworks, pony rides, Chinese music and cockfights were all promised back in 1938.

So was ice-pick throwing for men and rolling-pin throwing for married women.

Fourth of July, 1942. Forget the rolling pins. Tucson, like the rest of the country, was at war.

That night we got the "Tucson at War parade," featuring everyone from soldiers to air-raid wardens to road-repair squads, all marching in formation.

But the biggest crowd-pleaser turned out to be "seven giant bombers from Davis-Monthan Field," doing simulated bombing runs over the stadium.

Peacetime or war, the pyrotechnics continued at Arizona Stadium until 1979, when liability worries sent the little dazzlers skittering elsewhere.

For years now, that's meant "A" Mountain to most.

HOLIDAYS
5

Carolers on horses

Santa wore cowboy boots, the lone "reindeer" was really a mare and sleigh bells jingled against a backdrop of saguaros and prickly pear.

It's been close to 50 years since a ragtag group of kids mounted their horses and burros and went a'caroling through the sparsely settled neighborhoods of the Catalina Foothills.

"We'd heard of people Christmas caroling and thought, 'Why don't we go?' " said Tucsonan Margaret Canning, who got to wear the Santa suit.

Older sister Harriet, then a freshman at the University of Arizona, did the organizing.

"I was a horse lover and rode on the UA quadrille team," said Harriet Canning Perkins, who would later move to Puyallup, Wash. "I did it with a couple of university students. We got the younger kids involved."

But first they had to get their parents' blessing.

"Our parents said it was all right," said Canning. "After all, we had the horses, and since it was winter, the snakes weren't out."

Which is how it came to be that for several years in a row back in the mid-1950s, the sounds of young voices wafting through the clear desert nights of late December supplanted the usual coyote cacophony.

"I think the coyotes went and hid," said Canning, with a boisterous laugh.

Originally from Tennessee, the Canning family — parents Graeme and Mary Margaret, sisters Harriet, Margaret and Andrea — moved out West in the late '40s.

"My grandfather had bought some property down by the university and when he died, my father came out here to develop it," said Canning.

By the early '50s, the family was firmly ensconced in a new foothills home off Campbell Avenue, a couple of miles north of River Road.

"There were six houses on our street and nothing north of us," said Canning, who continued to live in the house as an adult.

Rustic is the best way to describe the old neighborhood.

Most of the roads were dirt, everyone had septic tanks, and there were no phones. When they did get a phone, it was on an eight-party line.

Just about everyone had horses. "Hardly anyone had fences and we would ride all over," said Canning.

To the north of them sprawled a still-working cattle ranch.

"Every once in a while, the cattle would get loose and come down and steal the hay out of our corral," said Canning. "We'd chase them on back on our horses."

School was held at the old Catalina Foothills School on River Road, which would later become the headquarters for the Catalina Foothills School District.

Back in the early '50s, however, it was still a two-room schoolhouse, grades one to eight.

"We had two teachers and about three kids in a grade," said Canning, who counted among her classmates future actor Ted Danson, who lived just up the street.

"I was in third grade, he was in first grade," she said.

Sometimes the Canning girls' father took them to school, sometimes they went by horseback, trotting down Camino de Escuela.

The girls had several horses to choose from, including mares Tip and Sandy, a half-thoroughbred named Wrinkles and a burro dubbed Little Fellow.

Only Sandy, however, would tolerate the sleigh bells, said Canning. Or the antlers.

"We'd put the bells around her. Then we'd hook deer horn antlers right to her bridle."

"They were whitetail deer horns," said Perkins. "We covered them with aluminum foil."

Depending on whom you talk to, Canning was privileged — or forced — to wear the Santa suit.

"I wore the beard and the whole thing," she said.

"We made her," said Perkins.

Meanwhile, the rest of the kids had to settle for jeans, jackets and cowboy hats.

"We were not real organized, to put it mildly," said Canning. "But we did braid the horses' manes and tails with red and green ribbon."

They also slung saddlebags onto the backs of their mounts, in hopes of sweet reward.

"Sometimes we got Christmas candy. Sometimes people would come out and hand us hot chocolate. But we never got off our horses," said Canning.

"A lot of people offered to make donations, but we took no money," said Perkins.

The first year they only went out one night — Christmas Eve — enlisting no more than six kids, none younger than 10.

"People were shocked," said Canning. "Nobody had ever done that before. At first, it was like, 'Who's that out there bothering me?' But then it was like, 'Oh, gee. This is really nice.' It was a complete turnaround."

So pleased were the neighbors, in fact, that the old eight-party line was soon jammed with callers.

"People would call my mother and tell her we had just been there. Or they'd hear from their neighbors that we had been there and wonder why we hadn't come to their house," said Canning.

Through sandy arroyos and up and down washboard roads they clip-clopped, traveling as far south as the university farms on Roger Road, as far east as Hacienda del Sol Road.

"We only went to houses where we saw a light," said Canning.

No lanterns or flashlights, however, did the carolers take. "We went by the light of the moon and stars," said Canning.

After arriving at a house, the horseback carolers would form a semicircle, then launch into their repertoire — beginning with "Jingle Bells," followed by "The First Noel," "Silent Night" and ending with "We Wish You a Merry Christmas."

"No, we never practiced," said Canning. "But we did get better as the night went along."

By 10 or 11 p.m., they were back home, horses brushed and put back into the corral at the bottom of the hill.

"My mother always had hot cider, hot chocolate, cookies and hot dogs for everybody," said Perkins, who remembered both Ted Danson and his sister trotting along on those rides. "Everybody came back to our house."

The following year, the carolers went out two nights in a row. "We started getting calls in November," said Canning. "People wanted to make sure we didn't pass them by."

Would-be carolers swelled their ranks to about a dozen singers that second year. Who got in, however, depended less on vocalization skills than on horse deportment, said Canning.

"We had one girl who wanted to go, but her horse did not like the sound of the bells. And when we got in the semicircle, it would bite and kick the other horses. You had to have a horse that would tolerate sleigh bells and close quarters with other horses."

One year, one of the local papers even came out and took the group's photo.

But times were changing. "Some of the kids moved away," said Perkins.

"The foothills were getting filled up," said Canning. Fences started going up. It became harder and harder to find a decent horse trail. "My father eventually got rid of the horses."

Three years, that's all it lasted, said Perkins.

"There was a group of adults that tried to get it started again," said Canning. "But as kids, we didn't want to be organized. We didn't want to be told what houses to sing at.

"We liked it more when we could just ride out there and pick our own houses."

And so once more, Christmas Eve came to be serenaded only by the yip and yodel of the coyote.

HOLIDAYS
6

Christmas miracles

Richard Wood, a few weeks before the crash.

This is the story of a Christmas miracle, a snowfall that couldn't be, and a cat named Tuffy, who truly was.

In the waning hours of Dec. 23, 1941, Richard Wood, then age 9, was fast asleep.

Not far above him, a four-engine bomber with 19 men aboard was silently gliding through the icy air, heading for an emergency landing at what was then called Davis-Monthan Field.

"I assume I didn't hear it because no motors were going," said Wood, who also soundly slept through the ensuing crash — right through the roof of a house less than two blocks away.

Wood, who would grow up to be a meteorologist, figured it was ice on the wings. "It probably iced up on the approach to D-M," he said.

The plane struck two power poles before hitting the four-room adobe house. Its right wing sheared off the upper half of the home, causing it to collapse.

Inside were four people who had just retired for the night: a Mr. and Mrs. Osborne Otteson, a Mrs. T.E. Callaghan and her 3-year-old child.

Here's where the miracle comes in: None suffered so much as a scratch, save for Mr. Otteson, who was treated for minor injuries.

What's more, while several of the crew members had fractures and other injuries, none was life-threatening.

Yet another survivor would be pulled from the still-crumbling home early that Christmas Eve morn: Tuffy, the family cat, rescued by Pvt. David Lindsay of the 32nd Air Base Squadron.

"I don't know who was scared the most, Tuffy or me," Lindsay would tell Star reporters.

When young Wood woke up that morning at his Midtown home on East Pima Street, he found one more miracle outside his window: snow.

During the night, the first snow of any merit since 1937 had blanketed Tucson.

"We had 2 or 3 inches," said Wood, who spent the day throwing snowballs at his sister and visiting the crash scene.

"It was all roped off," he said. "You couldn't see too much."

Naturally, the next day's papers were filled with stories about the crash. There was also a short story about the snowfall, rather cryptically written.

"(Censored) Blankets Tucson For First Time Since 1937," ran the Christmas Day headline.

Beneath it, all mention of snow also drew the word "censored," along with this explanation:

"Since wartime regulations have inhibited the dissemination of any information regarding the weather, the substance which local residents discovered upon their lawns and housetops when they arose yesterday morning must remain a military secret."

The story went on to describe children "engaging in (censored) fights and building (censored) men."

"It was just three weeks after World War II broke out," said Wood. "I remember asking my mother what war means."

He soon found out — at least on the home front. The next year, the family moved to Southern California, where Wood's widowed mother and brother-in-law found work in the defense plants.

The family later moved to Washington, D.C.

In 1973, Wood returned to Tucson, heading up its National Weather Service office until 1980. Following assignments in Maryland and Albuquerque, he retired to Tucson in 1987.

From 1988 to 1992 he wrote a weekly weather column for the Star, including one, of course, about the censored snow.

Later, Wood would become editor of the Gale Group Weather Almanac, and Weather of U.S. Cities.

A lot of Decembers have come and gone since then. But he never forgot Christmas Eve, 1941 — and its many miracles.

The More Things Change

The dam in lower Sabino Canyon created a popular and convenient fishing hole in the '30s.

We learned to dial without an operator, made plans to dam up Sabino Canyon and brought Howard Hughes — or at least his plant — to town. Oh yeah, we also created the world's biggest gem show.

THE MORE THINGS CHANGE
1

Water, Water Everywhere

A flick of the fingers, a turn of the wrist. And there you have it. Cool, clean water.

All you want. And all taken for granted, yea though we live in the desert.

It's a good bet, however, that such nonchalance was rare among those who preceded us in this valley, oh, a hundred or so years ago. But then that's what usually happens when you buy your water from a leather bag stung across the back of some burro.

Tucsonans drawn to the waters of Carrillo's Gardens in 1887. The resort is now the site of Carrillo Intermediate Magnet School.

The burros "filled up" at "El Ojito," or "Little Eye Springs" — Tucson's principal source of water, gurgling just west of a more recent Tucson landmark, the Wishing Shrine on South Main Avenue.

Even before the walls of the presidio went up in 1775, El Ojito was here, slaking the thirst of everyone from Father Eusebio Kino to Capt. Juan Bautista de Anza.

Once the "Americanization" of Tucson began following the Gadsden Purchase in 1854, the springs became even more crucial to a town with few private wells.

Mornings would find several burros lined up at the springs, each waiting its turn. Water vendors would then lead the burros through the streets of town, crying "agua" for sale.

By the late 1870s, the burro had been supplanted by progress — in this case a wooden water cart also lined with animal skins to hold the precious liquid.

Owned by two entrepreneurs, Joe Phy and Adam Saunders, the cart rolled down the same rutted streets where once the burros had clopped.

Nickel a bucket was the going rate, payable upon delivery or else at the end of the week. Water vendors simply penciled the tab on the doorjambs. Erasures, it was reported, were few.

Needless to say, few of the precious drops were wasted on laundry, shrubbery or the human body. Hence, the public bath houses to the north of Little Eye Springs.

Known first as Simpson's Baths and later as Spring Garden, the baths, which were also operated in later years by Phy and Saunders, proved a more sociable alternative to the usual Saturday night "spit-in-a-rag" routine.

From former Arizona Daily Star reporter and historian Bernice Cosulich comes this description of the baths:

"Customers who waited their turns to pay 25 cents for a bath could sit on benches under the trees in the patio as their children swayed in swings. In a small building there was a boiler under which a fire constantly burned to heat the water.

"A series of bath houses was nearby, each with its small rooms just large enough for zinc or tin tubs, pegs for clothes and towels, and a shelf for soap and collar buttons. Partitions did not interrupt conversations, and the latest gossip flowed more freely than the few buckets of water allotted each customer.

"There were no social barriers among those who used the baths. Prominent families gathered there with whiskey-soaked miners who had come in from the hills for a prolonged spree. Cowboys and legislators steamed the alcohol from their bodies, and soldiers just back from a campaign against the Apaches relaxed their saddle-weary muscles."

The town's first piped-in water arrived at 4 p.m. Sept. 16, 1882; after a valve on Main Street was opened and a "six-inch stream came bursting forth," reported the next day's Star, which went on to rhapsodize:

"We may truly say that Tucson has witnessed the third great event in her steady, solid growth. First, the railroad; then artificial light by gas. But the crowning event — that which will make pleasant homes surrounded by shrubbery, lawns and gardens — is the grand water supply, which brings health and its many attending advantages."

Events leading up to that momentous occasion actually began a year earlier, when Sylvester Watts set up a water farm and pumping system on the banks of the Santa Cruz River. Wells were sunk in the land, and a wooden flume in the bed of the river sped the water to town.

A year after Tucson first experienced the marvel of piped-in water, Bettina Steinfeld — Albert's wife — became the first in town to own a bathtub with running water.

But as any student of plumbing knows, what's piped in must eventually be piped out. By the late 1890s, Tucsonans were beginning to tire of stepping around what was routinely flowing down the streets of town. City fathers, taking note, created a water and sewage commission, to, as they say, look into the problem.

Not everyone, however, recognized that there was indeed a problem, as Tucson pioneer Mose Drachman recounted in his memoirs:

"Strange as it may seem, some of our prominent citizens were opposed to the installation of a sewer system. I remember one in particular. His argument was that he did not want a sewer — he had just completed a very fine cesspool.

"The conditions here in the city were deplorable as one can imagine — think of a town of four or five thousand without a sewer system. In spite of opposition, we finally got a sewer put down Congress Street.

"Then we started out to get one on Stone Avenue. Again we ran into opposition from people who owned corner property. They said they already had a sewer on Congress Street and what did they want with one on Stone Avenue.

"We were constantly fighting over these public improvements."

Well, the city got its sewer system all right. It also got the water company. On July 24, 1900, Tucson Water Co. — still owned by Watts and a Mr. H.A. Lawton — became the City of Tucson Water Works. Price tag: $110,000.

As the time of the sale, the company had 225 customers, who paid an average monthly bill of $2.

When Tucson began its sewer system, also in 1900, raw sewage irrigated grain crops around what is now Oury Park. The town's first sewage treatment plant was still 28 years away.

Just as we had effluent back then, we also had water conservation. Despite the Star's glowing oasis-in-the-desert predictions, the town's water supply — or rather its inadequate pumping capacity — soon brought forth some rather ominous-sounding conservation measures.

Arizona Daily Star Aug. 4, 1916's headline: "Mayor is going after those who waste water — police instructed to keep eyes peeled for all-night irrigators."

Thirteen years earlier, on June 19, 1903, the Star also reported what may have been the first "Beat the Peak" campaign, as citizens were urged to sprinkle and irrigate only between the hours of 5 and 8, a.m. and p.m.

By 1909 the trend begun by Bettina Steinfeld and her bathtub was also having its effect. Reported the Star: "People who take baths cause a drain much greater than is believed."

So great was the problem of excess water use that residents were ordered to turn off their faucets whenever the fire whistle blew.

As of 1921, the list of water customers had grown to the point that the city was forced to hire a second meter reader, part time, with the stipulation that the rest of the employee's time be spent repairing city cars.

Disputes over rate hikes — some as much as 50 percent — also occurred during the late 1920s, leading one city attorney to give this legal opinion: "It (city water) was not bound to do so for a uniform or reasonable price, but had the right to charge all it could get."

Today, it's the county, rather than the city that administers our sewer system. As for what comes out of our faucets, we've come a long way from the burros with the water bags.

THE MORE
THINGS CHANGE
2

Direct-Dialing

You say you don't own a computer, your TV doesn't come with remote control and you have no idea how to send e-mail?

Never mind.

You're still more technologically adroit than the entire population of Tucson 60 years ago.

Before 1949, the only way to make a phone call in this burg was to give the operator your number.

Then direct-dialing hit town. Think learning a new computer system is scary?

Try dialing your own.

So daunting was the task that the phone company held an open house, complete with dial-your-own lessons.

A phone company "educator" taught Tucsonans to dial.

The Tucson Kiwanis and Optimists also got detailed demos during their luncheons.

Witness this account in the Jan. 6, 1949, Star, with phone company "educator" Marguerite Lupton using a large phone dial mock-up in front of some obviously worried Optimists:

"Miss Lupton, step by step, explained how to use a dial, translating her words into action by dialing the massive dial on the giant model.

"Lifting the receiver, Miss Lupton got and called attention to the normal dial tone. The next move is to dial the number you want, being careful to permit the dial to return to neutral after each of the five digits.

"As she twirled each digit, the demonstrator lit up, right across the board."

Miss Lupton and her demonstrator must have been mighty busy.

For the Star noted future appearances in schools, other civic groups and "wherever large groups gather to learn the intricacies of the dial system."

Fresh hell would follow.

By the mid-'50s, Tucsonans were getting lettered prefixes, swelling their phone numbers from five to seven digits.

Among the useless bits of minutiae still stuck in my brain is my parents' old number: MA3-8035.

Never mind that just a few years later, those prefixes were phased out in favor of the seven-digit numbers we have today.

Result: Lots of Tucsonans wound up with new numbers.

Not so, however, for those at the Dalton residence.

"I'm guessing we had the same number since 1947," said Estella Dalton, who found the earliest listing in a 1949 phone book.

"When I called up the phone company to ask them how long the line had been in use, they said they didn't have the records anymore."

It was Estella's aunt, Dora Dalton, who first had the line put in at their Barrio Anita home.

Back then, the outside world came ringing in on a basic black phone.

"We have weathered boyfriends, girlfriends, fire, threatening calls, obscene calls and never changed the number," said Estella, who moved back to the house a few years ago to care for her ailing aunt.

"After my aunt passed away, I asked to keep the same phone number," Estella said. The phone company charged her $50 for the privilege.

Alas, the black phone is no more. "In 1974 the wiring gave out," Estella said. "They didn't have the parts anymore."

Later, her phone would be beige — with buttons.

Incidentally, the Arizona Weekly Star, as today's Star was then known, installed its first telephone the same year phone service came to town: 1881.

Teenage boys handled the switchboard. Apparently none had been schooled in customer service.

For while lauding the "progressive spirit of the times," the Star also shot this warning across its editorial bow:

"We take this occasion to caution the operator that we won't stand any back talk whenever it becomes our painful duty to admonish him."

Good grief. No wonder we went to dial phones.

THE MORE
THINGS CHANGE
3

Marjorie Long

Her name is synonymous with putting roofs over people's heads.

Yet her mother's first home in Tucson was a tent — and a rather humble one at that.

"My grandfather sent for my grandmother and the two kids — one was my mother — and they pitched a tent at what is now a park on Fourth Avenue, south of Speedway," said Marjorie Long.

Yes, that's "Long." As in Long Realty, founded by her father-in-law, Roy H. Long, in 1926.

Two years earlier, Marjorie was born into a family whose own roots in Tucson stretch back to the early 1900s.

Marjorie Long, the matriarch of the Long Realty family.

Grandfather Burton Bovee, a tubercular from Pennsylvania, arrived in 1901.

Not long after, he sent for his family: wife Katherine, infant son Daniel and daughter Clara, age 2.

Soon, Burton Bovee signed on with the fledgling Desert Laboratory, atop Tumamoc Hill.

"Mother said there wasn't one side of the Tucson Mountains or the lower Catalinas that he didn't explore. He discovered a number of species of cactus."

By then, the family had abandoned the tent for a house on West Congress Street.

Meandering close by was the still-wet Santa Cruz, where young Daniel would gather watercress along the banks.

Objective: sales to the working girls in Tucson's red-light district. "My uncle used to say that money put him through dental school," said Marjorie.

In 1923, her father, Clarence Perrin, married her mother, Clara. "Nine months and five days later, I was born."

On her first birthday, her father, then working for the Southern Pacific Railroad, passed the Arizona State Bar Exam. "You didn't need to go to law school then," said Marjorie.

Hers was small-town childhood at its best. Home was the southwest corner of Stone Avenue and Helen Street.

Chickens scratched and rabbits scurried in the back yard. Meanwhile, the whole world rolled down Stone Avenue.

"I used to put a purse tied with string in the middle of the road, then hide behind a tree," said Marjorie. When drivers circled back for a closer look, she'd yank on the string.

She remembered Indians rumbling into town, wagons loaded with wood and baskets for sale. Then there were the picnic lunches, munched under the mulberry trees in the park at Stone Avenue and Speedway.

"I never worried about safety. I'd walk home from the U of A at night through that park."

In the spring of '43, her first year at the University of Arizona, she met Barry Long.

They courted for a time before he left for military training.

That summer, Marjorie also signed up for the war effort, working the swing shift as a mechanic's helper at Ryan Field.

She and Barry married in '44, just before he shipped off to the European Theater as a combat engineer. She went to work in the SP's dispatch office.

Barry came back, got his civil engineering degree and began building houses in boomtown Tucson. When his father retired in '52, he took over the real estate company.

"They had one office and five salespeople," said Marjorie, who raised four sons: Russell, Randy, Steven and Roy H. Long II.

In 1980, Barry retired and the couple moved to the Willcox area, where they grew apples — thousands of 'em. "It was a wonderful time but it was a money-guzzler," said Marjorie.

By 1994, they were back in town, where Marjorie earned her real estate license. Barry, who rejoined her in the business, died in 1998.

Like many long-timers, she cherished the town that was. But she also looked to the future.

"Tucson's a wonderful place, but you can't keep standing still," she said. Or live in a tent.

THE MORE
THINGS CHANGE
4

Jury duty for women

They were serving in the armed forces. They were riveting airplanes together in defense plants. They were holding down titles ranging from attorney to congresswoman.

But up until March 9, 1945, women were not allowed to serve on juries in Arizona.

You read it right.

Never mind that Arizona gave women the vote the same year it became a state in 1912 — eight years before it became the law of the land.

Somehow women were still deemed too delicate of temperament to listen to gory testimony.

Arizona wasn't alone. Writing in The Journal of Arizona History's Winter 2002 edition, Tucson author Jan Lo Vecchio noted that only 12 states automatically allowed women to sit on juries after the 19th Amendment gave women the vote in 1920.

One year later, the fight to get women inside the jury box in this state began, with bills being regularly introduced and defeated in the Arizona Legislature just about every year between 1921 and 1945.

Critics, wrote Lo Vecchio, argued that women were "too emotional to make logical decisions." Furthermore, they needed protection from the "filth" of courtroom testimony.

Not every man agreed with this sort of thinking, Lo Vecchio said. "One year, the bill was totally sponsored by male legislators."

Thanks to the lobbying of several hundred members of the Arizona Federation of Business and Professional Women's Clubs and the determination of several female legislators, wrote Lo Vecchio, the bill was finally passed and signed into law on March 9, 1945.

Even so, some in power were still looking out after the fairer sex, sticking in a provision that allowed women to request that their names be stricken from the jury list.

"Ordinary housewives do not want jury duty. They have too much other work caring for their homes and families," Pima County Superior Court Judge Evo DeConcini told a Tucson Citizen reporter.

Apparently many women failed to take advantage of this little "out." For on April 25, 1945, 100 women in Pima County were called to make up a jury panel sitting through the summer and fall.

Here's how the Citizen rather archly introduced that little fact, in a news story, no less:

"Dawned this day. A tragic one for the men of Tucson or for quite a goodly number of them.

"Tonight those men will wander home, tired, and hungry. Will they find the house in order and the odor from a well-prepared, home-cooked meal assailing their noses when they enter?

"They will not. Instead, they will learn that wife or sister or daughter is detained downtown and if the jury is deadlocked, heaven alone can tell when the women will return to their homes and firesides."

Dear me.

Braving their husbands' horrors at coming home to find a cold stove or an unironed shirt, four women on April 26, 1945, joined eight men in Superior Court to weigh the fate of one Charles Lewis, who was duly found guilty of the crime of robbery.

Deliberation took a mere 12 minutes. So much for women not being able to make up their minds — yet another argument against them serving on juries.

Even so, women were still allowed to opt out of jury duty by pleading domestic duties, a fact that, ironically, started grating on men not granted that option.

Somehow in just a few short years, the mind-set went from "women shouldn't serve on juries" to "why shouldn't women serve on juries just like the men?"

The Arizona Supreme Court agreed. In 1953 it ruled the provision unconstitutional.

Now we're all snared. Equally.

THE MORE THINGS CHANGE
5

How Tucson Got Its Plant

It took the sale of a pig farm and the humoring of a general who was prone to jumping on the beds of the Pioneer Hotel. But when it was over, the country's most famous recluse had made his decision.

Howard Hughes would bring his guided missile plant to Tucson. "Manna from heaven" read a Star headline in February 1951.

All it took was securing the options on 32,000 acres, enough secrecy to fuel the plots of a hundred "Get Smart!" episodes and the willingness of a still-new-to-the-game real estate man who knew how to keep his mouth shut and his suitcase packed.

"For 10 days I never slept in my own bed," said Roy P. Drachman, the man who helped wheel and deal Hughes Aircraft Co. (now Raytheon) into town.

The story begins with whom Drachman knew: Axel Johnson, an old friend who by 1950 was working at Hughes' plant in Culver City, Calif.

"The feelers were out that Hughes was going to build a plant in the Southwest," said Drachman. "Axel told me this in early 1950." Drachman promptly introduced his friend to C. Edgar Goyette, manager of the Tucson Chamber of Commerce.

Industrialist Howard Hughes gave Roy Drachman, right, only a few hours to secure the land.

Using Johnson as a "fifth column," Drachman and Goyette began a secret campaign, extolling Tucson's virtues through brochures mailed to various Hughes officials.

"On Jan. 12, 1951, I got a call from Del Webb," Drachman recalled. "He told me to be in Phoenix at 2 p.m. that afternoon to meet a TWA flight coming in from L.A." Aboard were two men from the Hughes plant. Webb, by the way, would wind up building Hughes' Tucson plant.

Drachman obligingly drove the visitors around Phoenix — which never had a clue, he says — showing them land and growth patterns. He did the same thing in Tucson and Albuquerque.

The lookers from Culver City kept coming back. "I drove them around Tucson. They wanted to know why so many of our streets were unpaved. They were not impressed," said Drachman. "They went into a supermarket and priced items. They wanted to talk to people at the university, to see how cultured we were."

Only five men in town knew what was brewing: Drachman; Goyette; Monte Mansfield, who was president of the Tucson Airport Authority; Mayor

Joe Neimann; and Board of Supervisors Chairman J. Homer Boyd. "It was on the hush-hush," said Drachman. "It was easy to cover up back then. Everyone wanted to see Tucson grow." The secret meetings lasted for several days. "These Hughes people would never go to an office," said Drachman. "They were nuts. We'd have to meet in a hangar."

Meanwhile, Phoenix finally caught on to what was happening. "A blue-ribbon committee up there met with the Hughes officials," said Drachman.

In the end, it all came down to the land. "In Phoenix, the land was more valuable because it was farmland," said Drachman. "In Tucson, most of it was desert so it was cheaper."

A site adjacent to the Tucson Municipal Airport seemed a logical choice for the plant. Gen. Ira Eaker, who'd retired from the Air Force and gone to work for Hughes after World War II, entered the picture as head of the search committee.

"One night we met at Monte Mansfield's house," Drachman recalled. "It was 11 at night. Eaker said the boss — he always called Hughes the boss — had decided to build a plant in Tucson, provided he could buy one mile of land on the north and east sides by 2 o' clock the next afternoon.

"Monte turned to me and said, 'You've got a job to do.' "

Drachman immediately went to the phone and got Pima County Assessor Leo Finch out of bed. "I told him I wasn't drunk in a bar but I needed the records of ownership on that land by 6 the next morning."

Most of the land was owned in large sections, including a pig farm at the end of one runway. By 2 p.m. Drachman had his options secured — for $100,000.

"Then, of course, they said they wanted more land, for the people coming in," said Drachman. "But it was just Hughes buying up land for speculation. People in the office kept asking me, 'What the hell is going on?' "

Within two weeks, Drachman had options to buy some 32,000 acres scattered around Tucson, some of it prime foothills land that went for $150 an acre.

Secrecy still prevailed. "We all went under assumed names," said Drachman. "Eaker always called me from a pay phone, never from his home. We had everything in code for each plat of land."

One night the general came to town and took a suite at the Pioneer. "We had maps of Tucson spread out all over the room," Drachman recalled. "In the middle of the discussion, Eaker asked me, 'Is this room secure?' Then he and others climbed on the beds and started looking through the lights and ceiling, searching for hidden microphones. They looked behind the curtains, too."

Still feeling somewhat insecure, the group concluded business at the Minerva Café on Congress Street. "It was 10:30, 11 at night," said Drachman. "Nobody was there."

Feb. 2, 1951, the official announcement was made: Hughes was coming to town. It would be, reported the Star, "The biggest industrial development in the city's history."

Fifty-three minutes after the formal announcement from Washington, bulldozers were clearing a site for the $9 million plant.

Meanwhile, Drachman began exercising his options. When it was all over, Hughes had bought 20,000 acres for $1.9 million "It averaged $95 an acre," said Drachman.

Ah, yes. The land that Hughes was so loath to part with in later years. "He was just odd. He just wouldn't sell," said Drachman. "After Hughes became a total recluse and others started running the company, they did sell off about 8,000 acres. I don't think he ever knew."

Six years after Hughes died in 1976, the remaining 12,000 acres were finally sold — and then resold for even higher profits. The land that Howard Hughes bought for just under $2 million in 1951 would later be worth, estimated Drachman, $750 million to $1 billion.

Despite all the behind-the-scenes maneuvering, Drachman never met Howard Hughes in person, though he did talk to him several times on the telephone.

"He called himself Jack Thompson, but I knew it was Hughes," said Drachman remembering the time he followed orders to arrange a suite of room for Hughes and his party at the old El Conquistador Hotel, complete with limo, special telephone and lunch.

Twice Hughes postponed the visit for a day. Then he canceled.

Drachman visited the sprawling plant south of town only once or twice. "I'm more for putting things together," he said. "I like the action, not necessarily going to the thing later."

THE MORE
THINGS CHANGE
6

Now Arriving — Tucson's Airport

An old control tower at the Tucson Municipal Airport.

Many Tucsonans were still saddling up Old Paint the year airplanes started swooping down here with some regularity.

That was in 1919, the year the Old Pueblo got its first municipal airport. Incidentally, it was the first of its kind in the country.

It began when an aviation committee made up of members of the City Council and Chamber of Commerce picked an 82-acre site smack-dab where the Tucson Rodeo Grounds sprawls today.

Within a few years, however, the site was fast becoming squeezed for space. So city fathers looked eastward, to where 1,080 acres lay ready for acquisition.

They paved a runway, moved in a hangar from Nogales, and, in 1927, called upon Charles Lindbergh to dedicate what was then the world's largest municipal airport. Davis-Monthan, they called it, named for two Tucson aviators who had met an earlier demise in the cockpit.

Standard Airlines, which would later become American, began serving Tucson the following year. Bob Scruggs, American manager in 1939, recorded a typical day out at the old Davis-Monthan Field:

"Sweep the lobby, ensure that toilet paper was in the unisex john, sell two tickets, make reservations, unload incoming baggage and their passengers, deliver to the curb, reload outgoing passengers, their baggage, two sacks of mail and one sack of express, raise the flag at 0800 and take it down at sundown (if not working the radio communications station.)"

Passenger Peggy Wilder, who ventured into the wild blue yonder above Tucson in 1933, would later recall a most memorable flight: "I don't believe there were flight attendants on those planes. The second officer took care of the passengers."

The plane, a Ford Tri-Motor, would take her from Tucson to Cleveland — via Douglas, El Paso, and the Texas towns of Big Spring, Abilene, Fort Worth and Dallas. After changing planes in Dallas, the flight then hopped along to Oklahoma City, Tulsa and St. Louis.

"We would leave Tucson at 5:30 in the afternoon and get to Washington, D.C., or New York at 7:30 the next morning," remembered Fred Stofft, one of those responsible for starting up the airport we know today.

Eight years later, with war clouds looming, Tucson had offered its 16,000 acres next to the municipal airport for a military field. But already it was becoming apparent that the military would eventually shove civilian landings elsewhere.

To prepare for that day, the city in 1940 bought 4,000 acres south of town and reserved another 2,500 acres for a new civilian field.

Here is where Consolidated Vultee Aircraft Corp. would build three huge hangars for workers modifying B-24s during the war.

Both the civilian and military airfields managed to coexist at Davis-Monthan during World War II. But by 1947, American Airlines and several other civilian endeavors were ordered to transfer to the new municipal airport.

"The old Consolidated Vultee property was available," said Stofft, who was then president of the Chamber of Commerce. "We decided to band together and lease the property from the city of Tucson."

Those doing the banding together were 15 men who made up the first Tucson Airport Authority — movers and shakers in this town such as Monte Mansfield, Harold Steinfeld, Henry Jaastad and Leon Levy.

Coming up with greenbacks to finance Tucson Airport Authority's efforts to operate a new airport were 25 businessmen, who put up $1,000 each.

In the last months of '48, three tenants moved onto the new site: American Airlines, the U.S. Weather Bureau and an office of the Civil Aeronautics Administration.

More tenants — of a less traditional nature — would follow. "We had an ironing board factory, a lumberyard, a toy factory, a ladies' clothing manufacturer and a roller-skating rink, open to the public," remembered Charles Broman, who started as assistant airport manager in 1948 and retired as its top executive in 1979.

Making money was the name of the game. And one of the airport's main sources of revenue was gasoline sales. Every gallon of gas sold generated 2 cents for the airport.

Pilots from all over the country also received rubber dollars extolling the "T-line," which went from Tallahassee to Topeka to Tucson. Gas sales tripled between 1949 and 1950.

Also attracting business was the airport's tower, striped in colors of red, orange, yellow, green and blue. "You thought of things to do that made your little town known," explained Broman, who got in on at least three of the tower paintings.

Everything from the roller rink to the passenger terminal to administrative offices was housed in one or the other of the three Consolidated Vultee hangars.

"The east side of one hangar was the terminal. It was a temporary thing that stayed until 1962," said Broman, whose chores included sweeping the cement floors and painting new stripes on the runway.

Passengers embarked on old DC-3 props — out of doors, of course. During the rainy season, Broman recalled, water would flow into the old terminal and passengers ran barefoot to and from flights.

In 1958, the old striped tower was replaced by an 11-story structure that flashed out "Tucson" in red, white and blue neon. Five year later, the airport finally got its new terminal. Passengers no longer had to rush barefoot through a former aircraft hangar.

THE MORE
THINGS CHANGE
7

Sabino Canyon

In the old days, it took half a day to reach Sabino Canyon.

From the Clovis and Hohokam cultures to today's Reebok-shod, iPod-attuned "nature lover," Sabino Canyon has felt the trod of many.

So far it's survived unruly crowds, bumper-to-bumper traffic, and — believe it or not — at least three separate movements to flood the upper reaches of the canyon with a dam stretching more than 250 feet high.

Fewer and fewer are the Tucsonans who remember the canyon as it once was — before parking lots, before gates, before warning signs.

"In 1922, it used to take a half-day to drive out there on a little rickety dirt road," remembered J. Lester Hearn. "When you got to what is now Wilmot and Speedway, the road took a left turn."

He remembered swimming in canyon pools so clear they were drinkable, then heading back to Tucson in reverse.

"The grade was so steep that if you were in a Model-T, the gasoline wouldn't run from the gas tank under the seat of the car to the carburetor, so we'd have to get out, turn the car around and back up."

Here's hoping someone was keeping a lookout for what was on the other side of that hill. For by 1926, reported the Tucson Citizen, a record 483 cars in one day were counted chugging to and from Sabino Canyon.

A decade later, progress and the need to keep men working during the Depression spur road work into the canyon itself.

It begins in November 1934 with "a handful of men, a wheelbarrow, two shovels and a pick," reads an early newspaper account.

Two years and who know how many dynamite sticks later, the federal government's Works Project Administration has managed to lay down a winding canyon road linked by nine one-way bridges.

But the way the WPA, and a few forward-thinking citizens see it, the work is far from over.

Sept. 11, 1936. City, county and state officials crowd council chambers to hear plans to apply to the federal government for construction of a 250-foot-high dam in upper Sabino Canyon.

"No Protests Made At All-day Hearing," reports the Star, as government officials and a who's who of local movers and shakers stands up to be counted in favor of the dam — and the potential for another source of water for a growing Tucson.

Also heard that day is the voice of one W.H. Daily, who remarks that when he first set foot in Tucson in 1898, "They were talking about building a Sabino Canyon dam and now we are still talking about it."

Daily goes on to tell how the earlier dam and accompanying power plant were turned down by a "boneheaded city council."

Not a chance this time around. By early '37, headlines are trumpeting: "Mighty Sabino Canyon Dam Approved by U.S. Army, Is No. 1 Pima County Project."

The article goes on to describe the dam approved by the Army Corps of Engineers as a "constant angle structure of reinforced concrete rearing itself 250 feet in the box of upper Sabino basin.

"Behind the dam will lie a 9,500-acre-foot lake, representing a clear body of water more than a mile and three quarters in length."

Estimated cost: slightly more than $1 million, $750,000 of which will be shouldered by the WPA, designated builder of the dam. Tucson and Pima County must pick up the rest of the tab.

Skittishness soon sets in. In May of '37, a Star editorial reminds readers that federal engineers have recommended that the dam not be approved for flood control but only as a recreation project.

The article goes on to question whether $750,000 in WPA money truly does exist for the project, and lauds the Pima County Board of Supervisors for refusing to give the go-ahead on the final mile of road leading up to the proposed dam site.

Nevertheless, the leaders of Tucson's Chamber of Commerce forge ahead. Al Condron, secretary of the chamber, travels to Washington D.C., where he spends weeks trying to get the project on the official WPA job list.

When he returns, it is with the news that Pima County's $300,000 share of the tab, to be financed through a bond issue, has now doubled. Pima County must now pay 60 percent of the cost.

A meeting is held. It does not go well. "Profane Duet Buries Sabino Dam Proposal," trumpets the Star in an Aug. 5, 1937, headline.

The story reads as obituary: "The Sabino Canyon dam project drew its last breath yesterday morning and died for want of approval on the part of the Chamber of Commerce board of directors. It was interred amid a burst of lost tempers, which saw J.J. O'Dowd (board president) fling his resignation at the board and stalk from the meeting."

Echoing O'Dowd's sentiments is chamber member William B. Misbaugh, who tells the gathering: "Old Pueblo is a good name for this G... damned place. I don't see how you ever expect to do anything, accomplish anything here. You shy away from anything new."

More fireworks soon follow. The next day, Condron also resigns from the Chamber of Commerce. In a parting shot, he attributes the defeat to a certain "Mussolini attitude" among some local officials, "conniving with a very small minority of Pima County tax payers."

"It tore the community apart," recalled Roy P. Drachman. "Al Condron left town and never came back, and he had lived here since 1912."

Evelyn Condron confirmed the story about her father-in-law, who died in 1984. "Bitter? He may have been. I think he finally got over it."

As for the plan itself, Drachman said: "It would have covered a lot of beautiful area. I don't recall anyone talking about that. The main question was 'Would there be enough water?' There were no environmentalists then."

Before the decade is through, the canyon does get a dam of sorts, in lower Sabino. The small lake behind it is regularly stocked with fish. Even more regularly, the lake silts up.

All through the '40s and '50s, the lake is dredged of tons of silt and leaf mold. Public-spirited gardeners are urged to help with the cleanup.

"The leaf mold being removed is ideal for enriching gardens and is being piled up on the right hand side of the entrance road for anyone who cares to come and get it," exhorts a 1951 newspaper article.

That same year, Sabino Canyon is closed and gated for the first time at night. Gate-crashers promptly tear down the barriers. Time after time.

In '52, talk is bandied about of charging an admission price. However, "quick and irate protests" plus funds from the county's parks budget keep the canyon free for the hordes, now numbering 200,000 a year.

Record rainfall destroys much of man's handiwork in the canyon in 1954. House-size boulders smash through nine bridges. News accounts also describe raging torrents, which "peeled the road off the face of the cliffs."

Reports the Star: "The popular playground has returned to its inaccessible wilderness state — temporarily at least."

Temporarily is right. By 1959, the ghost of the old upper Sabino dam is once again rattling its chains. Once again, engineers say it can be done. Once again, the Star editorializes — this time in more negative tones. Once again, nothing comes of it.

By the late 1960s, the canyon is a cacophony of honking horns and squealing tires. Auto exhaust hangs among the tree boughs. The Forest Service puts a 200-car lid on canyon capacity.

But another decade will pass before cars are banned and shuttle trams start riding the road — a road, incidentally, that would end a mile before the "mighty dam" that never was.

THE MORE
THINGS CHANGE
8

Gem and Mineral Show

The gem and mineral is world-class and world-famous.

They unstopped the toilets, strung their own lights and guarded the gems with a shotgun — all inside a drafty old Quonset hut.

And that was *after* the event had proved to be roaring success.

The first year's show was held in a school cafeteria. "After all the bills were paid, we came in about $10 ahead. The janitor was working for free, so we gave it to him."

Those were the words of Betty Caudle, who along with her husband, Dan, helped start up what the whole world now knows as the Tucson Gem and Mineral Show — an event that pumps millions of dollars each year into the local economy while luring visitors from just about every country with rocks.

It began, of all places, in Phoenix.

In January of 1955, Dan and Betty Caudle, members of the then-8-year-old Tucson Gem and Mineral Society, were attending a gem and mineral show in Phoenix.

There, they met up with gem and mineral dealer Bob Roots, who urged them to start a gem show in Tucson.

"He said he would line up all the dealers," said Dan, who became chairman of Tucson's first show.

The Caudles, along with fellow "rockhounds" Harold Rupert and Clayton Gibson, managed to talk the Tucson Gem and Mineral Society into sponsoring the show — as long as none of the society's money was used, that is.

The organizing committee got permission to hold the two-day affair in the cafeteria of Helen Keeling Elementary School. "Our kids went there," said Betty. The school parents' group also offered to sell refreshments.

With just a few weeks to plan it all out, members hurriedly cobbled together a few glass display cases. The rest of the cases were borrowed from accommodating shop owners around town.

Betty was in charge of publicity. "I made up signs and put them in every store window in Tucson," she said.

Then she hit the airwaves. "I went on some radio show with a big bag of Apache tears and said any parents or kids who wanted to come to the show could get one. That drew a lot."

The show, featuring the displays of fewer than a dozen dealers, was free, of course. Despite rainy weather, close to 1,500 attended the two-day event.

"We had so many people, we knew we had to have it somewhere else the next year," said Betty. The Tucson Gem and Mineral Society also agreed to fund the show from then on.

The next year, they set up shop in what then passed for the town's only exhibition hall — a Quonset hut out at the Pima County Fairgrounds on South Sixth Avenue.

"There was no heat, it was cold, the toilets were always stopping up, and the roof leaked," said Dan.

Not only that, existing ceiling lights were woefully inadequate when it came to illuminating the brilliant mineral displays down below.

"We had no money, so we bought aluminum-foil-shaped reflectors, strung wire and hung light bulbs over every case," said Dan, a retired electrician.

Everyone pitched in — covering the walls with butcher paper to hide the dirt and kick marks, dusting the cases, sweeping floors and working on the plumbing.

Security was all in-house as well. "I took my shotgun, locked the doors and slept there for several years in a row," said Dan.

As for refreshments, the Keeling parents' group moved its food operation to the hut, where it would continue every year until 1972. "All the profits went to the school," said Dan.

About 2,500 swarmed to the two-day show in 1956, its second year in operation.

"The third year, we charged 25 cents," said Betty. "The membership thought that was outrageous." But even bigger crowds showed up.

Still, it was years before more than the front half of the Quonset hut was needed. But as the show grew, more and more dealers and wholesalers clamored for space.

One year — and one year only — the show committee responded to that demand by renting out the nearby cow barn.

"We went in and raked out all the manure and cleaned the stalls. But what we didn't bargain for was the green sawdust that covered the floor 4 inches deep," said Bill Schupp, who along with his wife, Milly, chaired the show for several years.

Some of the displays were more curious than valuable. In 1957, Erna Clark set a "dinner of rocks." Explained Milly: "They're rocks that look like food. They're common."

Less common was Mary Aspaas and her "singing rocks," which also drew the crowds for several years.

"She was quite unique," said Milly. "She collected the rocks and broke them for the tones." The rocks were then "played," somewhat like a xylophone.

Glittery showstoppers started cropping up as well, including a $2 million display of diamonds shown off during the 1965 event.

Four years earlier, it was emeralds that stole the show. "They were worth $40,000," said Bill. "I kept them under the bed for two weeks."

The real turning point for the show, however, came not in mineral but rather in human form, also back in '61. That was the year the show's organizers were able to snare a visit by Paul Desautels, then assistant curator of mineralogy at the Smithsonian Institution.

"We got a list of museums with mineral collections and wrote them," said Milly. "We offered to pay travel and exhibit expenses. Paul Desautels wrote back and said we were the only ones to ever do that."

Actually, expense money was so short that Desautels wound up bunking with the Schupps and using Milly's old car for transportation.

No matter. For year after year, he returned to Tucson, bringing with him cases of minerals for display, giving lectures and judging competitive events.

More importantly, Desautels told the rest of the world about this marvelous little gem and mineral show being held every winter in a Quonset hut in the middle of the desert.

By 1969, Desautels was describing Tucson's exhibition as "The New York Stock Exchange of the mineral world."

That sort of talk soon had other heavyweights of the mineral world flocking to the show as well. Among them: Peter Embrey, curator of the British Museum of Natural History, who was allowed to bring along an exhibit from the museum, something never before permitted.

"I had to call London at 3 in the morning and talk to the board of trustees to get permission," said Dan. "They said he could bring only what he could hand-carry."

Despite the warm Western "hanging" by members of the Tucson Vigilantes upon his arrival, Embrey, too, returned year after year. Curators from various museums in France, Denmark, Spain, Russia and China also started making the trek to Tucson.

"Now we have so many curators of museums coming here that they schedule their own meeting," said Betty.

In 1971, the show put up its glass cases for the

last time in the dust of the old Quonset hut. "It had gotten so crowded that our 20-foot aisles had gone into 10 feet," said Dan.

But the crowds were even more intense the following year, the show's first in the new Tucson Community Center.

Seems the people-pleaser was the Tucson Ring Meteorite, a 1,400-pound meteorite that had plunged to Earth near Tucson but had been housed at the Smithsonian since 1863.

"It drew such a mob of people that you couldn't even walk the floor," said Dan. "People were saying they wouldn't come back the next year."

But of course they did. And the year after that as well.

Today, the little endeavor that began in an elementary school cafeteria is touted by many as the largest gem and mineral show in the world. Others are not so sure, citing a similar show in Munich, Germany.

Betty Caudle, however, entertained no such doubt about who's No. 1 in the world of gem and mineral shows.

"We have a friend who was coming back from Europe who saw a sign about that Munich show in an airport there." The sign, said Betty, was billing the Munich show as "The Tucson of Europe."

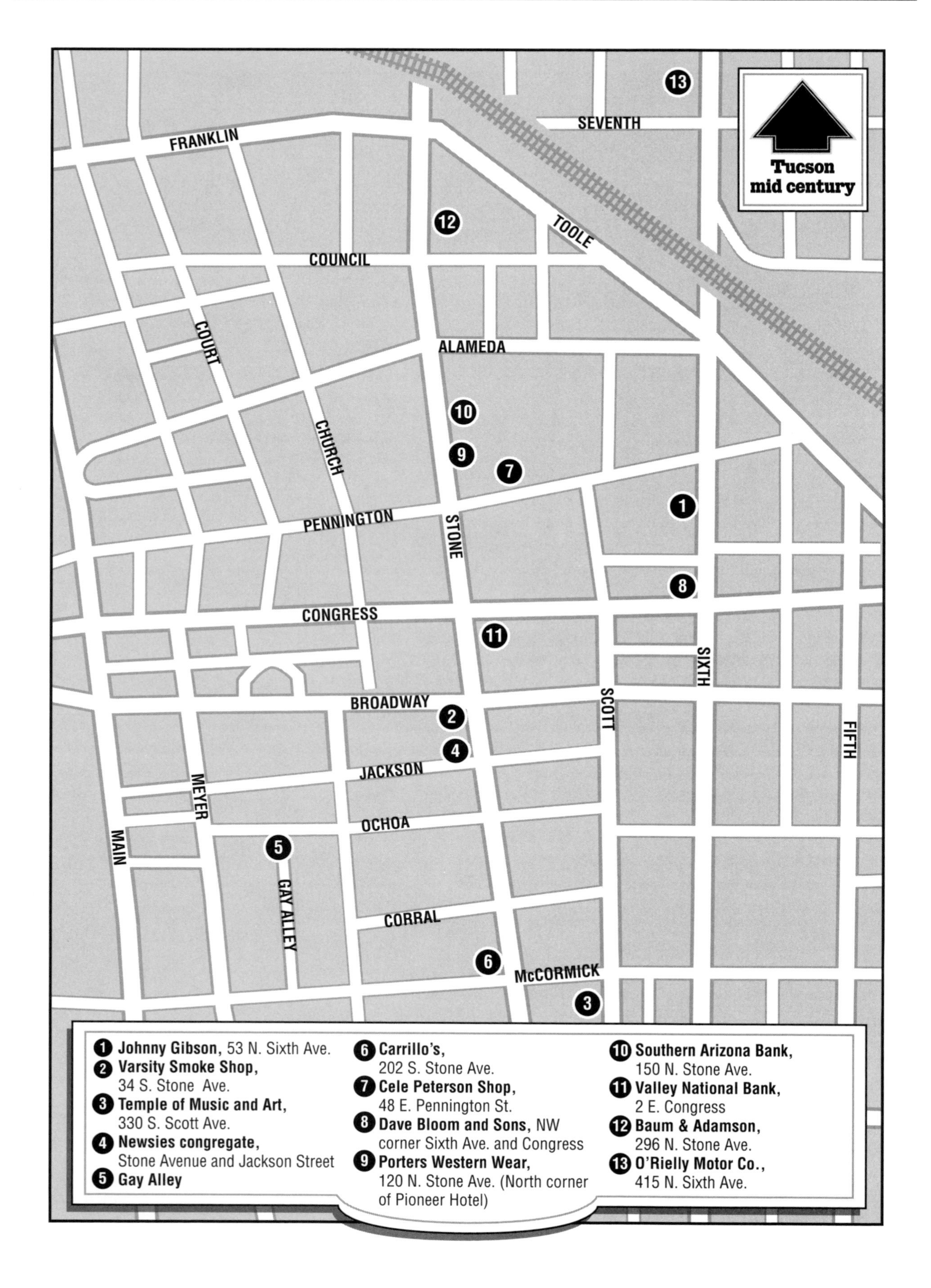

1. **Johnny Gibson,** 53 N. Sixth Ave.
2. **Varsity Smoke Shop,** 34 S. Stone Ave.
3. **Temple of Music and Art,** 330 S. Scott Ave.
4. **Newsies congregate,** Stone Avenue and Jackson Street
5. **Gay Alley**
6. **Carrillo's,** 202 S. Stone Ave.
7. **Cele Peterson Shop,** 48 E. Pennington St.
8. **Dave Bloom and Sons,** NW corner Sixth Ave. and Congress
9. **Porters Western Wear,** 120 N. Stone Ave. (North corner of Pioneer Hotel)
10. **Southern Arizona Bank,** 150 N. Stone Ave.
11. **Valley National Bank,** 2 E. Congress
12. **Baum & Adamson,** 296 N. Stone Ave.
13. **O'Rielly Motor Co.,** 415 N. Sixth Ave.

Photo Credits

Let the Good Times Roll: Kiddyland, Bonnie Jakimowich; Gay Alley, Arizona Historical Society/Tucson/#18196; Del Rio Ballroom, Ermelinda Gutierrez; Wayne Webb, Webb family; Tucson Rink, Ann Fee; Beau Brummell Club, Beau Brummell Club; Hi Corbett Field, Arizona Daily Star; Louis Leon, Louis Leon; Tucson Boys Chorus, Ray Manley; Polar Bar, Derald Fulton; Valley of the Moon, Daily Star; Rodeo Grounds, Arizona Historical Society/Tucson/#44294.

Merchants: College Shop, Karen Fisher Levine; Valley National Bank, Arizona Historical Society/Tucson/#BN28933; Chinese Grocers, Arizona Historical Society/Tucson/#PC 193-F7-A; Carrillo's, Carrillo family; Southern Arizona Bank, Arizona Historical Society/Tucson/#B32409; Le Cave's, Daily Star; Rincon Barber Shop, Joel C. White; O'Rielly Motor Co., Buck O'Rielly; Arizona Inn, Patty Doar; Jacobs Assay, Jacobs family; Porters, Arizona Historical Society/Tucson/ #B5 202.782; Ted Walker Trailers, Julie Waddell; Roh's, Roh family; Baum & Adamson, Arizona Historical Society/Tucson/#PC 193-F.7A; Cele Peterson, Cele Peterson.

Bear Down, Arizona: Shirlee Bertolini, Shirlee Bertolini; Oasis, Daily Star; Polo Team, UA Special Collections; Varsity Inn, UA Special Collections; Arizona State Museum, UA Special Collections; Cavalry Training, UA Special Collections; Bob Svob, Bob Svob; The Big Game, Daily Star; Polo Village, Miriam Pattison; The Library, UA Special Collections; Louie's Lower Level, UA Special Collections.

Hometown Notables: Johnny Gibson, Johnny Gibson; Newsies, Tucson Citizen; Duke Dillas, Arizona Historical Society/Tucson/#B93806; Bill Richey, Daily Star; Madeline Berger, Mathew H. Lemen Jr.; Boilermaker Dick, Beatrice Amado Kissinger; Charley Thornton, Western Ways; Georges DeMeester, Daily Star; Maria Urquides, Daily Star; Iceman, Arizona Historical Society/Tucson/#62801; Chuck Waggin, Carol Amesbury.

War and Disasters: Supreme Cleaners, Daily Star; Train Wreck, Arizona Historical Society/Tucson/#B92181; Myers & Bloom, Daily Star; Class of '42, Tucson High Class of 1942; Plane Crash, Daily Star; Hacienda, Jeanne Glasgow; Chatter, Arizona Historical Society/Tucson/#Cover; Death of a President, UA Special Collections; Wartime Housing, Lacagnina family.

Western Ways: Rancho Nezhone, Mission Palms Apartments; Botanical Gardens, Tucson Botanical Gardens; Oracle Junction Service Station, Charley McDaniel; Westward Look, Arizona Historical Society/Tucson/#MS 1255F.499A; Tanque Verde Valley, Arizona Historical Society/Tucson/#B131-48 MS452; Desert Museum, Arizona-Sonora Desert Museum; King Anvil Ranch, Daily Star; Picacho Peak Pilot Light, Irma Duttle; Link and Lutie, Daily Star; Tumbleweed Ranch, Virginia Roberts; Tohono Chul, Tohono Chul Park; Binghampton, Bingham family.

Institutions: Mount Calvary, Willie E. Fears; Laguna School, Daily Star; Mount Calvary, Arizona Historical Society/Tucson/#78838; Fort Lowell School, Daily Star; St. Mary's School of Nursing, Carondelet Health Network; Escuela, Arizona Historical Society/Tucson/#13535; Pima County Hospital, Jack Sheaffer; TMC, Tucson Medical Center; Square and Compass, Children's Clinics.

Teen Times: Drag Racing, Gary "Red" Greth; Elvis, Daily Star; Johnie's, Connie Wright; The Ramblers, Frank Catalano; Hot Rods, Gary "Red" Greth; Lewallen Brothers, Lewallen family; Junior Assembly, Jim Turner.

Holidays: Christmas Crowd, Daily Star; Arizona Stadium Fireworks, UA Special Collections; Mardi Gras, Jim Pfersdorf; Celebrations, Daily Star; Christmas Miracles, Richard Wood.

The More Things Change: Sabino Canyon, Arizona Historical Society/Tucson/#7239; Water, Arizona Historical Society/Tucson/#18997; Marjorie Long, Daily Star; Airport, Tucson Airport Authority; Gem and Mineral Show, Daily Star.

Another TUCSON

By Bonnie Henry

Tucson has far too many memories to contain in a single book. Which is why you won't find much mention of Steinfeld's or Jácome's, the Fox-Tucson Theatre or the Pioneer Hotel in "Tucson Memories." But you will find these stories and more in Bonnie Henry's "Another Tucson." Published in 1992, the book is available online at cafepress.com/azstarnet or by calling 1-877-809-1659. If ordering by phone, the order number is: 13596486. You can find Bonnie's recent columns at azstarnet.com/bonnie